DEEPER TRUTH DICTIONARY OF BIBLE TYPES

by: Samuel N. Greene, Ph. D.

Glory Publishing, Inc.
GloryPublishingInc.com

About the Author & Narrow Way Ministries Int'l:
www.NWMin.org

All Scriptures used in this book were taken from the King James Version.
Also, we have decided not to capitalize any names of the devil and his kingdom.

Printed in the United States of America
ISBN: 978-1-937199-35-7

Foreword

This book was written with a true heart so that God's people could understand and begin to fathom the depths, riches, mysteries, and majesty of God. Dr. Greene has spent over forty years studying, teaching, and plumbing the depths of Scripture. This book came out of his many years of experience, but the author truly is the Holy Spirit, the giver of all truth. This book will help the reader in understanding the keys to Biblical revelation as well as in understanding the mysteries of God. Once one understands these keys, that Bible names, colors, numbers, objects, directions, animals, etc. all carry within them hidden truths that open up and unlock the Scriptures to them, then they can apply these keys and will come to know the Word in a far more richer and meaningful way. If this happens, then the writer will be blessed because God's precious sheep will know their wonderful Savior and His Word like never before.

This Bible Dictionary of Scriptural types and symbols is humbly written and set forth with a number of perspectives in mind. One perspective is to glorify and exalt the Lord Jesus Christ, who is the anti-type, the symbol, and the fulfillment of all truth. Jesus is the person behind all that is taught. All things revealed in Scripture point to, speak of and find their ultimate fulfillment in Jesus, who is the Living Word:

"In the volume of the book it is written of me" (Hebrews 10:7)
Search the Scriptures... they are they which testify of me" (John 5:39)
"To Him give all the prophets witness..." (Acts 10:43)
"In the beginning was the Word, and the Word was with God and the Word was God" (John 1:1)
"And the Word was made flesh and dwelt among us" (John 1:14)
"I am the Way, the Truth and the Life" (John 14:6)

The Scripture also declares that in Him dwell the revelation of God:

"...that in all things He might have the preeminence" (Colossians 1:18)
"According to the eternal purpose, which he purposed in Christ Jesus our Lord" (Ephesians 3:11)
"In Him dwelleth all the fullness of the Godhead bodily" (Colossians 2:9)
"Who (Jesus) is the image of the invisible God" (Colossians 1:15)
"For it pleased the Father that in Him should all fullness dwell" (Col. 1:19)
"Who being the brightness of His glory and the express image of his person" (Hebrews 1:3)

Another perspective is to give believers the heart of the Word, the hidden meanings, the deeper truth.

"Have not I written to thee excellent [excellent in the Hebrew means three-fold or weighty] *things in counsels and knowledge. That I might make thee know the certainty of the words of truth"*(Proverbs 22:20-21)
"...I looked, beheld a hand was sent unto me and lo a roll of a book was therein, and he spread it before me and it was written within and without... (Ezekiel 2:9-10)."
"...Unto you it is given to know the mystery of the kingdom of God, but unto them that are without all these things are done in parables (Mark 4:11)."
"It is the glory of God to conceal a thing: but the honor of kings is to search out a matter (Proverbs 25:2)."

The third perspective is to encourage and promote the searching of the Word of God, and to instill a greater love for the truth.

"These were more noble than those in Thessalonica, in that they received the word with all readiness of mind, and searched the scriptures daily, whether those things were so." (Acts 17:11)
"For when for the time ye ought to be teachers, ye have need that one teach you again" (Hebrews 5:12)
"Strong meat belongeth to them... who by reason of use" (Hebrews 5:14)
"But his delight is in the law of the Lord, and in his law doth he meditate day and night" (Psalm 1:2)

The fourth perspective would be to give an answer to them who seek the truth, for those who long to know His heart.

"...to give an answer to every man that asketh you" (I Peter 3:15)
"...Aquila and Priscilla had heard, they took him unto them, and expounded unto him the way of God more perfectly" (Acts 18:26)
"A wise man will hear and increase learning... To understand a proverb and the interpretation: the words of the wise and their dark sayings" (Proverbs 1:5-6)

The fifth perspective is to show that the Word of God is more precious than anything this world can offer. That it is far deeper and full of substance than man will ever know.

Last, but not least, this book is written simply to be a tool of blessing to the body of Christ. It is meant to aid them, to save them extra hours of study, so that they can give themselves to the meat of the Word.

Acknowledgements

First of all, I acknowledge the Holy Spirit, the great revealer of truth for the forty five years He has taught me and revealed the Word of God to me. If I were to give credit to certain people, it would be a book in and of itself. I have sat at the feet and learned in the books of hundreds of men and women of God. Truly they are too numerous to mention. Special thanks though must be given to two men who wrote definitive works on types and shadows, Walter Wilson and Kevin Conner.

I want to thank my wife for sharing me for days on end with Jesus in studying the Scriptures. I want to thank my assistant, Andrew Jensen, for all his great help, faithfulness, and support. I also want to thank my precious congregation for allowing me the privilege to obey the Lord. Lastly, thanks to all who helped in typing, editing, and putting this book together, which took me twelve years to write. I pray this book will be a blessing to all who read it and helps them to understand the Word of God more. To God be the glory.

Jesus is Precious!

Dr. Samuel Greene

DEEPER TRUTH DICTIONARY
Table Of Contents

Chapter 1
God's Hidden Truths In Scripture

A truly remarkable principle is that underneath all the obvious literal Word of God, lies deep and revelatory truths found only by those who "search the Scriptures." Those who dig deeper will find precious hidden truths lying beneath the surface. To understand the deep things of God we must have a love for the truth, and a great desire for searching the Scriptures. If we are not disciples, then we cannot expect God to share His deepest secrets with us.

Therefore, the first step in understanding types and shadows, or Biblical symbolism, is that you must be a student of the Word. Once God sees you have applied yourself diligently, searched for Him, and given yourself to know and understand His ways, then He will see that your are faithful and He will begin to commit to you His secrets.

The Scriptures declare "*It is the glory of God to conceal a thing: but the honour of kings is to search out a matter*" (Proverbs 25:2). This is for the serious Bible student, one who isn't satisfied with just a cursory look into the Word. As in Acts 17:11, "*These were more noble than those in Thessalonica, in that they received the word with all readiness of mind, and searched the scriptures daily, whether those things were so.*" The Bible also says "*Study to shew thyself approved unto God, a workman that needeth not to be ashamed, rightly dividing the word of truth*" (II Timothy 2:15). So for all who are true students and lovers of the Word, you will find this chapter illuminating.

I.   Hidden Treasures – God conceals hidden truths in His Word.

    A.   Proverbs 25:2 – "*It is the glory of God to conceal a thing: but the honour of kings is to search out a matter.*" – For His glory God conceals or hides truth from the insincere, worldly, unspiritual heart (Psalms 92:5-6). His hidden realities are not for the carnally, lukewarm minded, but for those who, with their whole heart, seek Him, search for, and love His truth.

        1.   Those who seek find

            a.   Psalms 111:2 – "*The works of the LORD are great, sought out of all them that have pleasure therein.*"
            b.   Matthew 7:7 "*Ask, and it shall be given you; seek, and ye shall find; knock, and it shall be opened unto you...*"

c. Proverbs 2:1-6 "*¹My son, if thou wilt receive my words, and hide my commandments with thee; ²So that thou incline thine ear unto wisdom, and apply thine heart to understanding; ³Yea, if thou criest after knowledge, and liftest up thy voice for understanding; ⁴If thou seekest her as silver, and searchest for her as for hid treasures; ⁵Then shalt thou understand the fear of the LORD, and find the knowledge of God. ⁶For the LORD giveth wisdom: out of his mouth cometh knowledge and understanding.*"

B. God has hidden glorious truths in the Scriptures that only those who search them out find them.

If you and I would simply "search the Scriptures", we can and will find the deep precious and hidden truth God has placed there. He does this for His glory's sake. He is only interested in giving these gems to those who have proved themselves worthy. God's truth is too powerful a weapon to be found in the hands of a novice or one who is not a true disciple or who does not have a great foundation in the Word! God's way of teaching is to build the Word of God in the lives of His people, "*line upon line, line upon line; here a little, and there a little*" (Isaiah 28:10). In other words, revelation is progressive and if you don't have the background of truth or as the Bible calls it a "foundation" you will not be able to know or understand the deeper things of God.

1. Proverbs 22:20-21 – "*²⁰Have not I written to thee excellent things in counsels and knowledge, ²¹That I might make thee know the certainty of the words of truth; that thou mightest answer the words of truth to them that send unto thee?*" – The Hebrew word for excellent means "threefold" or "weighty." We see from this that there lies even in passage of Scripture many facets and aspects of truth. As we uncover one layer we find another, building one upon another.

2. Ezekiel 2:9-10 – "*⁹And when I looked, behold, an hand was sent unto me; and, lo, a roll of a book was therein; ¹⁰And he spread it before me; and it was <u>written within and without</u>...*" – Written within and without – There is a deeper revelation than seen initially.

3. Daniel 12:4 and 9 (Revelation 22:10) – "*...O Daniel, shut up the words, and seal the book, even to the time of the end: many shall run to and fro, and knowledge shall be increased...*" There are things God has sealed that won't be revealed until the end.

4. Exodus 26:33, II Corinthians 3:13-18 – A veil divides the holy from the most holy. Paul says, there is also a veil over the Scriptures. God is protecting His holy things from those who would not understand or appreciate them.

5. Psalms 40:7, John 5:39 – In the volume of the book, hidden deep within the Word is a revelation of Jesus.

6. Mark 4:10-12 – For those that are without (the unsaved, the carnally minded, the unspiritual) God only speaks to in parables (truths veiled in a story).

7. Matthew 13:10-17 – In seeing that which is written without (the letter) they still don't see the Spirit of the Word, that which is written within.

8. Luke 24:45 – *"Then opened he their understanding, that they might understand the scriptures,"*

9. Matthew 16:17 – *"And Jesus answered and said unto him, Blessed art thou, Simon Barjona: for flesh and blood hath not revealed it unto thee, but my Father which is in heaven."*

10. Amos 3:7 – *"Surely the Lord GOD will do nothing, but he revealeth his secret unto his servants the prophets."*

11. Revelation 2:17 – *"He that hath an ear, let him hear what the Spirit saith unto the churches; To him that overcometh will I give to eat of the hidden manna..."*

C. God hides and keeps secrets.

The Hebrew word for "hide" and "secret" is the same word. It means to conceal, to hide, to cover. It's interesting to note that the Greek word for "revelation" means to take the cover off.

1. Isaiah 45:15 – *"Verily thou art a God that hidest thyself, O God of Israel, the Saviour."*

2. Job 34:29 – *"When he giveth quietness, who then can make trouble? and when he hideth his face, who then can behold him? whether it be done against a nation, or against a man only:"*

3. Job 26:9 – *"He holdeth back the face of his throne, and spreadeth his cloud upon it."* – God spreads His glory over the face of His throne. Only those that can endure the glory will ever see His face. Examples:

   a. Genesis 3:24
   b. Isaiah 33:13-17 (Isaiah 57:15)
   c. Psalms 24:3-6
   d. Exodus 33:20, Revelation 22:4

      e.   Ezekiel 44:10-14, Ezekiel 44:15-16

3. Amos 3:7
4. Habakkuk 3:3-4
5. Job 23:8-11
6. There are times and occasions when God even hides Himself from us, but eventually His purpose will be worked out. However to the rest, He cannot be seen (Luke 24:15-17, John 21:4, John 20:14)
7. Deuteronomy 29:29 *"The secret things belong unto the LORD our God: but those things which are revealed belong unto us and to our children for ever, that we may do all the words of this law."*

    a.   Revelation 5:1
    b.   I Corinthians 2:9-16
    c.   Matthew 16:13-19
    d.   Philippians 3:15 *"Let us therefore, as many as be perfect, be thus minded: and if in any thing ye be otherwise minded, God shall reveal even this unto you."*
    e.   I Samuel 3:7 & 21
    f.   Daniel 2:20-22 & 28 & 30 &47
    g.   Amos 3:7
    h.   Revelation 1:1 *"The Revelation of Jesus Christ, which God gave unto him..."*
    i.   Galatians 1:12 *"For I neither received it of man, neither was I taught it, but by the revelation of Jesus Christ."*
    j.   Ephesians 3:3-5 (Luke 2:26-27)
    k.   Matthew 11:25

8. We need the Spirit of Revelation, Ephesians 1:17-20 – *"[17]That the God of our Lord Jesus Christ, the Father of glory, may give unto you the spirit of wisdom and revelation in the knowledge of him: [18]The eyes of your understanding being enlightened; that ye may know what is the hope of his calling, and what the riches of the glory of his inheritance in the saints..."*

II.   Old Testament Truths are Types and Shadows of Examples to Us

I know that this may be elementary to some, but I feel the need to cover a few points before we look into the Scriptures. You have heard the saying "The Old Testament is the New Testament contained, and the New Testament is the Old Testament revealed." The Scriptures are clear that God uses the natural stories of the Old Testament to teach us spiritual truths. They are examples, types, symbols, and shadows to the New Testament believer. So, though we believe these things literally happened, we know that God uses them to speak eternal and glorious truths to us. The Old Testament is so rich when it comes to deeper revelation if we know this principle.

A.   Here is a list of Scriptures that tell us plainly God uses these Old Testament passages to reveal great truths.

1.   Romans 15:4 – *"For whatsoever things were written aforetime were written for our learning, that we through patience and comfort of the scriptures might have hope."*

2.   I Corinthians 10:6 – *"Now these things were our examples, to the intent we should not lust after evil things, as they also lusted."*

3.   I Corinthians 10:11 – *"Now all these things happened unto them for ensamples: and they are written for our admonition, upon whom the ends of the world are come."*

4.   Hebrews 10:7 – *"Then said I, Lo, I come (in the volume of the book it is written of me,) to do thy will, O God."*

5.   Luke 24:27 – *"And beginning at Moses and all the prophets, he expounded unto them in all the scriptures the things concerning himself."*

6.   Galatians 3:24 – *"Wherefore the law was our schoolmaster to bring us unto Christ, that we might be justified by faith."*

7.   Hebrews 10:1 – *"For the law having a shadow of good things to come, and not the very image of the things, can never with those sacrifices which they offered year by year continually make the comers thereunto perfect."*

8.   Hebrews 9:9 – *"Which was a figure for the time then present, in which were offered both gifts and sacrifices..."*

9.   Colossians 2:16-17 – *"Let no man therefore judge you in meat, or in drink, or in respect of an holyday, or of the new moon, or of the sabbath days: Which are a shadow of things to come; but the body is of Christ."*

10.   I Corinthians 15:46 – *"Howbeit that was not first which is spiritual, but that which is natural; and afterward that which is spiritual."*

11.   Hosea 12:10 – *"I have also spoken by the prophets, and I have multiplied visions, and used similitudes, by the ministry of the prophets."*

Chapter 2
The Mysteries Of God

I suppose one of the most amazing revelations of Scripture is that God wants us to know His mysteries. He has given us certain "keys of revelation" that we can use to unlock spiritual truths. These keys, however, are not just given to anybody, but are given to those who show an earnest and heartfelt love for the Word of God. Understanding that names, numbers, places, colors, animals, and objects are sometimes speaking of something other than the natural revelation will open to us a treasure house of truth. But be assured, God wants us to know the "mysteries, hidden from the ages." He is holding nothing back. These mysteries are there for those who are willing to search and go after it. He wants us to know His mysteries and here are the Scriptures confirming this.

There is no question that God is a mystery. It is true that He conceals and hides Himself. A person has to want to know Him. They have to have a desire to seek Him. Thankfully, God has put in every man a desire to know Him. Many do not know Him; because, they don't want to believe or stop sinning, or they just reason Him away with philosophy. They say show me and I'll believe, but God says to believe and then you'll see. Trust me, no one will be able to stand before the Lord at the judgment and say, there wasn't something deep inside of themselves crying out for more, crying out to know and experience God! This mystery isn't supposed to remain one. If we seek Him the Bible says we shall find Him.

While much of religion relishes in and speaks of the divine mystery as if it is to be accepted that way, we as the people of God have been given the right, the honor, and the privilege of understanding and unlocking God's great secrets and mysteries. Jesus declares in Mark 4:11, "*unto you it is given to know the mystery of the kingdom of God*" as well as Paul states that we are called to be "*stewards of the mysteries of God*" (I Corinthians 4:1). God, whose "ways are unsearchable and past finding out", keeps things from the casual Christian who doesn't see their need to search the Scriptures, or their need to worship God intimately, or simply spend time with Him to get to know Him. He will not share His secrets, His deep spiritual truths, or allow us to see His great depth as a person to the casual Christian. These secrets will remain a mystery to them.

This brings us to the Greek word for mystery which is *musterion*, which means that which is only known by the initiated. Before God will open the deep and hidden places of His Word or person, we must first be initiated into the deeper things of God. By this I mean we have a proven track record of being a true disciple, a student of His Word, are devout worshippers that worship Him in Spirit and in Truth, have set our face like flint to know Him intimately, are delighted just to be a servant, and are one whose whole desire is the Lord. At some given point in all our lives, He, after judging us, testing us, proving us, will initiate us into the Divine mysteries, secrets, and hidden truths of God. The Scripture says in Jeremiah 29:13, "*And ye shall seek me, and find me, when ye shall search for me with all your heart*", and in Isaiah 55:6, "*Seek ye the LORD while he may be found, call ye upon him while he is near*", as well as in Psalms 27:4, "*One thing have I desired of the LORD, that will I seek after...*" In other words, we must prove to God that we are serious. Then and only then will He open His heart to us and reveal the deep, hidden truths and secrets of His Word and His person. These will be shown the divine mysteries; these will have an understanding of God's secrets and see God's hidden truths in Scripture.

I. I Timothy 3:16 – "*And without controversy great is the mystery of godliness...*"

A. It is true God is a mystery

1. Job 11:7-8 – "*Canst thou by searching find out God? canst thou find out the Almighty unto perfection? It is as high as heaven; what canst thou do? deeper than hell; what canst thou know?*"
2. Job 15:8 – "*Hast thou heard the secret of God?*"
3. Proverbs 25:2 – "*It is the glory of God to conceal a thing...*"

God purposely hides and conceals rich truth in the Scriptures. He does this because He doesn't want just the casual reader whose heart isn't really after the Lord discovering deep profound revelation. They would not know what to do with it, or they simply wouldn't understand or care. God only reveals Himself to those who truly love Him and seek Him.

4. I Corinthians 2:14-16 – "*But the natural man receiveth not the things of the Spirit of God: for they are foolishness unto him: neither can he know them, because they are spiritually discerned. But he that is spiritual judgeth all things, yet he himself is judged of no man. For who hath known the mind of the Lord, that he may instruct him? But we have the mind of Christ.*"
5. Romans 16:25 – "*...according to the revelation of the mystery, which was kept secret since the world began*"
6. Colossians 2:2 – "*...to the acknowledgement of the mystery of God, and of the Father, and of Christ*"
7. Matthew 13:35 – "*That it might be fulfilled which was spoken by the prophet, saying, I will open my mouth in parables; I will utter things which have been kept secret from the foundation of the world.*"

15

8.   Job 26:9 – *"He holdeth back the face of his throne, and spreadeth his cloud upon it."*
9.   Isaiah 45:15 – *"Verily thou art a God that hidest thyself, O God of Israel, the Saviour."*
10. Habakkuk 3:4 – *"...and there was the hiding of his power."*
11. Psalms 81:7 – *"...I answered thee in the secret place of thunder..."*

C.   It has been given to us to know the mysteries of God.

1.   Mark 4:11 – *"And he said unto them, Unto you it is given to know the mystery of the kingdom of God: but unto them that are without, all these things are done in parables:"*
2.   I Corinthians 4:1 – *"Let a man so account of us, as of the ministers of Christ, and stewards of the mysteries of God."*
3.   Ephesians 3:9-10 – *"And to make all men see what is the fellowship of the mystery, which from the beginning of the world hath been hid in God, who created all things by Jesus Christ: To the intent that now unto the principalities and powers in heavenly places might be known by the church the manifold wisdom of God,"*
4.   Ephesians 1:9 – *"Having made known unto us the mystery of his will, according to his good pleasure which he hath purposed in himself"*
5.   I Corinthians 2:9-10 – *"But as it is written, Eye hath not seen, nor ear heard, neither have entered into the heart of man, the things which God hath prepared for them that love him. But God hath revealed them unto us by his Spirit: for the Spirit searcheth all things, yea, the deep things of God."*
6.   Daniel 2:22 – *"He revealeth the deep and secret things: he knoweth what is in the darkness, and the light dwelleth with him."*
7.   Proverbs 2:1-5 – *"My son, if thou wilt receive my words, and hide my commandments with thee; So that thou incline thine ear unto wisdom, and apply thine heart to understanding; Yea, if thou criest after knowledge, and liftest up thy voice for understanding; If thou seekest her as silver, and searchest for her as for hid treasures; Then shalt thou understand the fear of the LORD, and find the knowledge of God."*
8.   Isaiah 45:3 – *"And I will give thee the treasures of darkness, and hidden riches of secret places, that thou mayest know that I, the LORD, which call thee by thy name, am the God of Israel."*
9.   Proverbs 3:32 – *"...but his secret is with the righteous."*
10. Psalms 25:14 – *"The secret of the LORD is with them that fear him; and he will shew them his covenant."*

11. Deuteronomy 29:29 – *"The secret things belong unto the LORD our God: but those things which are revealed belong unto us and to our children for ever, that we may do all the words of this law."*
12. Isaiah 48:6 – *"...I have shewed thee new things from this time, even hidden things, and thou didst not know them."*
13. Colossians 1:26 – *"Even the mystery which hath been hid from ages and from generations, but now is made manifest to his saints:"*

D. Those that seek Him, find Him – God is not going to give meat unto babes. It can only be given to those who are ready and prepared for it, who have proven themselves worthy to know God's secrets. We must be true disciples and students of the Word who have a passion and zeal to know Him instantly.

1. We must be able to handle God's revelation.

   a. Hebrews 5:12-14 – *"For when for the time ye ought to be teachers, ye have need that one teach you again which be the first principles of the oracles of God; and are become such as have need of milk, and not of strong meat. For every one that useth milk is unskilful in the word of righteousness: for he is a babe. But strong meat belongeth to them that are of full age, even those who by reason of use have their senses exercised to discern both good and evil."*
   b. Luke 12:42 – *"...to give them their portion of meat in due season?"*
   c. I Corinthians 3:2 – *"I have fed you with milk, and not with meat: for hitherto ye were not able to bear it, neither yet now are ye able."*
   d. Matthew 11:15 – *"He that hath ears to hear, let him hear."*
   e. Mark 4:33 – *"...spake he the word unto them, as they were able to hear it."*

2. We must seek, search, and study to be approved or initiated

   a. Ecclesiastes 1:13 – *"And I gave my heart to seek and search out by wisdom concerning all things that are done under heaven: this sore travail hath God given to the sons of man to be exercised therewith."*
   b. Isaiah 34:16 – *"Seek ye out of the book of the LORD, and read..."*

  c. Isaiah 41:17 – *"When the poor and needy seek water, and there is none, and their tongue faileth for thirst, I the LORD will hear them..."*

  d. Isaiah 55:6 – *"Seek ye the LORD while he may be found, call ye upon him while he is near:"*

  e. Jeremiah 29:13 – *"And ye shall seek me, and find me, when ye shall search for me with all your heart."*

  f. Amos 5:4 – *"...Seek ye me, and ye shall live:"*

  g. Zephaniah 2:3 – *"Seek ye the LORD, all ye meek of the earth, which have wrought his judgment; seek righteousness, seek meekness..."*

  h. Matthew 6:33 – *"But seek ye first the kingdom of God..."*

  i. Matthew 7:7 – *"...seek, and ye shall find; knock, and it shall be opened unto you:"*

  j. Hebrews 11:6 – *"...and that he is a rewarder of them that diligently seek him."*

  k. II Timothy 2:15 – *"Study to shew thyself approved unto God, a workman that needeth not to be ashamed..."*

  l. Ecclesiastes 7:25 – *"I applied mine heart to know, and to search..."*

  m. Proverbs 2:4 – *"...searchest for her as for hid treasures"*

  n. Acts 17:11 – *"...and searched the scriptures daily..."*

II. God Has Mysteries

A. Those listed in Scripture

1. Revelation 10:7 – *"But in the days of the voice of the seventh angel, when he shall begin to sound, the mystery of God should be finished, as he hath declared to his servants the prophets."* – **The mystery of the plan of God.**

2. I Timothy 3:16 – *"And without controversy great is the mystery of godliness: God was manifest in the flesh, justified in the Spirit, seen of angels, preached unto the Gentiles, believed on in the world, received up into glory."* – **The mystery of Godliness**

3. Mark 4:11 – *"And he said unto them, Unto you it is given to know the mystery of the kingdom of God: but unto them that are without, all these things are done in parables:"* – **Mystery of the Kingdom of God**

4. I Corinthians 4:1 – *"Let a man so account of us, as of the ministers of Christ, and stewards of the mysteries of God."* – **The mysteries of God**

5. I Corinthians 15:51 – *"Behold, I shew you a mystery; We shall not all sleep, but we shall all be changed."* – **The mystery of His coming and our transformation**

6. I Corinthians 2:7 – *"But we speak the wisdom of God in a mystery, even the hidden wisdom, which God ordained before the world unto our glory."* – **The wisdom of God is a mystery**

7. I Timothy 3:9 – *"Holding the mystery of the faith in a pure conscience."* – **The mystery of the faith**

8. Ephesians 6:19 – *"And for me, that utterance may be given unto me, that I may open my mouth boldly, to make known the mystery of the gospel."* – **The mystery of the gospel**

9. Ephesians 5:32 – *"This is a great mystery: but I speak concerning Christ and the church."* – **The mystery of the bride and the Bridegroom.**

10. Ephesians 1:9 – *"Having made known unto us the mystery of his will, according to his good pleasure which he hath purposed in himself:"* – **The mystery of His will**

11. Colossians 4:3 – *"Withal praying also for us, that God would open unto us a door of utterance, to speak the mystery of Christ, for which I am also in bonds."* – **The mystery of Christ**

12. Colossians 2:2 – *"That their hearts might be comforted, being knit together in love, and unto all riches of the full assurance of understanding, to the acknowledgement of the mystery of God, and of the Father, and of Christ."* – **The mystery of God the Father**

13. Ephesians 3:3-4, 9 – *"³How that by revelation he made known unto me the mystery; (as I wrote afore in few words, ⁴Whereby, when ye read, ye may understand my knowledge in the mystery of Christ)...⁹And to make all men see what is the fellowship of the mystery, which from the beginning of the world hath been hid in God, who created all things by Jesus Christ."* – **The mystery of Christ**

14. Romans 16:25-26 – *"²⁵Now to him that is of power to stablish you according to my gospel, and the preaching of Jesus Christ, according to the revelation of the mystery, which was kept secret since the world began, ²⁶But now is made manifest, and by the scriptures of the prophets, according to the commandment of the everlasting God, made known to all nations for the obedience of faith:"* – **The revelation of the mystery kept secret since the world began**

15. I Corinthians 14:2 – *"For he that speaketh in an unknown tongue speaketh not unto men, but unto God: for no man understandeth him; howbeit in the spirit he speaketh mysteries."* – **mysteries in the Spirit**

16. II Thessalonians 2:7 – *"For the mystery of iniquity doth already work: only he who now letteth will let, until he be taken out of the way."* – **The mystery of iniquity**

17. Revelation 1:20 – *"The mystery of the seven stars which thou sawest in my right hand, and the seven golden candlesticks. The seven stars are the angels of the seven churches: and the*

seven candlesticks which thou sawest are the seven churches."
– **The mystery of the seven stars**

18. Revelation 17:5, 7 – *"⁵And upon her forehead was a name written, MYSTERY, BABYLON THE GREAT, THE MOTHER OF HARLOTS AND ABOMINATIONS OF THE EARTH...⁷And the angel said unto me, Wherefore didst thou marvel? I will tell thee the mystery of the woman, and of the beast that carrieth her, which hath the seven heads and ten horns."* – **The mystery of Babylon**

19. Romans 11:25-26 – *"²⁵For I would not, brethren, that ye should be ignorant of this mystery, lest ye should be wise in your own conceits; that blindness in part is happened to Israel, until the fulness of the Gentiles be come in. ²⁶And so all Israel shall be saved: as it is written, There shall come out of Sion the Deliverer, and shall turn away ungodliness from Jacob."* – **The mystery of Israel and the fullness of the Gentiles**

Chapter 3
Understanding The Principle Of Revelation

In Psalms 51:6 David cries, *"Behold, thou desirest truth in the inward parts: and in the hidden part thou shalt make me to know wisdom."* This obviously shows God wants us to have truth in our deepest heart, or our spirit. Because God is a spirit, He speaks and communicates to men by His Spirit, speaking spirit to spirit. Proverbs 20:27 says, *"The spirit of man is the candle of the LORD, searching all the inward parts of the belly"* and Psalms 42:7 says *"Deep calleth unto deep at the noise of thy waterspouts..."* Also, I Corinthians 6:17 shows us that *"he that is joined unto the Lord is one spirit"* and in I Corinthians 2:14 it says, *"But the natural man receiveth not the things of the Spirit of God: for they are foolishness unto him: neither can he know them, because they are spiritually discerned."* Even though this is true, we see in life that men will lean more to their soulish and natural mind to try to understand God, His Word, and His voice.

But in Romans 8:6-9 Paul says, *"⁶For to be carnally minded is death; but to be spiritually minded is life and peace. ⁷Because the carnal mind is enmity against God: for it is not subject to the law of God, neither indeed can be. ⁸So then they that are in the flesh cannot please God. ⁹But ye are not in the flesh, but in the Spirit, if so be that the Spirit of God dwell in you..."* This shows us that the deep things of God can only be understood spiritually, as in I Corinthians 14:14, *"For if I pray in an unknown tongue, my spirit prayeth, but my understanding is unfruitful."* We see this oh so very clearly in Matthew 16:14-17 when Jesus asks His disciples, *"who do you say I am"* and Peter answers that He is the Christ, the Son of the living God. Upon hearing Peter, *"Jesus answered and said unto him, Blessed art thou, Simon Barjona: for flesh and blood hath not revealed it unto thee, but my Father which is in heaven"* (verse 17). This was a direct revelation of God to Peter's spirit man.

We are no different from Peter. For the Bible says in I John 5:10, *"He that believeth on the Son of God hath the witness in himself."* I John 2:20 says *"ye have an unction from the Holy One, and ye know all things."* I John 2:27 reads *"the anointing which ye have received of him abideth in you, and ye need not that any man teach you: but as the same anointing teacheth you of all things, and is truth, and is no lie, and even as it hath taught you, ye shall abide in him."* In addition, Job 6:13 it says *"Is not my help in me?"* If we would only learn how to listen to our spirit man, we could learn so much! God speaks to His people primarily in two ways, first and foremost by His Word, and secondly to our human spirit. We must train ourselves to learn how to hear Him spiritually.

In Hebrews 5:14 Paul says, *"But strong meat belongeth to them that are of full age, even those who by reason of use have their senses exercised to discern both good and evil."* God longs to be able to speak to us like this; but far too often He finds us lacking spiritually, not only in our ability to understand His voice, but especially in His Word. As found in I Corinthians 3:1-2, *"And I, brethren, could not speak unto you as unto spiritual, but as unto carnal, even as unto babes in Christ. I have fed you with milk, and not with meat: for hitherto ye were not able to bear it, neither yet now are ye able"*, as well as in Hebrews 5:11-13 in speaking about Melchisedec, Paul says, *"Of whom we have many things to say, and hard to be uttered, seeing ye are dull of hearing. For when for the time ye ought to be teachers, ye have need that one teach you again which be the first principles of the oracles of God; and are become such as have need of milk, and not of strong meat. For every one that useth milk is unskilful in the word of righteousness: for he is a babe."* We see also Peter saying in I Peter 2:2, *"As newborn babes, desire the sincere milk of the word, that ye may grow thereby"*.

As we begin to desire God's Word and as we are fed with the milk of the Word (or basic and rudimentary doctrine), then only can we begin to understand this principle of revelation. As Jesus said in John 8:31-32, *"...If ye continue in my word, then are ye my disciples indeed; And ye shall know the truth, and the truth shall make you free."* True disciples are those Christians who study the Scriptures, pray fervently, worship liberally, and simply spend time in His presence getting to know Him and His Word. Truly only they can then begin to understand the revelation of God.

I.   Hebrew And Greek Words For Revelation, Reveal

    A.   Hebrew – *galah* – to uncover, discover, to make something openly known
    B.   Greek – *apokalupto* – to take off the cover, to disclose, to uncover, to unveil
    C.   Basic dictionary definition – a disclosure, to make something known that is hidden or secret

II.   Some Principles Of Revelation

    A.   It has always been the cry of men's hearts for God to reveal Himself and His purpose to them.

        1.   Psalms 119:18 – *"Open thou mine eyes, that I may behold wondrous things out of thy law."*

2. I Samuel 3:1 – *"And the child Samuel ministered unto the LORD before Eli. And the word of the LORD was precious in those days; there was no open vision."*

3. Psalms 25:3-4 – *"³Yea, let none that wait on thee be ashamed: let them be ashamed which transgress without cause. ⁴Shew me thy ways, O LORD; teach me thy paths."*

4. Psalms 27:4 – *"One thing have I desired of the LORD, that will I seek after; that I may dwell in the house of the LORD all the days of my life, to behold the beauty of the LORD, and to inquire in his temple."*

5. Exodus 33:13,18 – *"¹³Now therefore, I pray thee, if I have found grace in thy sight, shew me now thy way, that I may know thee, that I may find grace in thy sight: and consider that this nation is thy people...¹⁸And he said, I beseech thee, shew me thy glory."*

6. Philippians 3:7-12 – *"⁸...I count all things but loss for the excellency of the knowledge of Christ Jesus my Lord: for whom I have suffered the loss of all things, and do count them but dung, that I may win Christ..."*

B. God is very deep (in thought, person, and in His Word)

1. Psalms 42:7 – *"Deep calleth unto deep at the noise of thy waterspouts: all thy waves and thy billows are gone over me."*

2. Daniel 2:22 – *"He revealeth the deep and secret things: he knoweth what is in the darkness, and the light dwelleth with him."*

3. I Corinthians 2:10 – *"But God hath revealed them unto us by his Spirit: for the Spirit searcheth all things, yea, the deep things of God."*

4. Romans 11:33 – *"O the depth of the riches both of the wisdom and knowledge of God! how unsearchable are his judgments, and his ways past finding out!"*

5. Ephesians 3:8 – *"Unto me, who am less than the least of all saints, is this grace given, that I should preach among the Gentiles the unsearchable riches of Christ;"*

6. Job 5:8-9 – *"⁸I would seek unto God, and unto God would I commit my cause: ⁹Which doeth great things and unsearchable; marvellous things without number:"*

7. Psalms 145:3-7 – *"³...his greatness is unsearchable..."*

8. Psalms 139:17-18 – *"¹⁷How precious also are thy thoughts unto me, O God! how great is the sum of them! ¹⁸If I should count them, they are more in number than the sand..."*

9. Psalms 92:5 – *"O LORD, how great are thy works! and thy thoughts are very deep."*
10. Psalms 40:5 – *"Many, O LORD my God, are thy wonderful works which thou hast done, and thy thoughts which are to us-ward: they cannot be reckoned up in order unto thee: if I would declare and speak of them, they are more than can be numbered."*
11. I Timothy 1:17 – *"Now unto the King eternal, immortal, invisible, the only wise God..."*
12. Job 38:16 – *"Hast thou entered into the springs of the sea? or hast thou walked in the search of the depth?"*

Revelation is the making known of God's person, nature, will, and deeds in Scripture. The creation bears witness to the wisdom and power of its Creator. This natural knowledge of God is limited in its extent, but it is sufficient to convince human beings of the existence of God and the need to respond to Him.

The Old Testament bears witness to God's revelation in the history of Israel and in the inspired testimony of the prophets and other writers of the time period. This knowledge of God prepares the way for the full disclosure of God in Jesus Christ in the New Testament. The New Testament fulfills and completes the revelation which began in the Old Testament. Jesus Christ is the focus of this self-revelation of God.

Finiteness and sin make it impossible to gain adequate knowledge of God through human effort alone. God in His mercy makes Himself known through the incarnation of the Son and the illumination of human minds to understand Him. God requires and imparts a frame of mind that receives and responds to what He has made known.

C. The Vastness Of God

1. Job 5:8-9 – *"⁸I would seek unto God, and unto God would I commit my cause: ⁹Which doeth great things and unsearchable; marvellous things without number:"*
2. Psalms 145:3 – *"Great is the LORD, and greatly to be praised; and his greatness is unsearchable."*
3. Romans 11:33 – *"O the depth of the riches both of the wisdom and knowledge of God! how unsearchable are his judgments, and his ways past finding out!"*
4. Ephesians 3:8-9 – *"⁸Unto me, who am less than the least of all saints, is this grace given, that I should preach among the Gentiles the unsearchable riches of Christ; ⁹And to make all*

men see what is the fellowship of the mystery, which from the beginning of the world hath been hid in God, who created all things by Jesus Christ:"

5. Job 26:9 – "He holdeth back the face of his throne, and spreadeth his cloud upon it."

6. Isaiah 55:6-11 – "...*8For my thoughts are not your thoughts, neither are your ways my ways, saith the LORD. 9For as the heavens are higher than the earth, so are my ways higher than your ways, and my thoughts than your thoughts...*"

7. Psalms 77:19 – "Thy way is in the sea, and thy path in the great waters, and thy footsteps are not known."

8. Job 26:13-14 – "*13By his spirit he hath garnished the heavens; his hand hath formed the crooked serpent. 14Lo, these are parts of his ways: but how little a portion is heard of him? but the thunder of his power who can understand?*"

9. Psalms 36:6 – "Thy righteousness is like the great mountains; thy judgments are a great deep: O LORD, thou preservest man and beast."

10. Psalms 92:5 – "O LORD, how great are thy works! and thy thoughts are very deep."

11. Daniel 2:20-22 – "*20Daniel answered and said, Blessed be the name of God for ever and ever: for wisdom and might are his: 21And he changeth the times and the seasons: he removeth kings, and setteth up kings: he giveth wisdom unto the wise, and knowledge to them that know understanding: 22He revealeth the deep and secret things: he knoweth what is in the darkness, and the light dwelleth with him.*"

12. I Corinthians 2:9-16 – "*9But as it is written, Eye hath not seen, nor ear heard, neither have entered into the heart of man, the things which God hath prepared for them that love him. 10But God hath revealed them unto us by his Spirit: for the Spirit searcheth all things, yea, the deep things of God...*"

13. Ephesians 3:14-21 – "*...16That he would grant you, according to the riches of his glory, to be strengthened with might by his Spirit in the inner man; 17That Christ may dwell in your hearts by faith; that ye, being rooted and grounded in love, 18May be able to comprehend with all saints what is the breadth, and length, and depth, and height; 19And to know the love of Christ, which passeth knowledge, that ye might be filled with all the fulness of God...*"

14. Job 11:7-9 – "*7Canst thou by searching find out God? canst thou find out the Almighty unto perfection? 8It is as high as heaven; what canst thou do? deeper than hell; what canst thou*

know? *9The measure thereof is longer than the earth, and broader than the sea."*

15. Isaiah 40:28 – *"Hast thou not known? hast thou not heard, that the everlasting God, the LORD, the Creator of the ends of the earth, fainteth not, neither is weary? there is no searching of his understanding."*

16. Exodus 33:20 – *"And he said, Thou canst not see my face: for there shall no man see me, and live."*

    a. John 6:46 – *"Not that any man hath seen the Father, save he which is of God, he hath seen the Father."*
    b. John 1:18 – *"No man hath seen God at any time; the only begotten Son, which is in the bosom of the Father, he hath declared him."*
    c. I John 4:12 – *"No man hath seen God at any time..."*

17. Job 9:10-12 – *"10Which doeth great things past finding out; yea, and wonders without number. 11Lo, he goeth by me, and I see him not: he passeth on also, but I perceive him not. 12Behold, he taketh away, who can hinder him? who will say unto him, What doest thou?"*
18. Job 23:3-14
19. Job 36:22-29
20. Job 37:5, 23
21. Psalms 139:1-6
22. Ecclesiastes 3:11
23. Isaiah 40:12-25
24. John 1:1-5
25. Psalms 111:2

D. God desires to open and reveal Himself, His purpose, will and Word to us.

1. Isaiah 35:5 – *"Then the eyes of the blind shall be opened, and the ears of the deaf shall be unstopped."*
2. Isaiah 42:7 – *"To open the blind eyes, to bring out the prisoners from the prison, and them that sit in darkness out of the prison house."*
3. Isaiah 50:5 – *"The Lord GOD hath opened mine ear, and I was not rebellious, neither turned away back."*
4. Revelation 5:2-9 – *"...4And I wept much, because no man was found worthy to open and to read the book, neither to look thereon. 5And one of the elders saith unto me, Weep not:*

behold, the Lion of the tribe of Juda, the Root of David, hath prevailed to open the book, and to loose the seven seals thereof..."

5. Revelation 10:2, 8 – *"²And he had in his hand a little book open: and he set his right foot upon the sea, and his left foot on the earth...⁸And the voice which I heard from heaven spake unto me again, and said, Go and take the little book which is open in the hand of the angel which standeth upon the sea and upon the earth."*

6. Nehemiah 8:5 – *"And Ezra opened the book in the sight of all the people; (for he was above all the people;) and when he opened it, all the people stood up:"*

7. Romans 16:25-26 – *"²⁵Now to him that is of power to stablish you according to my gospel, and the preaching of Jesus Christ, according to the revelation of the mystery, which was kept secret since the world began, ²⁶But now is made manifest, and by the scriptures of the prophets, according to the commandment of the everlasting God, made known to all nations for the obedience of faith"*

E. God wants us to have revelation – He wants those who care to have an understanding of Him

1. Mark 4:11 – *"...Unto you it is given to know the mystery of the kingdom of God..."*

2. I Corinthians 4:1 – *"Let a man so account of us, as of the ministers of Christ, and stewards of the mysteries of God."*

3. Revelation 1:1 – *"The Revelation of Jesus Christ, which God gave unto him, to shew unto his servants things which must shortly come to pass; and he sent and signified it by his angel unto his servant John:"*

4. Ephesians 1:17 – *"That the God of our Lord Jesus Christ, the Father of glory, may give unto you the spirit of wisdom and revelation in the knowledge of him:"*

5. Ephesians 3:3-5 – *"³How that by revelation he made known unto me the mystery; (as I wrote afore in few words, ⁴Whereby, when ye read, ye may understand my knowledge in the mystery of Christ) ⁵Which in other ages was not made known unto the sons of men, as it is now revealed unto his holy apostles and prophets by the Spirit;"*

F. Only God can give true revelation

1. Deuteronomy 29:29 – *"The secret things belong unto the LORD our God: but those things which are revealed belong unto us and to our children for ever, that we may do all the words of this law."*
2. I Corinthians 2:9-12 – *"¹⁰But God hath revealed them unto us by his Spirit..."*
3. Matthew 16:13-19 – *"¹⁷...flesh and blood hath not revealed it unto thee, but my Father which is in heaven..."*
4. Daniel 2:20-22, 28-30, 47
5. Amos 3:7 – *"Surely the Lord GOD will do nothing, but he revealeth his secret unto his servants the prophets."*
6. Galatians 1:12 – *"For I neither received it of man, neither was I taught it, but by the revelation of Jesus Christ."*
7. Matthew 11:25 – *"At that time Jesus answered and said, I thank thee, O Father, Lord of heaven and earth, because thou hast hid these things from the wise and prudent, and hast revealed them unto babes."*
8. Philippians 3:15 – *"Let us therefore, as many as be perfect, be thus minded: and if in any thing ye be otherwise minded, God shall reveal even this unto you."*

G. The aloneness of true revelation

1. Mark 4:10-39
2. Jeremiah 15:17 – *"I sat not in the assembly of the mockers, nor rejoiced; I sat alone because of thy hand..."*
3. II Corinthians 12:7 – *"And lest I should be exalted above measure through the abundance of the revelations, there was given to me a thorn in the flesh, the messenger of Satan to buffet me, lest I should be exalted above measure."*
4. Proverbs 23:23 – *"Buy the truth, and sell it not; also wisdom, and instruction, and understanding."*

H. The need for Jesus to be revealed in us

1. Galatians 1:16 – *"To reveal his Son in me, that I might preach him among the heathen; immediately I conferred not with flesh and blood:"*
2. I Samuel 3:21 – *"And the LORD appeared again in Shiloh: for the LORD revealed himself to Samuel in Shiloh by the word of the LORD."*

3. Romans 1:17 – *"For therein is the righteousness of God revealed from faith to faith: as it is written, The just shall live by faith."* (Isaiah 28:9-13)
4. Hebrews 11:1-3
5. John 1:1, 14 – *"¹In the beginning was the Word, and the Word was with God, and the Word was God...¹⁴And the Word was made flesh, and dwelt among us, (and we beheld his glory, the glory as of the only begotten of the Father,) full of grace and truth."*
6. Colossians 2:2-3 – *"²That their hearts might be comforted, being knit together in love, and unto all riches of the full assurance of understanding, to the acknowledgement of the mystery of God, and of the Father, and of Christ; ³In whom are hid all the treasures of wisdom and knowledge."*

Chapter 4
In The Volume Of The Book – Jesus

I. All Of The Types and Shadows In The Scriptures Will Ultimately Find Their Fulfillment In Jesus.

    A. Psalms 40:7 – *"Then said I, Lo, I come: in the volume of the book it is written of me"* – Everything that God will ever say whether in doctrine or preaching, behind it, everything that it will point to, all that it will emphasize, will be Jesus. *"...in the volume of the book it is written..."* of Him.

        1. Hebrews 1:2 – *"Hath in these last days spoken unto us by his Son, whom he hath appointed heir of all things, by whom also he made the worlds;"* God is speaking to us by, about and through His Son in these last days.

            a. He is the Word, John 1:1, 14 – *"¹In the beginning was the Word, and the Word was with God, and the Word was God... ¹⁴And the Word was made flesh, and dwelt among us, (and we beheld his glory, the glory as of the only begotten of the Father,) full of grace and truth."*

            b. I John 5:7 – *"For there are three that bear record in heaven, the Father, the Word, and the Holy Ghost: and these three are one."*

            c. Revelation 19:13 – *"And he was clothed with a vesture dipped in blood: and his name is called The Word of God."*

        3. John 5:39 – *"Search the scriptures; for in them ye think ye have eternal life: and they are they which testify of me."* – The Scriptures testify of Him.

        4. Luke 24:27 – *"And beginning at Moses and all the prophets, he expounded unto them in all the scriptures the things concerning himself."*

        5. Acts 26:22-23 – *"²²Having therefore obtained help of God, I continue unto this day, witnessing both to small and great, saying none other things than those which the prophets and Moses did say should come: ²³That Christ should suffer, and that he should be the first that should rise from the dead, and should shew light unto the people, and to the Gentiles."*

        6. Acts 8:5, 35 – *"⁵Then Philip went down to the city of Samaria, and preached Christ unto them...³⁵Then Philip opened his mouth, and began at the same scripture, and preached unto him Jesus."*

7. II Peter 3:18 – "*18 But grow in grace, and in the knowledge of our Lord and Saviour Jesus Christ. To him be glory both now and for ever. Amen.*" – Grow in the knowledge of Him.
8. I Corinthians 1:30 – "*But of him are ye in Christ Jesus, who of God is made unto us wisdom, and righteousness, and sanctification, and redemption...*" – wisdom is a Person

B. It's all about knowing Him

1. Philippians 3:10 – "*That I may know him, and the power of his resurrection, and the fellowship of his sufferings, being made conformable unto his death;*"
2. I John 5:20 – "*And we know that the Son of God is come, and hath given us an understanding, that we may know him that is true, and we are in him that is true, even in his Son Jesus Christ. This is the true God, and eternal life.*"
3. Exodus 33:13 – "*Now therefore, I pray thee, if I have found grace in thy sight, shew me now thy way, that I may know thee, that I may find grace in thy sight: and consider that this nation is thy people.*"
4. Jeremiah 9:23-24 – "*23Thus saith the Lord, Let not the wise man glory in his wisdom, neither let the mighty man glory in his might, let not the rich man glory in his riches: 24But let him that glorieth glory in this, that he understandeth and knoweth me, that I am the Lord which exercise lovingkindness, judgment, and righteousness, in the earth: for in these things I delight, saith the Lord.*"

C. It's all about giving Him glory

1. John 3:30 – "*He must increase, but I must decrease.*"
2. Deuteronomy 32:3 – "*Because I will publish the name of the Lord: ascribe ye greatness unto our God.*"
3. Psalms 115:1 – "*Not unto us, O Lord, not unto us, but unto thy name give glory, for thy mercy, and for thy truth's sake.*"

4. Beware of those seeking a name

a. Genesis 11:4 – "*And they said, Go to, let us build us a city and a tower, whose top may reach unto heaven; and let us make us a name, lest we be scattered abroad upon the face of the whole earth.*"
b. John 7:18 – "*He that speaketh of himself seeketh his own glory: but he that seeketh his glory that sent him, the same*

is true, and no unrighteousness is in him." – Let's not get caught up in gifts or things, or even the work rather than the Lord.

D.   We would see Jesus

1.   John 12:21 – *"The same came therefore to Philip, which was of Bethsaida of Galilee, and desired him, saying, Sir, we would see Jesus."*
2.   Hebrews 2:9 – *"But we see Jesus, who was made a little lower than the angels for the suffering of death, crowned with glory and honour; that he by the grace of God should taste death for every man."*

This is what the world, the body of Christ, etc., wants to see. We've had enough of seeing men. It's time to exalt, glorify and put King Jesus first. Let's let Him shine. Instead of trying to shine ourselves, let Him shine and be glorified through and in you. The Scripture declares, *"out of Zion the perfection of beauty, <u>God</u> hath shined."*

E.   An example in Scripture, Luke 7:24-26 – *"24And when the messengers of John were departed, he began to speak unto the people concerning John, What went ye out into the wilderness for to see? A reed shaken with the wind? 25But what went ye out for to see? A man clothed in soft raiment? Behold, they which are gorgeously apparelled, and live delicately, are in kings' courts. 26But what went ye out for to see? A prophet? Yea, I say unto you, and much more than a prophet."*

1.   Who do we come to see?

a.   *"Reed shaken with the wind"* – Many people flock to see *demonstrations* of the Holy Ghost in miracles, signs, and wonders. Often times Jesus is misplaced in all of this. We exalt gifts more than the Giver.
b.   *"Man clothed in soft raiment"* – When we come together it's not to admire or judge people because of their attire. Clothing means nothing when it comes to real kingdom living. We must wear decent clothes and that is it. This also speaks of hyper prosperity teaching that goes too far.
c.   *"A Prophet"* – There has been a proliferation of personal prophecies in this last move. That's good; but, we must remember, *"We have a more sure Word of prophecy."*

People run from one meeting to another seeking a prophecy. If we would seek Jesus, <u>He</u> would speak to us. Finally, let us remember one simple principle. Jesus is the person and central theme behind all that we read, study, teach, preach, proclaim, and prophesy. Let us glorify Jesus, the living expression of God's Word, and not get lost in dogma, doctrine and principles, thereby leaving out the truth all of these things point to. For the Word of God always points to and glorifies, testifies of and exalts Jesus, our great and marvelous redeemer. Praise His holy name!

Chapter 5
Understanding Types And Shadows

I.   The Figurative Language of the Bible

     A.   Pictures In Word – The Bible was written to us to share God's thoughts and heart. But, God's thoughts are too wonderful for us human beings to fully understand. To help us, God many times in the Scriptures, draws for us "pictures in words" so we can see more clearly the spiritual truths of His thoughts and heart.

         1.   Hosea 7:8 – *"Ephraim, he hath mixed himself among the people; Ephraim is a cake not turned."* Another translation, *"What wonder Ephraim should throw in his lot with the Gentile: No better than a griddle-cake in Ephraim, baked only on one side."*

         2.   Psalm 18:2 – *"The Lord is my rock, and my fortress, and my deliverer; my God, my strength, in whom I will trust; my buckler, and the horn of my salvation, and my high tower."* Another translation, *"The Lord is my firm foundation, my fort and my liberator; my God, my trustworthy defense, my protector, my strong deliverer and my place of retreat."*

         3.   Deuteronomy 32:3 – *"My doctrine shall drop as the rain, my speech shall distil as the dew, as the small rain upon the tender herb, and as the showers upon the grass"* Other translations, *"May my instruction soak in like the rain"*, *"Let my speech distil as the dew"*, *"...like mists on the green growth"*, *"...and light rain on the turf."*

         4.   Psalm 119:05 – *"Thy word is a lamp unto my feet, and a light unto my path."*

         5.   I Peter 1:24 – *"For all flesh is as grass, and all the glory of man as the flower of grass. The grass withereth, and the flower thereof falleth away."* Other translation, *"All mankind is like herbage and all their beauty like it's flowers."*, *"...All earthly like is but grass, and all its splendor like the flower of the field"*, *"The herbage dries up and it's flowers drop off."*

         6.   John 1:29 – *"The next day John seeth Jesus Coming unto him, and saith, Behold the Lamb of God, which taketh away the sin of the world."*

         7.   Joshua 1:3 – *"Every place that the sole of your foot shall tread upon, that have I given unto you, as I said unto Moses."* Another translation, *"Every foot of ground you tread I assign to you, as I promised Moses."*

8. I Thessalonians 2:7 – *"But we were gentle among you, even as a nurse cherisheth her children."* Another translation, *"On the contrary I showed myself among you as gentle as a mother when she tenderly nurses her own children."*

9. Nahum 1:3 – *"The Lord is slow to anger, and great in power, and will not at all acquit the wicked: the Lord hath his way in the whirlwind and in the storm, and the clouds are the dust of his feet."* Other translations, *"In hurricane and in tempest is his path, and clouds are the dust at this feet"*, *"He shows his power in the terrors of the cyclones and raging storms: clouds are billowing dust beneath his feet!"*

B. Many of the things God intends for us to know can only be explained to us in such picture language. God describes heavenly things by using natural things

1. Romans 1:20 – *"For the invisible things of him from the creation of the world are clearly seen, being understood by the things that are made, even his eternal power and Godhead; so that they are without excuse."*

2. I Corinthians 15:46 – *"Howbeit that was not first which is spiritual, but that which is natural; and afterward that which is spiritual."*

3. Psalm 19:1-3 – *"¹The heavens declare the glory of God; and the firmament sheweth his handiwork. ²Day unto day uttereth speech, and night unto night sheweth knowledge. ³There is no speech nor language, where their voice is not heard."*

4. Matthew 13:1-7 – *"The same day went Jesus out of the house, and sat by the sea side. And great multitudes were gathered together unto him, so that he went into a ship, and sat; and the whole multitude stood on the shore. And he spake many things unto them in parables, saying, Behold, a sower went forth to sow; And when he sowed, some seeds fell by the way side and the fowls came and devoured them up: Some fell upon stony places, where they had not much earth: and forwith they spring up, because they had no deepness of earth: And when the sun was up, they were scorched; and because they had no root, they withered away. And some fell among thorns; and the thorns sprung up, and choked them:"* Jesus teaching in parables

5. Hebrews 8:5 – *"Who serve unto the example and shadow of heavenly things as Moses was admonished of God when he was about to make the tabernacle: for, See, saith he, that thou*

make all things according to the pattern shewed to thee in the mount."

6. I Chronicles 28:12 – *"And the pattern of all that he had by the spirit, of the courts of the house of the Lord, and of all the chambers round about, of the treasuries of the house of God, and of the treasuries of the dedicated things."*

7. II Corinthians 12:2, 4 – *"²I knew a man in Christ about fourteen years ago, (whether out of the body, I cannot tell: God knoweth;) such an one caught up to the third heaven...⁴How that he was caught up into paradise, and heard unspeakable words, which it is not lawful for a man to utter."*

C. Figurative language is used to hide deep truth. Figurative language may hide the truth, as well as make it clear. It hides it from the unbelieving, and pierces and makes it clear to those who seek to know the mind of God.

1. Mark 4:11-12 – *"And he said unto them, Unto you it is given to know the mystery of the kingdom of God; but unto them that are without, all these things are done in parables: That seeing they may see, and not perceive; and hearing they may hear, and not understand; lest at any time they should be converted, and their sins should be forgiven them."*

2. Matthew 11:25-26 – *"At that time Jesus answered and said, I thank thee, O Father, Lord of heaven and earth, because thou has hid these things from the wise and prudent, and has revealed them unto babes. Even so, Father, for so it seemed good in thy sight."*

3. II Corinthians 4:3 – *"But if our gospel be hid, it is hid to them that are lost:"*

4. Proverbs 1:5-6 – *"⁵A wise man will hear, and will increase learning; and a man of understanding shall attain unto wise counsels: ⁶To understand a proverb, and the interpretation; the words of the wise, and their dark sayings."*

5. I Corinthians 4:1 – *"Let a man so account of us, as of the ministers of Christ, and stewards of the mysteries of God."* – The Greek word for "mystery" is "musterion", which means that which is known by the initiated.

The way to understand the hidden truth of the Lord is to be born again and filled with the Spirit, and to have a love for searching the Scriptures.

II. How To Determine If Figurative Language Is Used.

    A.   Principles to determine if figurative language is used

        1.   Decide first whether the word, or passage under consideration, is being used by the Spirit as a type
        2.   Not all objects are types
        3.   Read the passage in context
        4.   Compare with other passages, I Corinthians 2:13 – *"Which things also we speak, not in the words which man's wisdom teacheth, but which the Holy Ghost teacheth; comparing spiritual things with spiritual."* Other translations:

            "And we tell and explain this mystery in words not taught by human learning."
            "And we speak of these gifts, not in language taught by human philosophy."
            "...in the very words given us by the Holy Spirit."
            "Explaining spiritual things to spiritual men."
            "Matching what is spiritual with what is spiritual"

        5.   Search the Scriptures

           a.   II Timothy 2:15 – *"Study to shew thyself approved unto God, a workman that needeth not to be ashamed, rightly dividing the word of truth."* Other translations:

                "Earnestly seek to commend yourself to God."
                "Do yourself to present yourself to God as one approved."
                "Aim first at winning God's approval."
                "a workman with no reason to be ashamed."
                "ever cutting a straight path for the message of the truth."
                "Skillfully handling the Word..."
                "...because of his straightforward dealing with the word..."

           b.   Isaiah 34:16 – *"Seek ye out of the book of the Lord, and read: no one of these shall fail, none shall want her mate: for my mouth it hath commanded, and his spirit it hath gathered them."* Other translations:

                "Turn back, when the time comes, to this record of divine prophecy, and read it afresh: you shall learn, then that none of these signs are lacking, none waited for the coming of the next."

"...for with his own mouth he has ordered it and with his own breath he has brought them together."

    c.   II Peter 1:20 – *"Knowing this first, that no prophecy of the Scripture is of any private interpretation."* – Other translations:

"...understanding this, at the outset, that no prophetic scripture."
"But above all, remember that no prophesy in Scripture."
"can be understood through one's own powers."
"allows a man to interpret it by himself."
"is a matter of one's own interpretation."
"was ever thought up by the prophet himself."

    d.   Matthew 18:16 – *"But if he will not hear thee, then take with thee one or two more, that in the mouth of two or three witnesses every word may be established."* Other translations:

"But if he refused to listen, call in one or two other people."
"That every word may be confirmed by the evidence of two or three witnesses."

    e.   II Corinthians 13:1 – *"This is the third time I am coming to you. In the mouth of two or three witnesses shall every word be established."* – Other translation, *"This will be my third visit to you. Any charge must be sustained by the evidence of two or three witnesses."*

6.   When it is obvious that the thing being spoken of is pointing to something else, or there is a witness that there is something more, then you have a type.
7.   The Holy Spirit, our teacher, may, by the spirit of revelation, tell you what the object or type means.
8.   Don't force the Word to say something it is not saying. If there is no peace or grace as you're reading or studying, or no witness then simply leave it alone. Let the Word explain itself. Let the Word say what it wants, not what you want. (This is how we get into error, trying to make the Word say more than it has said.)
9.   See whether this type is referred to anywhere else in Scripture.

10. How was the type first used in Scripture? The first time you find anything in the Bible, determines a great deal about that thing or principle. It is called the "law of first reference." There in seed form is usually all the truth about that principle hidden within it. For instance take Genesis 1-3 the story of creation.

11. In the context of the passage is it obvious that in symbolic form God is speaking on end-time truth? As you go through the passage or study, all of it must be true to the symbolic point or truth it is revealing.

Finally, let's remember the Bible is rich with symbolic and typical language, far more than most people realize. Hopefully, this book will help you to understand the great depth of God's Word and the richness of every passage.

Chapter 6
Figurative Languages I: Types

I. Types

    A. Definition of a type

        1. A figure or example of something future, more or less prophetic.

        2. A type is any person or thing, providing a visual picture, representing something or someone, yet to appear.

        3. An emblem, a symbol, a representation of something that is called the anti-type.

        4. A prophetic symbol, prefiguring another.

TYPE ←——————→ ANTI-TYPE

FIGURATIVE ←——————→ TRUE

SYMBOL ←——————→ REVELATION

EXAMPLE ←——————→ REALITY

    B. Greek word for type is "*tupos*" – to strike, make an impression, a die as struck, a resemblance, a sampler, a model for imitation, a blow then the mark left by the blow. It is translated in the King James as **print, figure, fashion, example, ensample, and pattern** in the Scriptures below:

        1. John 20:25 – "*The other disciples therefore said unto him, We have seen the Lord. But he said unto them, Except I shall see in his hands the **print** of the nails, and put my finger into the **print** of the nails, and thrust my hand into his side, I will not believe.*"

        2. Romans 5:14 – "*Nevertheless death reigned from Adam to Moses, even over them that had not sinned after the similitude of Adam's transgression, who is the **figure** of him that was to come.*"

        3. Romans 6:17 – "*But God be thanked, that ye were the servants of sin, but ye have obeyed from the heart that **form** of doctrine which was delivered you.*"

        4. Titus 2:7 – "*In all things shewing thyself a **pattern** of good works: in doctrine shewing uncorruptness, gravity, sincerity,*"

5. Hebrews 8:5 – *"Who serve unto the example and shadow of heavenly things, as Moses was admonished of God when he was about to make the tabernacle: for, See, saith he, that thou make all things according to the **pattern** shewed to thee in the mount."*

6. I Corinthians 10:11 – *"Now all these things happened unto them for **ensamples**: and they are written for our admonition, upon whom the ends of the world are come."*

7. Philippians 3:17 – *"Brethren, be followers together of me, and mark them which walk so as ye have us for an **ensample**."*

8. II Thessalonians 3:9 – *"Not because we have not power, but to make ourselves an **ensample** unto you to follow us."*

9. I Peter 5:3 – *"Neither as being lords over God's heritage, but being **ensamples** to the flock."*

10. Acts 7:44 – *"Our fathers had the tabernacle of witness in the wilderness, as he had appointed, speaking unto Moses, that he should make it according to the **fashion** that he had seen."*

11. I Corinthians 10:6 – *"Now these things were our **examples**, to the intent we should not lust after evil things, as they also lusted."*

12. I Timothy 4:12 – *"Let no man despise thy youth; but be thou an **example** of the believers, in word, in conversation, in charity, in spirit, in faith, in purity."*

C. Examples of types

1. Noah's Flood – Baptism (I Peter 3:20-21)
2. Jonah in Whale – Jesus in Hell (Matthew 12:39-41)
3. House of God – Our types of Jesus and His church: Tabernacle of Moses, Tabernacle of David, Temple of Solomon

4. Feasts of Israel – Experiences we must enter into

    a. Feast of Passover – Salvation
    b. Feast of Pentecost – Baptism of Holy Ghost
    c. Feast of Tabernacles – Fullness

5. Daysman – Mediator is Jesus (Job 9:33, I Timothy 2:5)
6. Brazen Serpent – Jesus on cross (Num. 21:8-9, John 3:14-15)
7. Scape goat – Jesus bore all sins (Lev. 16:10, 27, John 1:29, I Peter 2:21)
8. David – type of Jesus (Psalms 69:9, John 2:17)
9. Melchisedec – type of Christ (Hebrews 7:3)

II.   Other Aspects of Types

The "type" is perhaps the least understood but most important concept in the hermeneutics of Biblical prophecy. Typological prophecy occurs throughout the Bible and can be considered the "normal" way that the prophets, including Jesus, spoke of the future. Failure to take this method of speaking into account can lead to gross distortions of the prophetic message.

A popular claim in some quarters is that one holds to a "literal" or a "literal where possible" hermeneutic. Those who follow this model frequently look for some single, highly specific fulfillment to a prophecy, whether it is an event in the early ministry of Jesus or some alleged fulfillment to come in the "great tribulation" or millennium.

Such interpretations generally face three difficulties. First, they often fail to account for the contextual meaning of a given prophecy both in the historical context of the prophet's own generation and in the literary context of the book in which the prophecy is found. In short, the prophecies are thought to address some far-off situation but are all but irrelevant to the people who first heard them and to the central messages of the books in which they are found. Second, this hermeneutic obscures the fact that every reasonable interpretation of prophesy is to some degree literal and to some degree metaphorical. Third, this hermeneutic is not followed by the New Testament itself, in that it does not demand the literalism allegedly maintained by "single fulfillment" interpretations of prophecy. For example, Jesus did not regard it as a violation of valid interpretation to assert that John the Baptist could fulfill the prophecy that Elijah would come before the Messiah (Matthew 17:11-13: Mark 9:11-13), notwithstanding the fact that John was not "literally" Elijah. Like true allegory, predictions of singular events are rare in the Bible and are marked by explicit and precise language (I Kings 13:2, in which a prophet explicitly predicts that Josiah would profane the altar of Bethel.)

The typological interpretation of prophecy asserts that the prophets did not so much make singular predictions as proclaim certain theological themes or patterns and that these themes often have several manifestations or fulfillments in the course of human history.

As another example, Joel understands the "day of the Lord" (Joel 2:31) to be not a single event but a theological concept with multiple fulfillments, or perhaps better, multiple manifestations.

Typology also explains how many of the events in Jesus' life and ministry are fulfillments of Old Testament patterns. Like the nation of Israel, Jesus came out of Egypt (*Matthew 2:15*), spent forty days in the wilderness (comparable to the forty years of Israel's wandering), and gave his law on a mountain. Jesus individually fulfills the highest ideals of the role of Israel as God's servant and is in a sense the nation of Israel incarnate.

A. The word "type'" has only 2 basic ideas

    1. Pattern
    2. Product – that which is produced from the pattern, i.e., a product

The Greek word is used of types given by God as an indication of the future in the form of persons or things (Romans 5:14, I Corinthians 10:6). For example, Adam was the type of the one (Jesus) who was about to be the head of the new humanity.

B. Antitype – The Greek adjective "antitupos" has the meaning "corresponding to something that has gone before."

C. The Typological Approach to interpreting is different than the grammatical-historical approach, which focuses attention on only one period. This is the difference:

    1. The grammatical-historical interpretation focuses its attention on the periods in which the passage was written.
    2. The interpretation of types by necessity focuses its attention on the periods in which both the type and the antitype occurred.

Two things are necessary to be understood: The historical facts of the Old Testament and the basic characteristics of the New Testament about salvation. Typology should not become the fueling concept in Old Testament Exegesis.

D. Essential characteristics of typology

    1. The Biblical writers within the sphere of history always place the things compared. It comes out of the living stream of human existence.

2. Some notable point of resemblance or analogy must exist between the type and antitype. This "particular point" must be worthy of notice.
3. The contemporaries of the type did not necessarily recognize that it had special significance.
4. The point of correspondence is important for later generations because they can see that God's earlier action became significant in his later action.

E. Examples of Typology

1. David was a type of Christ (Psalm 69:9).
2. Melchizedek: That Melchizedek is a type of Christ is seen in the fact the writer of Hebrews draws one basic conclusion from the silence of the Old Testament narrative. In Hebrew 7:3, the "being made similar to the Son of God" indicates that Melchizedek is a type. For the writer of Hebrews, the points of correspondence consist in Melchizedek's superiority as a priest, his independence from all earthly relations, and the absence of any allusion to his death.
3. Passover – Exodus 12. Christ is called the Lamb of God, in John 1:29. Paul states in I Corinthians 5:7 that Christ is our Passover lamb.
4. Brass serpent – Numbers with John 3:14

F. Interpretation of the Old Testament in the New Testament

1. The New Testament writers quoted the Hebrew, and the Septuagint literally.
2. The New Testament writers also adapted certain words and phrases for themselves and quoted from memory and blended ideas from two or more passages. These adaptations may involve the substitution of one thing such as a pronoun for another, or perhaps the addition of a word or phrase.

In these interpretive alterations the main thrust of the original passage is left intact. In typology a statement may be applied to a higher level, but such transference does not obscure the correspondence or the identity of a meaning preserved in the comparison.

3. Old Testament language in new train of thought. In these instances the main thrust of the passage is changed. Compare Romans 10:6-8 with Deuteronomy 30:12-14.

G.   Allegorical interpretation

1.   The only instance is in Galatians 4:21-31
2.   The antitype is the ideal or spiritual realization of the type.
3.   The type may have its own place and meaning independently of that which it prefigures, i.e., brazen serpent
4.   The type may not have been realized to have a higher character at the time it occurred.
5.   The essence of a type must be distinguished from its accessories.
6.   The only real authority for the application of a type is to be found in the scriptures.
7.   Mere resemblance does not make it a type; it has to be designed to resemble the antitype.

H.   A type is different than an allegory

1.   In allegory, the historical truth may or may not be accepted.
2.   In a type, the fulfillment can only be understood in the light of the historical truth.

I.   A type is essentially prophetic in character

1.   A type differs in form with prophecy
2.   A type images or prefigures. Prophecy foretells coming realities

J.   Prophetic revelation through symbols

1.   There are, or may be, six kinds of symbols that are prophetic in character: persons, institutions, offices, events, actions, things.

2.   There are three fundamental principles in dealing with symbols

a.   The names of symbols are to be understood literally.
b.   The symbols always denote something different from themselves.
c.   Some resemblance is traceable between the symbol and the thing symbolized.

3.   The Scriptures interpret their own symbols in the immediate context or in the book which they occur

K. Methods of Prophetic Revelation

   1. Future events are revealed through types, symbols, parables, dreams, and prophetic ecstasy
   2. Prophetic revelation through types – a type is a person, event, or institution ordained by God in the Old Testament to have a relationship with corresponding persons, events, and institutions in the New Testament.

L. Rules for Correctly Interpreting Types

   1. First, discern what, if any parts of a Scripture are actually types, and their resemblance to the antitype.
   2. Remember again to read passage in context (verse prior to and after passage continuing type).
   3. Let the Scripture interpret itself. Confirm the passage (type) with other witnesses (out of the mouth of two or three witnesses).
   4. Doctrine should not be established on types alone. Types should confirm and illustrate the particular doctrine.
   5. Do not force Scripture to say something it isn't saying. If there isn't any flow of revelation, or there is a struggle and no confirming passages, let it go. Why push it? Don't distort Scripture with your opinion.
   6. We need to know when a type begins and ends. You may be using a person as a type in some instance of their life, but certainly we know not all of their life is a type.
   7. There is oftentimes more revelation in the type than in the antitype. Just be careful to balance it out with the real.
   8. There is oftentimes more in the antitype than in the type.
   9. The type must fit the antitype in all points in the passage, thereby giving confidence.
   10. Use common sense. Wicked things or people would never represent Jesus. Nor would the wicked things or people ever represent the works of God or His Son (murder, adultery, etc.).
   11. A type can represent more than one thing. For example, Noah and the flood can represent the wicked being judged, the righteous being saved, as well as a type of baptism.

M. Classification of Types:

1. Prophetical types - These are things or symbols that though they are something present, signify something to come and along with it warns, admonished, or prophesies (Aaron's rod, manna, scapegoat).
2. Historical types – These are things acted or done in the Old Testament that prefigured things in the New Testament (priesthood, tabernacles, feasts, etc.).
3. Typical persons – These are certain people in Scripture that are used to prefigure someone else in their office, life, dealings, etc. (Joseph, Aaron, Moses, David all speak of Jesus).
4. Typical events – These are historical events that symbolized or foreshadowed events to come (Feasts of Israel, flood of Noah).
5. Typical offices – These are certain offices used as types of offices to come (king, high priest, shepherd, etc.).
6. Typical institutions – Certain institutions are to be seen as foreshadowing those to come (Tabernacle of Moses, heavenly tabernacle).

N. Difference Between Type and Symbol

1. Type – A type is a prophetic symbol that prefigures something. It is a figure of that which is to come.
2. Symbol – A symbol may represent something past, present or future, and it will have certain characteristics that identify what it represents. It is one thing standing for another. Examples of symbols: colors, objects, numbers, animals. These are all symbols, not types.

Chapter 7
Figurative Languages II:
Symbols And Parables

The below Scriptures once again show us that the "Old Testament is the New Testament contained and the New Testament is the Old Testament explained." Many times the Bible is referring to something other than itself, speaking of some far greater and glorious subject, person or principle.

I Peter 1:11 – "*Searching what, or what manner of time the Spirit of Christ which was in them did signify, when it testified beforehand the sufferings of Christ, and the glory that should follow.*"
Hebrews 9:8 – "*The Holy Ghost this signifying, that the way into the holiest of all was not yet made manifest, while as the first tabernacle was yet standing*"
Ephesians 5:31-32 – "*³¹For this cause shall a man leave his father and mother, and shall be joined unto his wife, and they two shall be one flesh. ³²This is a great mystery: but I speak concerning Christ and the church.*"

In the previous chapter, we looked at types. This brings us to our next kinds of figurative language, symbols and parables.

I.   Symbols

    A.   Definition – an object that stands for something else; usually a visible image that represents a concept or a certain recognized meaning; a material object substituted for a moral or spiritual truth.

    B.   Facts about this term symbol

        1.   Though the word "symbol" is not specifically used in the Bible, it is implied throughout. It is good to remember that there are more symbols used in Scripture than any other type of figurative language.

        2.   Categories of symbols:

            a.   **Dreams or visions** (examples: Acts 10:9-17, Genesis 37:5-9, Genesis 28:10-19, Daniel 2, Genesis 41:1-32)
            b.   **Objects** (example: Rainbow – covenant of love and faithfulness, Genesis 9:13-16, Revelation 4:3) – *see chapter on Scriptural Definitions Of Objects*

c. **Colors** (example: Red – symbol of suffering, sacrifice, Isaiah 1:18-19, Revelation 6:4) – *see chapter on Symbolism Of Colors*

d. **Numbers** (example: Five – God's grace, Matthew 14:17-21, I Samuel 17:40) – *see chapter on Biblical Numerics*

e. **Directions** (example: East – coming of the Lord, glory of God, Matt. 24:27, Gen. 3:24) – *see chapter on Symbolism Of Directions*

f. **Creatures/Animals** (example: Ass – stubborn, rebellious, Psalms 32:9, Psalms 104:11)

g. **Names** (example: Samuel's name in Hebrew means – asked of God, heard of God)

h. **Places** (example: Eden – God's garden, paradise, kingdom, inheritance, Isaiah 51:3, Joel 2:3)

i. **Actions** (example: Sleeping – rest, slothfulness, or death, Matthew 25:5, Genesis 2:21)

j. **Events** (examples: Crossing the Red Sea, Swelling of Jordan, births, wars, circumcisions)

k. **Structures** (examples: Tabernacle of Moses, Noah's Ark, altars)

l. **Offices** (examples: Priests, prophet, husband, watchmen)

C. Symbols and similitudes

1. Trees of life and knowledge – *Genesis 2:9, 17, 3:3, 24, Revelation 22:2*

2. Rainbow – *Genesis 9:12-13*

3. Circumcision of the covenant of Abraham – *Genesis 17:11, Romans 4:11*

4. Passover, the sparing of the firstborn, and the atonement made by Christ – *Exodus 12:3-28, I Corinthians 5:7*

5. Of the divine presence, the pillar of cloud – *Exodus 13:21-22*

6. Thunder on Mount Sinai – *Exodus 19:9, 16*

7. Darkness, of God's inscrutability – *Exodus 20:21, Leviticus 16:2, I Kings 8:12, Psalms 18:11, 97:2, Hebrews 12:18-19*

8. The struck rock, of Christ – *Exodus 17:6, I Corinthians 10:4*

9. The sprinkled blood of the covenant – *Exodus 24:8*

10. Wine, of the atoning blood – *Matthew 26:27-29, Mark 14:23-25, Luke22:17-18, 20*

11. The brazen serpent, of Christ – *Numbers 21:8-9, John 3:14*

12. Sacrificial animals – *Genesis 15:8-11, John 1:29, 36*

13. Waving the wave offering and heaving the heave offering – *Exodus 29:24-28, Leviticus 8:27-29, 9:21*

14. The whole system of Mosaic rites – *Hebrew 9:9-10, 18-23*
15. Tabernacle – *Psalms 15:1, Ezekiel 37:27, Hebrews 8:2, 5, 9:1-12, 23-24*
16. Sanctuary – *Psalms 20:2*
17. Canaan, of the spiritual rest, Invitation to approach – *I Samuel 14:8-12*
18. Bow-shot, by Jonathan – *I Samuel 20:21-37*
19. Bow-shot by Joash – *II Kings 13:15-19*
20. Men meeting Saul – *I Samuel 10:2-7*
21. Rain and thunder – *I Samuel 12:16-18*
22. Split altar – *I Kings 13:3, 5*
23. Tearing of the veil – *Matthew 27:51, Mark 15:38; Luke 23:34*
24. Wounding – *I Kings 20:35-40*
25. Praying toward the temple – *I Kings 8:29; Daniel 6:10*
26. Harvest – *II Kings 19:29*
27. Isaiah's children – *Isaiah 8:18*
28. Nakedness – *Isaiah 20:2-4*
29. Almond rod – *Jeremiah 1:11*
30. Sticks and poles – *Ezekiel 37:7-8, Zechariah 11:7, 10-11, 14*
31. Food – *II Kings 19:29, Isaiah 37:30*
32. Shadow on Ahaz's dial – *II Kings 20:8-11, Isaiah 38:7-8*
33. Cooking – *Jeremiah 1:13, Ezekiel 4:9-15, 24:3-5*
34. Girdle – *Jeremiah 13:1-7; Acts 21:11*
35. Bottles – *Jeremiah 13:12, 19:1-2, 10*
36. Breaking of potter's vessel – *Jeremiah 19*
37. Good and bad figs – *Jeremiah 24*
38. Basket of fruit – *Jeremiah 24:1-3, Amos 8:1-2*
39. Wine – *Jeremiah 25:15-17, Matthew 26:27, Mark 14:23, Luke 22:17*
40. Yokes – *Jeremiah 27:2-3, 28:10*
41. Jeremiah's deeds of land – *Jeremiah 32:1-16*
42. Book cast into Euphrates – *Jeremiah 51:63*
43. Muteness – *Ezekiel 4:9-17*
44. Ezekiel's beard – *Ezekiel 5:1-4*
45. Change of domicile – *Ezekiel 12:3-11*
46. Eating bread with carefulness – *Ezekiel 12:17-20*
47. Eating and drinking in fear – *Ezekiel 12:18*
48. Vine – *Ezekiel 15:2, 19:10-14*
49. Death – *Ezekiel 24:16-19*
50. Boiling pot – *Ezekiel 24:1-5*
51. Mourning forbidden – *Ezekiel 24:15-18*
52. Two sticks – *Ezekiel 37:15-28*
53. Handwriting on the wall – *Daniel 5:5-6, 16-28*
54. Plumb line – *Amos 7:7-8*

55. Marrying a prostitute – *Hosea 1:2-9; 3:1-4*
56. Roll – *Zechariah 5:2-4*
57. Ephah – *Zechariah 5:6-11*
58. Jonas – *Matthew 16:4, Luke 11:29-30*
59. Star in the east – *Matthew 2:2*
60. Struck rock – *I Corinthians 10:4, Exodus 17:6*
61. Salt – *Colossians 4:6*
62. Bread – *Matthew 26:26, Mark 14:22, Luke 22:19*
63. Childhood – *Matthew 18:3, Mark 10:14-15, Luke 18:16-17*
64. Manna – *John 6:31-58*

D. Symbols of Holiness

1. High priest's holy garments were of white linen – *Leviticus 16:4, 32*
2. Choir singers arrayed in white – *II Chronicles 5:12*

E. Symbols of affliction and calamity

1. Job 3:5 – *Let darkness and the shadow of death stain it; let a cloud dwell upon it; let the blackness of the day terrify it."*
2. Psalms 143:3 – *"For the enemy hath persecuted my soul; he hath smitten my life down to the ground; he hath made me to dwell in darkness, as those that have been long dead."*
3. Nahum 2:10 – *"She is empty, and void, and waste: and the heart melteth, and the knees smite together, and much pain is in all loins, and the faces of them all gather blackness."*
4. Jude 13 – *"Raging waves of the sea, foaming out their own shame; wandering stars, to whom is reserved the blackness of darkness for ever."*
5. Revelation 16:10 – *"And the fifth angel poured out his vial upon the seat of the beast; and his kingdom was full of darkness; and they gnawed their tongues for pain,"*

F. Symbols of Deity (Exodus 14:10; Jeremiah 10:9; Ezekiel 1:26; 10:1 Exodus 25:3,4; 26:1; 28:28, 37; 38:18; 39:1-5,21,24,29,31, Numbers 4:5-12; 15:38-40, II Chronicles 2:7, 14; 3:14)

G. Symbols of various ideas

1. Iniquity – *Isaiah 1:18, Revelation 17:3-4, 18:12,16*
2. Royalty – *Judges 8:26, Daniel 5:7, 16, 29, Matthew 27:28*
3. Prosperity – *II Samuel 1:24, Proverbs 31:21, Lamentations 4:5*
4. Conquest – *Nahum 2:3, Revelation 12:3*

5. Colors figured largely in the symbolisms of the tabernacle furnishings and priestly vestments and functions as types and shadows of the atonement (Exodus 26:1,14; 25:5; 26:31; 36:35,37; 26:36; 27:16; 38:18,23; 28:4; 39:1;28:5,6; 39:2,3,5; 28:8;39:29; Leviticus 14:4, 6,49,51,52, Numbers 4:7,8,13, Isaiah 63:1-3, Hebrews 9:19-23)

II. Parables

A. Definitions

1. Hebrew – a pithy maxim, usually of a metaphorical nature, a similitude or oracle
2. Greek – a placing one thing beside another, a laying by the side of; a symbolic or figurative saying; a saying out of the usual cause

3. An actual definition

a. A short simple story designed to communicate a spiritual truth, religious principle, or moral lesson
b. A parable is like a simile in which one thing is compared to another, but it is much fuller and larger
c. A parable is a natural story with the purpose of teaching a hidden spiritual truth

B. Scriptures to define the Word parable

1. Psalms 78:2 – *"I will open my mouth in a parable: I will utter dark sayings of old:"*
2. Psalm 49:4 – *" I will incline mine ear to a parable: I will open my dark saying upon the harp."* Other translations:

"I will set my ear to catch the moral of the story."
"I disclose my hidden thought upon the harp."
"I will solve my riddle to the music of the lyre."

3. Mark 4:2 – *"And he taught them many things by parables, and said unto them in his doctrine."* – Another translation, *"He continued teaching them by many stories."*
4. Mark 4:10-13 – *"And when he was alone, they that were about him with the twelve asked of him the parable. And he said unto them, unto you it is given to know the mystery of the kingdom of God: but unto them that are without, all these things are*

done in parables: That seeing they may see, and not perceive; and hearing they may hear, and not understand; lest at any time they should be converted, and their sins should be forgiven them. And he said unto the, know ye not this parable? And how then will ye know all parables?"

5. Matthew 13:34-35 – *"All these things spake Jesus unto the multitude in parables; and without a parable spake he not unto them: That it might be fulfilled which was spoken by the prophet, saying, I will open my mouth in parables; I will utter things which have been kept secret from the foundation of the world."* Jesus spoke to the multitudes in parables. Actually this was His favorite method of teaching.

C. Examples of parables in the Old Testament

   1. II Samuel 12:1-4 – The poor man's ewe lamb
   2. Isaiah 5:1-7 – The vineyard yielding wild grapes
   3. II Samuel 14:1-23 – Joab and the wise woman

D. Examples of parables in the New Testament

   1. Mark 4:3-8 – The sower
   2. Matthew 13:24-30 – The tares
   3. Matthew 13:31-32 – The mustard seed
   4. Luke 15:11-32 – The prodigal son
   5. Luke 10:25-37 – The good Samaritan

Chapter 8
Figurative Languages III

I. Metonymy

    A. Definition of Word (Pronounced met-o-nmy-y)

        1. A metonymy is a subject represented by something that is connected with it.
        2. The change of one noun for another related noun
        3. The use of the name of one object or concept for that of another to which it is related or of which it is a part

    B. Scriptural examples

        1. Proverbs 25:15 – "*...a soft tongue breaketh the bone.*" Tongue means gentle words.
        2. I Corinthians 10:21 – "*Ye cannot drink the cup of the Lord and...*" Cup of the Lord is the communion cup.
        3. Isaiah 38:18 – "*For the grave cannot praise thee...*" People that are dead don't praise.
        4. Galatians 1:6 – "*I marvel that ye are so soon removed... unto another gospel.*" Another gospel here represents false teaching.
        5. Matthew 23:2 – "*The scribes and the Pharisees sit in Moses' seat.*" This seat represents authority, leadership, or ability to teach as Moses did.
        6. Lamentations 2:4 – "*...and slew all that were pleasant to the eye in the tabernacle of the daughter of Zion:*" The objects the eye desired
        7. II Samuel 12:10 – "*Now therefore the sword shall never depart from thine house;*" The sword means war, trouble, and hostility in his family.
        8. Deuteronomy 10:8 – "*...to stand before the Lord to minister unto him...*" Stand literally means to minister to the Lord, to be in His presence.
        9. Psalms 2:12 – "*Kiss the Son...*" To kiss the Son means to submit to Him, be ruled by Him.

II. Synecdoche

    A. Definition of Word (Pronounced syn-ek-do-kee)

        1. It could also be easily called transfer.

2. The exchange of one idea for another associated idea

    a. man – mankind
    b. break bread – eat meal

3. A figure by which one word received something from another which is intentionally associated with it by the connection of two ideas
4. A synecdoche is when a part of something is used to represent the whole of it, or a whole of something represents a part of it.
5. The difference between metonymy and synecdoche lies in this; that in metonymy, the exchange is made between two related nouns; while in synecdoche the exchange is made between two associated ideas.

B. Scriptural examples

1. Joel 2:28 – *"...pour out my spirit on all flesh"* All flesh – all kinds of people
2. John 15:5 – *"I am the vine, ye are the branches: He that abideth in me, and I in him, the same bringeth forth much fruit: for without me ye can do nothing."* Nothing in the sense of good things of the Lord
3. Deuteronomy 19:12 – *"...the hand of the avenger of blood..."* Blood – murder
4. I Corinthians 1:29 – *"That no flesh should glory in his presence."* Flesh – people
5. Genesis 22:17 – *"...and thy seed shall possess the gate of his enemies;"* Gate – cities
6. Psalm 102:14 – *"For thy servants take pleasure in her stones..."* Stones – restored temple or house of Zion
7. Philippians 3:19 – *"...whose God is their belly..."* Belly – themselves or what they can get

III. Simile

A. Definition of Word (Pronounced sim-i-le)

1. It could also be called resemblance.
2. A figure of speech in which two unlike things are explicitly compared ("she is like a rose")
3. A declaration that one thing resembles another or comparison by resemblance

4. A simile is a comparison in which something is said to be 'like' or 'as' something else

B. Scriptural examples

1. Psalm 1:3 – *"and he shall be like a tree planted by the rivers of water..."* Scriptural man – like a tree planted
2. Psalm 17:8 – *"Keep me as the apple of the eye..."* A man kept – like the pupil of an eye is kept
3. Psalm 5:2 – *"...with favour wilt thou compass him as with a shield."* A man surrounded by favor – like a shield protects
4. Matthew 24:37-39 – *"[37]But as the days of Noe were, so shall also the coming of the Son of man be..."* Flood of judgment then – flood of judgment at coming
5. Matthew 9:36 – *"and were scattered abroad, as sheep having no shepherd."* Men wandering without leadership – like sheep without a shepherd

IV. Metaphor

A. Definition of Word (Pronounced met-a-phor)

1. A declaration that one thing is or represents another, or comparison by representation (Example: *"A mighty fortress is our God"*)
2. A metaphor is a kind of comparison too; however, in this case something is said actually to be something else, not simply to be like it. Metaphors are so commonly used that we sometimes forget that they are picture language. They picture something that is real.

B. Spiritual examples

1. Psalms 23:1 – *"The Lord is my shepherd..."* He will be as a shepherd to us.
2. Psalms 91:4 – *"...his truth shall be thy shield and buckler."* His truth will protect and strengthen us.
3. Psalms 84:11 – *"For the Lord God is a sun and a shield..."* God is my light and defense.
4. John 10:9 – *"I am the door;..."* He is to us what a door is, an entrance.
5. John 6:35 – *"I am the bread of life..."* What bread does in supporting natural life, He is in supporting spiritual life.

V. Personification

   A. Definition of Word

      1. Things represented as persons
      2. A figure by which things are represented or spoken of as persons: or by which we attribute intelligence, by words or actions, to inanimate objects or abstract ideas.
      3. Things which are not alive being spoken of as if they were people (Psalm 98:8)

   B. Scriptural Examples

      1. I Corinthians 1:30 – *"But of him are ye in Christ Jesus, who of God is made unto us wisdom, and righteousness, and sanctification, and redemption:"* In other words, Jesus has become wisdom, righteousness, sanctification and redemption to us.
      2. Psalm 85:10 – *"Mercy and truth are met together; righteousness and peace have kissed each other."* Human actions are attributed to things.
      3. Revelation 18:5 – *"For her (Babylon) sins have reached unto heaven..."* Babylon here is being personified in a woman.
      4. Proverbs 1:20 – *"Wisdom crieth without; she uttereth her voice in the streets:"* Wisdom is spoken of as a woman.
      5. Isaiah 5:14 – *"Therefore hell hath enlarged herself..."* Shoel (hell) is spoken of as a woman.
      6. Psalm 19:1-3 – *"The heavens declare the glory of God; and the firmament sheweth his handiwork. Day unto day uttereth speech, and night unto night sheweth knowledge. There is no speech nor language, where their voice is not heard."* The heavens, the firmament is said to speak, while day also speaks, and night shows knowledge, each having a voice
      7. Genesis 4:10 – *"...the voice of thy brother's blood crieth unto me from the ground."* Once again, we see that an inanimate object is used to speak out.
      8. Matthew 6:3 – *"But when thou doest alms, let not thy left hand know what thy right hand doeth:"* Whose left hand knows what their right hand does? This is abstract.

VI. Allegory

A. Definition of Word

1. A symbolic representation of truth about human conduct or experience
2. To express or explain one thing under the image of another
3. An allegory is an enlarged metaphor, it is like a metaphor, in which something is said to be something else, but it too is fuller and longer than a metaphor
4. Dictionary definition – a representation of an abstract or spiritual meaning though concrete or material forms, figurative treatment of one subject under the guise of another.
5. Greek word – found in Galatians 4:24

Galatians 4:22-31 – "*22For it is written, that Abraham had two sons, the one by a bondmaid, the other by a freewoman. 23But he who was of the bondwoman was born after the flesh; but he of the freewoman was by promise. 24Which things are an* **allegory**: *for these are the two covenants; the one from the mount Sinai, which gendereth to bondage, which is Agar. 25For this Agar is mount Sinai in Arabia, and answereth to Jerusalem which now is, and is in bondage with her children. 26But Jerusalem which is above is free, which is the mother of us all. 27For it is written, Rejoice, thou barren that bearest not; break forth and cry, thou that travailest not: for the desolate hath many more children than she which hath an husband. 28Now we, brethren, as Isaac was, are the children of promise. 29But as then he that was born after the flesh persecuted him that was born after the Spirit, even so it is now. 30Nevertheless what saith the scripture? Cast out the bondwoman and her son: for the son of the bondwoman shall not be heir with the son of the freewoman. 31So then, brethren, we are not children of the bondwoman, but of the free.*"

This is perhaps the most memorable of Paul's allegories, however, it is found in Galatians 4:22-31: Hagar and Sarah, Ishmael and Issac. One of them (Ishmael) was born to the bondwoman Hagar, the other (Issac) was born to a freewoman, Sarah. Hagar and Ishmael are symbolic of the Old Covenant; the law from Mount Sinai that brings all people into bondage. Sarah and Issac are symbolic of the New Covenant: the gospel of grace from Mount Calvary that gives spiritual freedom. When Paul concluded by saying, "So then, brethren, we are not children of the bondwoman, but of the free[woman], he was urging his readers to reject the bondage of legalism – salvation by keeping the law – and to live by faith in Christ. Though this passage deals with <u>real</u> people, Paul used it to present an even greater truth. This story is not necessarily an allegory, but an inspired allegorization of a historical fact, for the sake of illustration and emphasis Paul is simply drawing lessons from this account of scripture. An allegory once again is a story, poem or word-picture in which a spiritual or poetical meaning is conveyed symbolically. It is a legitimate way of teaching and illustrating truth by way of comparison.

B.   General information about an allegory

1.   An allegory may sometimes be fictitious.
2.   The actual word "allegory" is only found once in scripture.
3.   Though it is only found once, this literary device is used extensively in Scripture.

C.   Important Facts About Allegories

1.   The word "allegory" is found only once in the King James Version. In Galatians 4:24, it translates the Greek verb "allegoreo," which means to say something different from what the words normally imply. The New Kings James Version translates it by the word "symbolic."
2.   As a literary device, an allegory may consist of only a few lines or it may be sustained through an entire book. According to traditional Jewish and Christian interpretation, the entire book of the Song of Solomon is an allegory of God and His wife, Israel (Jewish), or of Christ and His bride, the church.
3.   In the New Testament, Jesus' parable of the wheat and the tares (Matthew 13:24-30, 36-43) is a good example of allegory. The apostle Paul also used allegories when writing. In Ephesians 6:11-17, he urges his readers to "put on the whole armor of God" and then gives the symbolic spiritual designation for each article worn by the Christian soldier. And, in Corinthians 10:1-4, Paul gives an allegory that compares the experience of Moses and the Israelites to Christian baptism and the Lord's Supper.

D.   Scriptural Examples

1.   Isaiah 5:1-7 –Jerusalem and Judah are spoken of here as the vineyard of the Lord. And, He uses the vineyard to describe Israel and what judgment will come to it.
2.   Song Of Solomon – All of this book is a story referring to Jesus and His bride. It is a symbolic book.

3. Matthew 9:16-17
4. Ezekiel 13:8-16
5. Psalms 80
6. John 10:1-16

VII. Proverb

A. Definition of Word

1. Proverb in Hebrew – a similitude or representation; from a root – to rule, to control, to exercise mental superiority
2. Proverb in Greek – alongside of supposition, an adage, a fictitious illustration
3. Proverbs 1:6 – *"To understand a proverb, and the interpretation; the words of the wise, and their dark sayings."*
4. A wayside saying in common use, a saying most widely used
5. One can make up a proverb of his own or quote one already used. Most are older sayings.
6. A short, local or universal saying which has stood the test of time and contains special truth or wisdom.

B. Scriptural ones already being used at that time

1. II Peter 2:22 – *"But it is happened unto them according to the true proverb, The dog is turned to his own vomit again; and the sow that was washed to her wallowing in the mire."*
2. Luke 4:23 – *"And he said unto them, Ye will surely say unto me this proverb, Physician, heal thyself: whatsoever we have heard done in Capernaum, do also here in thy country."*
3. Jeremiah 31:29 – *"In those days they shall say no more, The fathers have eaten a sour grape, and the children's teeth are set on edge."*
4. II Samuel 20:18 – *"Then she spake, saying, They were wont to speak in old time, saying, They shall surely ask counsel at Abel: and so they ended the matter."*
5. Genesis 10:9 – *"He was a mighty hunter before the Lord: wherefore it is said, Even as Nimrod the mighty hunter before the Lord."*
6. Numbers 21:27 – *"Wherefore they that speak in proverbs say, Come into Heshbon, let the city of Sihon be built and prepared:"*
7. John 4:37 – *"And herein is that saying true, One soweth, and another reapeth."*

VIII. Shadow

A. Definition of Word

1. Shadow in Greek – a shade or a shadow
2. General definition of this term – This term shadow means the picture in the Old Testament gives a glimpse and is an outline of what was to be fulfilled in the New Testament. Natural things representing spiritual truths.

B. Used In Scripture Three Times

1. Colossians 2:17 – *"Which are a shadow of things to come; but the body is of Christ."* Another translation: *"All these things have at most a symbolic value."*

2. Hebrews 8:5 – *"Who serve unto the example and shadow of heavenly things, as Moses was admonished of God when he was about to make the tabernacle: for, See, saith he, that thou make all things according to the pattern shewed to thee in the mount."* Other translations:

    "...rendering divine service with a glimpse and shadow of..."
    "men who serve a mere outline"
    "These men are serving what is only a pattern..."
    "a service which is only a copy"

3. Hebrews 10:1 – *"For the law having a shadow of good things to come, and not the very image of the things, can never with those sacrifices which they offered year by year continually make the comers thereunto perfect."* Other translations:

    "The Law possessed a dim outline"
    "...Laws gave only a dim foretaste"

Chapter 9
Principle Of Names

Teaching by symbolism, allegory, and parable abounds throughout the Scriptures. It is true that if you ignore the meaning of names you will have passed up a storehouse of deep and revelational truths. Whole passages now take on greater depth and meaning. Sometimes a name will unlock the hidden, deep meaning of a passage. I believe that understanding Bible names and places is one of the keys to unlocking the Word of GOD.

This is not only so with normal Bible names and places but most importantly to understanding the revealed and/or covenant and redemptive names of GOD (see back of book for list of these names). He has chosen this way (by using the meaning of names) to reveal Himself, His characteristics and His divine nature that we might know Him better. I do not claim, however, that in every instance a name may have a specific or spiritual meaning, but nonetheless, it is necessary to *"seek that we may find"* (Mt. 7:7, Jer. 29:13) for Luke 11:10 says *"he that seeketh findeth."*

We will look also at the many places in Scriptures where a person's name changes. These are great truths revealing not only the change of a name but also a person's nature.

I.   Significance Of Bible Names

There is a significance pertaining to Names and the Interpretation of Names found in Bible times, both Pagan and Hebrew history confirming this. In Hebrew History, the Israelites had an awareness of the significance of the Name and the potential therein. Naming an object, person, or place meant more than just the utterance of a name over them. It established a dominion and possession over that subject.

    A.   Following are illustrations of these conclusions:

        1.   Adam named all the creatures which God brought to him (Genesis 2:19-20). Thus he exercises dominion over creation and relates all to his sphere of rule. The creatures were named according to their natures.

        2.   The Lord called Israel by name and claims the nation as His own (Isaiah 43:1).

        3.   The name of the Lord is also named upon Israel and thus they become His people (Isaiah 43:1; 63:19; II Chronicles 7:14). We are known because of His name (Ephesians 3:15, II Timothy 2:19, I Timothy 6:1).

4. The name of Yahweh is named over the Temple (Jer. 7:10).
5. The name of Yahweh is called upon the Ark of the Covenant. (II Samuel 6:2).
6. The city of Jerusalem is the city where the Name of God is named also (Jeremiah 25:29; Daniel 9:18). Thus the city is His city.
7. God knew Moses by name (Exodus 33:12, 17). Jeremiah is known by name (Jeremiah 15:16).

8. Names of progenitors are carried on in the descendants, for the children are to keep alive the name of their fathers (Genesis 21:12; 48:16. II Samuel 18:18).

    a. If a man dies without children, his relative is to carry on his name by marriage to the wife of the deceased (Deuteronomy 25:5-10 with Numbers 27:1-11).

B. Patriarchal Times show the significance of names and their interpretation.

1. Jacob called the place of angelic visitation, "Beth-EL," which means "House of God" (Genesis 28:17, 19).
2. Adam called his wife's Name, "EVE" which means "Mother of the living." (Genesis 3:20).
3. Noah's name means "Rest" (Genesis 5:29).
4. The tower of Babel was interpreted as "Gate of Confusion" (Genesis 11:9).
5. Isaac was named "Laughter" in connection with the laughter of Abraham and Sarah (Genesis 17:17; 18:12; 21:6).
6. Jacob and Esau had prophetic names given to them (Genesis 25:25-30, Hosea 12:3-4).
7. Jacob's twelve sons also were named with prophetic significances (Genesis 29:31 – 30:24).

C. Gentile Kingdoms knew the significance of interpreted names also.

1. Joseph is given a name, "Zaphnath-paaneah," which means "Saviour of the world" (Genesis 41:45). He lived according to this name, delivering the then-known world from famine.
2. Daniel and his companions had their names changed (Daniel 1:7). The new Babylonish names expressed their change of position to exalted dignity in the Kingdom, and the changing of their Hebrew names showing their dependant state. The

purpose was to cause them to forget the name of the True God and become identified with the Babylonian gods. Interpret the names and the truth is discovered.

D. Period of the prophets attest also to this symbolic use of names.

   1. Isaiah and his children were given symbolic names. Their names indicated that judgment is coming to Israel, yet a remnant would be saved (Isaiah 7:3; 8:3). Isaiah and his children were for "signs and wonders" (Isaiah 8:18).
   2. Hosea and his children were also given symbolic names suitable to the spiritual condition of Israel and God's dealings with the nation (Hosea 1:6, 9).
   3. In the name "Immanu-EL" there was a prophecy of salvation in a name (Isaiah 7:14; 9:5 with Jer. 23:6; Zechariah 6:12).

E. New names for the saints confirm this significance.

   1. God changed Abram and Sarai's names to Abraham and Sarah. That is, to "High Father, a Father of many nations," and his wife from "Contentious" to "Princess" (Gen. 17:5, 15).
   2. God changed Jacob's name to Israel, "Prince having power with God and with men and prevailing" (Genesis 32:28, 29).
   3. The new name meant not only blessing for the bearer but for others too (Genesis 12:2 and 48:20).
   4. The Son of God gave three of His disciples new names, these were a promise of what their character and nature would become in due time (Mark 3:16, 17; John 1:42).
   5. The Good Shepherd knows His sheep by name (i.e., by nature) (John 10:3).
   6. The overcomer will receive a new name in a white stone that only he himself can appreciate (Revelation 2:17).
   7. The names of the twelve Apostles and the names of the twelve Tribes of Israel are to be found in the Eternal City of God (Revelation 21:14, with Luke 10:20, Revelation 3:8, 13:8, 17:8, Phil. 4:3, Hebrews 12:23).
   8. The Name denotes the person, his identity, his nature and character.

Pagan History gives evidence of the connection of the truth relative to names and their interpretation. The belief was universal that the name of an object, person or angelic being was more than a mere label. The name expressed the personality.

Various customs and rites were used to find a suitable name for a child and when that name was invoked upon the child it set in motion the virtues and power contained in that name.

This was also believed relative to the name of the gods. Only as men knew the name of their god could they call upon him and experience his power. This was claimed to be so by the invocation of the name. When the name was invoked or pronounced, it set the god working in the behalf of the one invoking. Hence the reluctance of the gods to let men into the secret of their names because of the magical power connected with the name.

Thus the Romans and Greeks called on the name of their numerous gods, invoking their powers, essence and virtues in behalf of those invoking. They sought to know the nature and essence of their gods by their names. They believed by uttering the name the god would be brought under the power of the speaker as by a spell. Whatever a person desired of a god, he had but to speak "the name" and it would be fulfilled.

The Magicians of Egyptian, Persian, Syrian and Babylonian history, worked in this way. They claimed revelation of the name of the gods. They would ask "What is his name" and thus purport to have received an answer by which they could conjure up answers for the people subject to their magical powers. As the Magician invoked the magical name, "the name" would work of itself. The name meant the god himself.

II.   Defining Names In Scripture

A.   Names in Scripture

The very fact that the word "name" occurs more than a thousand times in the Bible attests to its theological importance. In the ancient world a name was not merely a label but was virtually equivalent to whomever or whatever bore it. I Samuel 25:25 is a key passage: "*Nabal: for as his name is, so is he; Nabal is his name, and folly is with him.*" Nabal's name literally means "fool." The Greek word "names" is correctly translated as "people" in Revelation 3:4 (NIV). Name often means (or is translated as) reputation (Mark 6:14; Revelation 3:1), authority/power (Matthew 7:22; Acts 4:7), character (Matt. 6:9). In the OT it is frequently found in parallelism with memory, remembrance, renown (Ex. 3:15; Job 18:17; Ps. 135:13).

Giving a name to anyone or anything was tantamount to owning or controlling it (Gen. 1:5, 8, 10; 2:19-20; II Sam. 12:28), and changing a name signified promotion to a higher status (Gen. 17:5; 32:28; to this day in orthodox Judaism a dying person's name is sometimes officially changed in the hope that a new name will bring health and a new life) or demotion to a lower status (II Kings 23:34-35; 24:17). Blotting out or cutting off the name of a person or thing meant destroying that person or thing (II Kings 14:27; Isa. 14:22; Zeph. 1:4; see also Ps. 83:4).

The name and being of God are often used in parallelism with each other (Ps. 18:49; 68:4; 74:18; 86:12; 92:1; Isa. 25:1; Mal. 3:16), stressing their essential identity. Belief in Jesus' names is the same as believing in Jesus Himself, as John 3:18 demonstrates. Prayer in Jesus' name, therefore, is not mystical reliance on a traditional formula but is praying in accord with Jesus' character, His mind, and His purpose. He is just like His name – a name that means Savior (Matt. 1:21), a name "that is above every [other] name" (Phil. 2:9).

1. Example of two names given and definition

    a. I Samuel 25:25 – Nabal – "Fool"
    b. Genesis 27:36 – Jacob – "Supplanter"

2. Name – reputation

    a. Mark 6:14 – *"And king Herod heard of him; (for his name was spread abroad..."*
    b. Revelation 3:1 – *"And unto the angel of the church in Sardis write; These things saith he that hath the seven Spirits of God, and the seven stars; I know thy works, that thou hast a name that thou livest, and art dead."*
    c. Matthew 10:22 – *"And ye shall be hated of all men for my name's sake..."*
    d. Revelation 2:3 – *"And hast borne, and hast patience, and for my name's sake hast laboured, and hast not fainted."*
    e. II Timothy 2:19 – *"Nevertheless the foundation of God standeth sure, having this seal, The Lord knoweth them that are his. And, Let every one that nameth the name of Christ depart from iniquity."*
    f. Genesis 48:16 – *"The Angel which redeemed me from all evil, bless the lads; and let my name be named on them, and the name of my fathers Abraham and Isaac; and let them grow into a multitude in the midst of the earth."*
    g. Psalms 8:9 – *"O Lord our Lord, how excellent is thy name in all the earth!"*
    h. I Kings 8:29 – *"That thine eyes may be open toward this house night and day, even toward the place of which thou*

hast said, My name shall be there: that thou mayest hearken unto the prayer which thy servant shall make toward this place."

3. GOD Gives Names

    a. Luke 1:13 – John
    b. Matthew 1:21 – Jesus
    c. Genesis 17:19 – Isaac

B. Defining a name

A name is a label or designation that sets one person apart from another. But in the Bible a name is much more than an identifier as it tends to be in our culture. Personal names (and even place names) were formed from words that had their own meanings. Thus, the people of the Bible were very conscious of the meaning of names. They believed there was a vital connection between the name and the person it identified. A name somehow represented the nature of the person.

This means that the naming of a baby was very important in the Bible. In choosing a name, the parents could reflect the circumstances of the child's birth, their own feelings, their gratitude to God, their hopes and prayers for the child, and their commitment of the child to God. The name Isaac reflected the "laughter" of his mother at his birth (Gen. 21:6). Esau was named "hairy" because of his appearance. Jacob was named "supplanter" because he grasped his brother Esau's heel (Gen. 25:25-26). Moses received his name because he was drawn out of the water (Exodus 2:10).

A popular custom of Bible times was to compose names by the shortened forms of the divine name El or Ya (Je) as the beginning or ending syllable. Examples of this practice are Elisha, which means "God is salvation"; Daniel – "God is my judge"; Jehoiakim – "the Lord has established"; and Isaiah – "the Lord is salvation."

Sometimes very specialized names, directly related to circumstances of the parents, were given to children. The prophet Isaiah was directed to name one of his children Maher-Shalal-Hash-Baz, meaning "speed the spoil, hasten the prey." This name was an allusion to the certain Assyrian invasion of the nation of Judah (Is. 8:3-4). Hosea was instructed to name a daughter Lo-Ruhamah, "no mercy," and a son Lo-Ammi, "not my people." Both names referred to God's displeasure with His people (Hos. 1:6-9).

The change of a name can also be of great importance in the Bible. Abram's name was changed to Abraham in connection with his new calling to be "a father of many nations" (Gen. 17:5). God gave Jacob the new name Israel ("God strives") because he "struggled with God and with men, and prevailed" (Gen. 32:28; 35:10).

In the giving or taking of new names, often a crucial turning point in the person's life has been reached. Simon was given the name Peter because, as the first confessing apostle, had the revelation that Jesus was the "rock" upon which the new community of the church would be built (Matt. 16:18). Saul was renamed Paul, a Greek name that was appropriate for one who was destined to become the great apostle to the Gentiles.

The connection between a name and the reality it signified is nowhere more important than in the names referring to God. The personal name of God revealed to Moses in the burning bush – "I AM WHO I AM" – conveyed something of His character (Ex. 3:14). According to Exodus 34:5-6, when the Lord "proclaimed the name of the Lord," He added words that described His character. The name of the Lord was virtually synonymous with His presence (Ps. 75:11). To know the name of God is thus to know God Himself (Ps. 91:14). For this reason, to "take the name of the Lord your God in vain" (Ex. 20:7) is to act in any way that is inconsistent with the profession that He is the Lord God.

The New Testament writers also emphasized the importance of names and the close relationship between names and what they mean. A striking illustration of this is Acts 4:12: "*For there is no other name under heaven...by which we must be saved.*" In this instance the name is again practically interchangeable with the reality it represents.

Jesus taught His disciples to pray, "*hallowed by thy name*" (Matt. 6:9). Christians were described by the apostle Paul as those who "*nameth the name of Christ*" (II Tim. 2:19). A true understanding of the exalted Jesus is often connected with a statement about His name. Thus, Jesus "*has by inheritance obtained a more excellent name*" than the angels (Heb. 1:4). According to Paul, "*God also has highly exalted Him and given Him the name which is above every name*" (Phil. 2:9).

C.   Other important facts about names

In Scripture a name is often an expression of the nature of its bearer, describing his character, position, function, some circumstance affecting him, or some hope or sorrow concerning him.

In the ancient Semitic world a name had much more religious, personal, family, historical or geographical significance than in our Western culture. The extensive genealogical tables in Scripture are indicative of the historical importance the Hebrews attached to ancestral origins and development regarding the names of individuals, families, tribes, and nations; thereby establishing inheritance rights, and substantiating pedigrees, lineage, and royal succession, especially of the Davidic Messiah (e.g., Gen. 5; 10; 11; 46; I Chr. 1-9; Mt. 1:1-17; Lk 3:23-38).

Since the name was considered to be descriptive of the essential nature of the person or thing, there was a conception of identity between the name and its bearer (Gen 2:19-20). To cut off one's name from the earth signified to remove him or his descendants from existence (Josh. 7:9; II Sam. 14:7; II Kgs. 14:27; Ps. 83:4). To act or speak or write in someone's name was to act as that person's representative, with his inspiration and power and authority (Ex. 5:23; Deut. 18:19; I Sam. 17:45; I Kgs. 21:8). Thus the literal expression "call one's name over or upon" a people or place indicated a claim to possession or ownership (II Sam. 12:28; Isa. 43:7; Jer. 7:10). The recipient might not use the name, but was made subject to the name's authority and was provided protection (II Chr. 7:14; Prov. 18:10; Isa. 4:1; Jer. 14:9).

Personal names were generally bestowed on the child at or shortly after birth. Before the Exile the name was often given the child for the significance attached to it, but after the Exile it was customary to name the individual after a relative, frequently the grandfather.

Many Bible names are Hebrew in origin, but some place-names of Palestine may be other than Hebrew, such as the non-Semitic word Ziklag., Greek and Latin names, such as Antipatris (Acts 23:31), Caesarea Philippi (Mt. 16:13), and Ptolemais (Acts 21:7), also occur.

Hebrew names may be composed of one element, such as Jacob ("supplanter") and Nabal ("fool"); several elements such as Penuel ("face of God") and Emmanuel ("God with us"); or even a whole sentence, as Jehoshua ("Yahweh is salvation"), Jehoshaphat ("Yahweh has judged"), and Elijah ("my God is Yah[weh]").

1. Personal names were used to identify or say something about:

    a. Personal, physical, or spiritual factors, such as Esau ("hairy") and Peter ("rock").

b. Faith and gratitude to God. Godly parents reflected their piety by compounding their children's names with elements of the two chief names for God, either El (from Elohim) or Jah or Yah (from Yahweh), e.g., Joel ("Yahweh is God"), Daniel ("El is my Judge"), Abijah ("Yahweh is my Father"), Nathanael ("El has given"), and Ishmael ("El hears").

c. Association with animals and plants, as Jonah ("dove"), Rachel ("ewe"), Peninnah ("coral"), and Tamar ("palm tree"), as a term of endearment or expression of a wish that the child might have the peculiar quality of said animal or plant.

d. Something important to the parent, as Jacob named his last son Benjamin ("son of the right hand"), although the dying Rachel had called him Ben-oni ("son of my sorrow").

e. Historical events at the time of birth, as Ichabod ("inglorious"), because *The glory is departed from Israel, for the ark of God is taken*" (I Sam. 4:21-22).

f. Prophecy concerning work to be done, as Jesus ("*He shall save His people.*" Mt. 1:21).

g. Relationship to a quality and/or a place, as Melchisedek ("king of righteousness"), king of Salem ("peace" Heb. 7:2) and Zerubbabel ("begotten in Babylon").

h. Tribal names, such as Cushi (II Sam. 18:21).

i. Events prophesied to occur, as in the names of Isaiah's children: Shear-jashub ("a remnant shall return," Is. 7:3) and Masher-shalal-hashbaz ("swift is the booty, speedy is the prey," Is. 8:3); and in the names of Hosea's children Jezreel ("God sows"; so named with dual significance because of past events and future blessing, Hos. 1:4-5, 11; 2:22-23), Lo-ruhamah ("not pitied," Hos. 1:6) and Lo-ammi ("not My people," Hos 1:9).

j. Function, as the name Eve ("life") was suggested to Adam because she was to be "the mother of all living" (Gen. 3:20), and in such names as Obil ("camel driver," I Chr. 27:30) and Onesimus ("useful," as a slave, Phm. 10-11).

2. Names for towns, places, and things – Geographical names may denote a number of different things, such as:

a. Physical conditions involved, such as the Salt Sea (Gen. 14:3), Lebanon ("white," because of its snow-covered summit), Jericho ("fragrance of palms, rose gardens, and balsams"), Engedi ("spring of the kid").

  b. Qualities, as Joppa ("beauty"), Shiloh ("tranquility") and Salem ("peace")
  c. Shape, as Chinnereth ("harp-shaped," i.e., Sea of Galilee, Num. 34:11), Shechem ("shoulder of a mount").
  d. Occupation as Gath ("winepress"), Bethlehem ("house of bread").
  e. Deity or religious custom, as Beth-dagon (Josh. 15:41), Ashtaroth (Deut. 1:4), Bethshemesh ("sun temple," Josh. 19:22).
  f. Important historical events, as Ebenezer ("stone of help," I Sam. 7:12), Bethel ("house of God," Gen. 28:16-19).
  g. Connection with a person or tribe, as Gibeah-Saul (I Sam. 11:4), Dan (Jud. 18:29).
  h. Animals and plants, as Aijalon ("deer field"), Bethhoglah ("house of the partridge"), Valley of Elah ("oak" or "terebinth").

3. Divine names and titles

It was considered all-important to learn the name of the divine being who appeared to one (e.g., Jacob, Gen. 32:29, and Manoah, Jud. 13:6, 16-21). Knowing His names and titles, such as Yahweh, Elohim, and Lord, made God living and real to His people. Sometimes the very concept "name" of God stood for the person of God himself (Lev. 24:11, RSV; Mt. 12:21). To know and believe God's name or that of Christ is equivalent to knowing and believing in God or Christ Himself (Ps. 9:10; 91:14; Isa. 64:2; Mal. 3:16; Jn. 1:12; 2:23; 3:18; I Jn. 3:23; 5:13).

4. The name of Jesus

The early Christians placed no magical value on the name of Jesus but used it as their forefathers had employed the names of God in Old Testament times. Jesus had taught His disciples that to do something for His name's sake was to do it for Him (Mt. 19:29). His name represented His power and authority, e.g., in working miracles (Mt. 7:22; Acts 4:7, 10). People were exhorted to call on His name for salvation (Acts 2:21; 4:12), and sinners were justified in or through His name (I Cor. 6:11; Acts 10:43). The gospel was to be preached in His name (Lk. 24:47), and eternal life comes in or through His name (Jn. 20:31). Jesus instructed His followers to pray to the Father in his name, i.e., on His authority (Jn. 16:23-24). "The name" alone is even used to refer to the Lord Jesus Christ ("His name," Acts 5:41; III Jn. 7).

The Israelites were fond of playing on names. The name to them was a sign of something quite outward. Hence names rarely became hereditary in Hebrew; they still retained their significance, being proper personal names, seldom passing into the unmeaning surname. They generally expressed some personal characteristic, some incident connected with the birth, some hope or wish or prayer of the parent, and henceforth the child embodied it, and for the parents' sake felt it like a personal vow and made his life an effort to realize it. This tendency to play on names and find analogies or contrasts in them is seen throughout the Bible (Ruth 1:20; I Sam. 25:3, 25). So we have "Dan [*judge*] shall judge his people" (Gen. 49:16) and many other instances.

The meaning of baptism in the name of Jesus varies slightly according to the Greek preposition used. In acts 2:38 Peter exhorted the Jews to repent and be baptized in or upon (*epi*) the name of Jesus Christ, resting upon His authority and being devoted to Him. Later Peter instructed Cornelius to be baptized in (*en*) the name of Jesus Christ, acting on His authority. Three passages use *eis* (Mt. 28:19; Acts 8:16; 19:5) plus the parallel phrase "baptized into Christ" (Rom. 6:3; Gal. 3:27). A study of these verses along with the verb *baptizō* and *eis* in I Cor. 1:13; 10:2; 12:13 indicates that the one baptized is identified with Christ and passes into new ownership or partnership with Him, with new loyalty and fellowship.

III. The Principle of Names in Scripture

Names were given to reveal GOD's purpose in the lives of His people, as well as what their character was and was yet to be, also to help better understand passages of Scripture, whom without a proper understanding of a name you would miss an entire revelation.

   A. Passages where without a true understanding of a name we would miss the entire revelation GOD is bringing forth.

   1. Hosea 2:15-16 – "*And I will give her her vineyards from thence, and the valley of Achor for a door of hope: and she shall sing there, as in the days of her youth, and as in the day when she came up out of the land of Egypt. 16And it shall be at that day, saith the Lord, that thou shalt call me Ishi; and shalt call me no more Baali.*"

a. Achor means trouble – Valley of trouble is our door of hope.
b. Baali – My Lord; Ishi – My husband – A revelation of the bride's ultimate end.
c. Place also where Achan was stoned, Joshua 7:9-26 – Deliverance from Babylon

2. Psalms 84:6 – *"Who passing through the valley of Baca make it a well; the rain also filleth the pools."* Baca means weeping, valley of misery – All must go through this as part of our discipleship.
3. Revelation 1:9 – *"John, who also am your brother, and companion in tribulation, and in the kingdom and patience of Jesus Christ, was in the isle that is called Patmos, for the word of God, and for the testimony of Jesus Christ."* Patmos means my killing. In other words you miss the true revelation of GOD unless you are willing to die.
4. Matthew 26:36 – *"Then cometh Jesus with them unto a place called Gethsemane, and saith unto the disciples, Sit ye here, while I go and pray yonder."* We must first know what Gethsemane means to properly understand these passages. Gethsemane means – oil or olive press. The understanding here is simple – without being pressed out of measure (the olive crushed for oil or anointing could ever flow, II Corinthians 1:8)
5. Genesis 26:18-23 – Isaac is journeying here trying to find a place to dwell. They are digging up spiritual ground to release living water, but the revelation of the journey to do this is tremendously seen behind the definition of the names of the places.

a. Esek – Strife, oppression, contention
b. Sitnah – Accusation, hatred, root – to like in wait, to be an adversary
c. Rehoboth – wide streets, open spaces, roominess

Even though we dig them up and bring forth living water, many times this is what happens between brothers and sisters. We can't seek to strive and have hatred. We just need to keep digging until we reach Rehoboth or the place where the Lord makes room for us.

6. Deuteronomy 10:6-14 – This shows the dealings of GOD in the lives of His people as they journey. Here they journeyed from a place of wells

a. Beeroth – Wells

b. Mosera – Bonds

c. Aaron – Light, mountain of strength

d. Eleazar – God helps – We have to learn to depend on GOD to be our help

e. Gudgodah – The slashing place, cavern of thunder – This obviously speaks of God's judgments in our lives.

f. Jotbath – Place of goodness, a land of rivers of waters. Here GOD leads us from slashing to a place of goodness.

7. Bethany, Luke 24:50 – *"And he led them out as far as to Bethany, and he lifted up his hands, and blessed them."*

a. Bethany – House of affliction, house of response, house of figs. Here we see the place the Lord will lead us to: prosperity and affliction, his twofold dealings in our lives.

b. This twofold principle found in Scripture

1) Goodness and severity of God (Romans 11:22)

2) Jeremiah 18:1-6 – Two hands of God

3) *"I know both, how to be abased, and I know how to abound..."* Philippians 4:12

4) Ecclesiastes 7:14 –*"In the day of prosperity be joyful, but in the day of adversity consider: God also hath set the one over against the other, to the end that man should find nothing after him."*

I. In Scripture a Name Change Absolutely Had To Mean a Change in Nature or Character

This is such an amazing truth. As we study these different accounts, take courage in your own life, God may be giving you a new name representing a name in you, a name you realize only He can give. Just as God has many names or facets of His name, so does a man. Below is a list of some dramatic name changes in Scripture

1. Genesis 17:5 – Abram to Abraham

a. Abram – Exalted father, high lofty thinker, father of height

b.   Abraham – Father of a multitude, father of many nations, father of mercy.

2.   Genesis 32:28 – Jacob to Israel

   a.   Jacob – He will supplant, deceiver, one who trips up
   b.   Israel – Champion, prince, he will be a prince with God, soldier   of God, God will rule, ruling with God, a God ruled man.

3.   Esther 2:7 – Esther to Hadassah

   a.   Esther – Star, she that is hidden
   b.   Hadassah – Myrtle

4.   John 1:42 – Simon to Peter

   a.   Simon – Hearkening, hearing with acceptance
   b.   Peter – A stone, a rock

5.   Acts 13:9 – Saul to Paul

   a.   Saul – Asked for, demanded, to require
   b.   Paul – Little

6.   Genesis 41:45 – Joseph to Zaphnathpaaneah

   a.   Joseph – May God add, increasing, to add
   b.   Zaphnathpaaneah – Savior of the age, savior of the world, giver of the nourishment, revealer of a secret, concealed treasure, treasure of the glorious rest.

7.   Daniel 1:7 – Daniel to Belteshazzar

   a.   Daniel – Judge of God, one who delivers judgment in the name of God, he that judges
   b.   Belteshazzar – The Lord's leader, Lord of the straitened treasure, preserve his life

8.   Judges 6:32, 7:1 – Gideon to Jerubbaal

   a.   Gideon – Feller, one who cuts down he that bruises, great warrior

      b.   Jerubbaal – Baal strives, he will contend with Baal, Baal will be contended with. Baal will be taught

9.   Ruth 1:22-23 – Naomi to Mara

      a.   Naomi – Pleasant, agreeable, attractive, my joy, my bliss, grace, beauty, pleasantness of Jehovah
      b.   Mara – Bitterness, sad, he was arrogant, rebellious

10.   Hosea 2:16 – Baal to Ishi

      a.   Baal – Lord, owner, master, possessor, controller
      b.   Ishi – My husband, to dwell, to abide

11.   Genesis 35:18 – Benoni to Benjamin

      a.   Benoni – Son of my sorrow
      b.   Benjamin – Son of the right hand, son of old age

12.   Genesis 17:5 – Sarai to Sarah

      a.   Sarai – Contentious, quarrelsome
      b.   Sarah – Princess, noble woman, a ruler, to lead, to right

13.   II Samuel 6:2-8 – Baale to Perez-uzzah

      a.   Baale - Lord, master, possessor, controller of everything
      b.   Perez-uzzah – Breach (comes from a root word that means strength)

14.   II Samuel 12:24-25 – Solomon to Jedidiah

      a.   Solomon – Peaceable, his peace, peaceableness
      b.   Jedidiah – The beloved of Jehovah, Jehovah is a friend

15.   II Kings 24:17 – Mattaniah to Zedekiah

      a.   Mattaniah – Gift of Jehovah
      b.   Zedekiah – Jehovah is might, Jehovah is righteousness

Chapter 10
Symbolic Animals

I.   God Uses Them To Speak To Us

As we have already seen, God uses animals (beasts) in the Bible symbolically to speak precious and marvelous truths to us. Let's take a moment to review some of those passages then press on to the spiritual definition of each animal. Let's not forget (Proverbs 25:2) *"It is the glory of God to conceal a matter, and the honor of kings to search out a matter."*

Job 12:7-10 says, *"7But ask now the beasts, and they shall teach thee; and the fowls of the air, and they shall tell thee: 8Or speak to the earth, and it shall teach thee: and the fishes of the sea shall declare unto thee. 9Who knoweth not in all these that the hand of the Lord hath wrought this? 10In whose hand is the soul of every living thing, and the breath of all mankind."*

A.   Foundation Scriptures – Where we see God use animals symbolically

1.   Romans 1:20 – Invisible understood by visible animals
2.   Genesis 2:19-20 – (Names reveal character in this case the symbolic character of animals.)
3.   Acts 10:9-15 – Beasts
4.   I Corinthians 15:32 – Beasts
5.   I Timothy 5:17-18 – Ox
6.   Philippians 3:1-3 – Dogs
7.   Revelation 4:5-11 – Four Beasts
8.   Revelation 5:6-14 – The Lamb slain
9.   Proverbs 6:6-10 – The ant
10. Song 6:9 – Dove (bride)
11. Matthew 3:16 – dove, Holy Spirit
12. Psalms 32:8-9 – Mule, horse
13. II Kings 2:23-25 – Two she bears
14. Mark 4:4, 15 – Fowls
15. Proverbs 14:4 – Oxen
16. Mark 11:2-11 – Colt
17. Proverbs 30:24-31 – Different animals mentioned
18. Revelation 12:7-9 – Dragon
19. Psalms 103:5 – Eagle
20. Revelation 12:7 – Eagle - Overcomer
21. John 10:7-16 – Sheep
22. Psalms 42:1-2 – Deer
23. Proverbs 9:1-2 – Beasts

24. I Peter 5:8 – Devil as lion
25. Proverbs 28:1 – Righteous as lions (Proverbs 34:9-10)
26. Revelation 5:5 – Jesus the lion of Judah
27. Joel 4 and Joel 2:23 – Locusts
28. Psalms 102:6-10 – Pelican, sparrow, owl
29. Jeremiah 12:5 (Zechis) Revelation 6:1-8) – Horses
30. II Peter 2:22 – (Matthew 7:6) (Mark 5:11-16) – Swine
31. Job 40:15-24 – Behemoth
32. Job 41:1-34 – Leviathan (Isaiah 27:1)
33. Romans 3:13 – Asps (snakes)
34. Judges 14:1-9, 14 – Bees
35. Song of Solomon 2:9, 8:14 – Roe, Hurt (Hebrew – Buck or young stag)
36. Matthew 23:24, Matthew 19:24 – Camel
37. II Kings 6:25 – Doves dung
38. Matthew 25:31-46 – Division of sheep and goats
39. Matthew 10:29-31 – Sparrows

These passages are truly just the tip of the iceberg, when it comes to God using animals symbolically to teach us. They are however, enough to show us that animals need to be seen at least two ways in Scripture, as their natural creation and as a spiritual type of something else.

Chapter 11
Symbolism Of Colors

I. Symbolism Of Colors

This is a fascinating and wonderful subject to consider. If one can get a true, Biblical understanding of what colors represent, it can unveil and broaden the revelation of a passage of Scripture, subject or doctrine. Understanding colors and their symbolism is essential to any true Bible student or disciple. All theologians agree that colors almost always represent something other than themselves. So to find out what they symbolize, we must truly search the Scriptures to see if we can find the right revelation for each color mentioned. As you read many commentaries and dictionaries of the Bible, or the few who have actually written about it, you find great disagreement as to what they truly represent. That is why we must let the Bible interpret itself, and not approach it with pre-conceived ideas or personal theories. We must let the Scriptures reveal to us what they mean and nothing else. It is true that some colors have several different types associated with them. We will examine all of these and prove them by the Word. We do not need men's ideas of what a color should represent or symbolize. We just simply need the true Biblical account of each color and then apply this to our study. Understanding color and their symbolism is a great key to help open up the Word to us. Hidden deep within the Word of God is revelation, wanting to be revealed, by the use of colors. Every teacher, pastor, prophet, and student of any kind will derive great benefit as they learn how to apply the key of symbolic colors.

Color as an abstract idea or concept is spoken of rarely in Scripture. The most common word translated color means – eye, or appearance, or aspect. It expresses color in terms of comparison with some other material This general lack of color terminology in the Bible may be a result of God's commandment to the Hebrews not to make any graven image or idols (Exodus 20:24). The Hebrew's were never known as an artistic or art-loving people. It may be because of their background as an enslaved people contributed to their lack of artistic and color appreciation. Rather than specific coloration, a colors brightness or dimness, lightness or darkness, brilliance or somberness is more emphasized in the Bible. Shade, rather than hue seems to be considered more important by the Biblical writers. Individual colors mentioned in the Word fall into two major types, natural colors and artificial colors. Artificial colors, such as paints and dyes were used widely in the ancient world. In Babylonia, bricks were made in several different colors, some resulting from different kinds of clay and others from special manufacturing processes. The

Israelites had an advanced textile industry. They were skilled not only in weaving but also in dying. Since dyes were made from vegetable sources or from shellfish, quality control was difficult. The completed colors were often impure and inexact. These problems were compounded by the fact that many dyes were closely guarded family recipes that were sometimes lost or changed.

The following artificial colors are mentioned in the Bible. Purple was the most precious of ancient dyes. The dye itself was derived from shellfish found in the Mediterranean Sea. It took a total of 250,000 mollusks to make one ounce of dye, which accounts for its great price. It was highly valued in Israel. Blue was also derived from small shellfish found in the Mediterranean. Red, scarlet, and crimson existed in several shades and the dye was extracted from the bodies of insects. All of the other colors were natural.

A.   Hebrew definitions for color, colors

1.   *Pac* – the palm of the hand, or sole of the foot; by implication a long sleeved tunic of many breadths
2.   *Ayin* – an eye literally or figuratively, a fountain as the eye of the landscape
3.   *Riqmah* – marked by a variation of color, specifically embroidery
4.   *Puwk* – to paint or dye
5.   *Tala* – to cover with pieces

B.   Greek, *Prophasis* – an outward showing

C.   Other facts about colors

Colors are made use of in religious symbolism among the Jews and in the Christian church. Specific directions were given in the Old Testament for the colors to be used in the building of the Tabernacle and in the garments for the priests. Colors are also introduced in giving moral or spiritual lessons and in describing scenes in the book of Revelation, as well as in the description of Jesus' transfiguration, or in Joseph's "coat of many colors", and as in Jezebel "painted her eyes" (II Kings 9:30). It is especially important to note the use of colors in describing the appearance of God (Ezekiel 1-3). All of the many colors are used in the building of God's houses, the Tabernacle of Moses, Tabernacle of David, and in the Temple of Solomon. Colors are also widely used in the Song of Solomon in describing the bridegroom and the bride. But the book of Revelation holds a wide degree of description of colors in defining Mystery Babylon, the church in the last days, and the future New Jerusalem. An understanding then of the symbolism of colors is essential to the understanding of these passages of Scripture. They carry with them great revelational truths. By applying this key of symbolism of colors, we then can come to have a greater and deeper revelation of the Word, and of God Himself. We will now look at all the colors mentioned in the Bible.

D.   Scriptures showing importance of understanding the symbolism of colors

1.   Isaiah 54:11 – *"O thou afflicted, tossed with tempest, and not comforted, behold, I will lay thy stones with fair colours, and lay thy foundations with sapphires."*

2.   Genesis 37:3, 23, 32 – *"Now Israel loved Joseph more than all his children, because he was the son of his old age: and he made him a coat of many colours."*

3.   II Samuel 13:18-19 – *"And she had a garment of divers colours upon her: for with such robes were the king's daughters that were virgins apparelled..."*

4.   I Chronicles 29:2 – *"Now I have prepared with all my might for the house of my God the gold for things to be made of gold, and the silver for things of silver, and the brass for things of brass, the iron for things of iron, and wood for things of wood; onyx stones, and stones to be set, glistering stones, and of divers colours, and all manner of precious stones, and marble stones in abundance."*

5.   Ezekiel 16:16 – *"And of thy garments thou didst take, and deckedst thy high places with divers colours, and playedst the harlot thereupon..."*

6.   Ezekiel 17:3 – *"...Thus saith the Lord GOD; A great eagle with great wings, longwinged, full of feathers, which had divers colours, came unto Lebanon..."*

7.   Ezekiel 1:4, 7, 16, 22, 27

8.   Ezekiel 8:2 – *"Then I beheld, and lo a likeness as the appearance of fire: from the appearance of his loins even downward, fire; and from his loins even upward, as the appearance of brightness, as the colour of amber."*

9.   Daniel 10:6 – *"His body also was like the beryl, and his face as the appearance of lightning, and his eyes as lamps of fire, and his arms and his feet like in colour to polished brass, and the voice of his words like the voice of a multitude."*

10. Revelation 17:4 – *"And the woman was arrayed in purple and scarlet colour, and decked with gold and precious stones and*

pearls, having a golden cup in her hand full of abominations and filthiness of her fornication:"

11. Jeremiah 4:30 – *"And when thou art spoiled, what wilt thou do? Though thou clothest thyself with crimson, though thou deckest thee with ornaments of gold, though thou rentest thy face with painting, in vain shalt thou make thyself fair; thy lovers will despise thee, they will seek thy life."*

12. Revelation 21:10-23 – New Jerusalem

E. Other Scriptures translated differently but are also translated color

1. Psalms 45:14 – *"She shall be brought unto the king in <u>raiment</u> of needlework.."*

2. Ezekiel 16:10, 13, 18 – *"I clothed thee also with <u>broidered work</u>..."*

3. Ezekiel 26:16 – *"...and put off their <u>broidered</u> garments: they shall clothe themselves with trembling; they shall sit upon the ground, and shall tremble at every moment, and be astonished at thee."*

4. Ezekiel 27:7, 16, 24 – *"Fine linen with <u>broidered work</u> from Egypt was that which thou spreadest forth to be thy sail..."*

5. Joshua 9:5 – *"And old shoes and <u>clouted upon</u> their feet, and old garments upon them; and all the bread of their provision was dry and mouldy."*

6. John 15:22 – *"...but now they have no <u>cloke</u> for their sin."*

7. Mark 12:40 – *"Which devour widows' houses, and for a <u>pretence</u> make long prayers: these shall receive greater damnation."*

8. I Thessalonians 2:5 – *"For neither at any time used we flattering words, as ye know, nor a <u>cloke</u> of covetousness; God is witness:"*

9. Philippians 1:18 – *"...notwithstanding, every way, whether in <u>pretence</u>, or in truth, Christ is preached; and I therein do rejoice, yea, and will rejoice."*

II. Colors in the Bible

A. **Green** – Life, prosperity

1. Hebrew definition – the color of vegetative life
2. Dictionary definition – color of growing foliage, between yellow and blue in the spectrum, full of life and vigor

3. Jeremiah 17:7-8 – *"Blessed is the man that trusteth in the LORD, and whose hope the LORD is. For he shall be as a tree planted by the waters, and that spreadeth out her roots by the river, and shall not see when heat cometh, but her leaf shall be green; and shall not be careful in the year of drought, neither shall cease from yielding fruit."*

4. Psalms 52:8 – *"But I am like a green olive tree in the house of God..."*

5. Song of Solomon 2:13 – *"The fig tree putteth forth her green figs..."*

6. Psalms 92:14 – Other translation – *"...they shall be full of sap and green"*

7. Psalms 23:2 – *"He maketh me to lie down in green pastures..."*

8. Genesis 1:30 – *"...I have given every green herb for meat..."* (Gen. 9:30)

9. Jeremiah 11:16 – *"The LORD called thy name, A green olive tree, fair, and of goodly fruit..."*

10. Song of Solomon 1:16 – *"Behold, thou art fair, my beloved, yea, pleasant: also our bed is green."*

B. **Silver** – Redemption

1. Leviticus 27:3-6, 13 – *"...even thy estimation shall be fifty shekels of silver...But if he will at all redeem it, then he shall add a fifth part thereof unto thy estimation."*

2. Numbers 3:44-51 – *"...And Moses gave the money of them that were redeemed unto Aaron and to his sons, according to the word of the LORD..."*

3. Matthew 26:15 – *"And said unto them, What will ye give me, and I will deliver him unto you? And they covenanted with him for thirty pieces of silver."*

4. Leviticus 5:15-17 – *"If a soul commit a trespass, and sin through ignorance, in the holy things of the LORD; then he shall bring for his trespass unto the LORD a ram without blemish out of the flocks, with thy estimation by shekels of silver..."*

5. Exodus 30:11-16

6. Genesis 44:2 – *"And put my cup, the silver cup, in the sack's mouth of the youngest, and his corn money. And he did according to the word that Joseph had spoken."*

C. **Blue** – Heaven, heavenly things

1. Dictionary definition – the pure color of a clear sky; the hue between green and violet in the spectrum
2. Exodus 24:10 – *"And they saw the God of Israel: and there was under his feet as it were a paved work of a sapphire stone, and as it were the body of heaven in his clearness."* Sapphire is a deep blue
3. Exodus 28:1-5 – The high priest wore an outer garment of solid blue over his white robe. He was the mediator between earthly and heavenly things
4. Ezekiel 10:1 – *"Then I looked, and, behold, in the firmament that was above the head of the cherubims there appeared over them as it were a sapphire stone..."*
5. Ezekiel 1:26 – *"And above the firmament that was over their heads was the likeness of a throne, as the appearance of a sapphire stone..."*
6. Exodus 26:1, 31-33
7. Numbers 15:37-40 - Israel wore a border of blue on their clothes to encourage them to remember the Lord in heaven, and the commandments that come to them from heaven. This was also to help them remember they had a heavenly walk and they needed to balance their natural life with it.

D. **Grey** – Maturity, honor, experience, old age

1. It is the same word in Hebrew that is translated "hoary"
2. Dictionary definition – a color between white and black; a neutral hue
3. Proverbs 20:29 – *"...and the beauty of old men is the gray head."*
4. Psalms 71:18 – *"Now also when I am old and grayheaded, O God, forsake me not; until I have shewed thy strength unto this generation, and thy power to every one that is to come."*
5. Proverbs 16:31 – *"The hoary head is a crown of glory..."*
6. Job 15:10 – *"With us are both the grayheaded and very aged men, much elder than thy father."*
7. Isaiah 46:4 – *"And even to your old age I am he; and even to hoar hairs will I carry you: I have made, and I will bear; even I will carry, and will deliver you."*
8. Leviticus 19:32 – *"Thou shalt rise up before the hoary head, and honour the face of the old man, and fear thy God: I am the LORD."*
9. I Samuel 12:1-2

E. **Brown** – That which is of the earth, flesh

    1. Hebrew definition – to be warm, sunburnt, or swarthy (black)
    2. Dictionary definition – a dark shade with a yellowish, reddish hue
    3. Genesis 30:32-35
    4. Genesis 30:40 – *"And Jacob did separate the lambs, and set the faces of the flocks toward the ringstraked, and all the brown in the flock of Laban; and he put his own flocks by themselves, and put them not unto Laban's cattle."*

F. **Red, Scarlet, Crimson** – Sacrifice, suffering, blood

    1. Dictionary definition – any of various colors, resembling the color of blood
    2. Numbers 19:2 – *"...that they bring thee a red heifer without spot, wherein is no blemish, and upon which never came yoke:"*
    3. Exodus 25:5 – *"And rams' skins dyed red, and badgers' skins, and shittim wood,"*
    4. Hebrews 9:19 – *"For when Moses had spoken every precept to all the people according to the law, he took the blood of calves and of goats, with water, and scarlet wool, and hyssop, and sprinkled both the book, and all the people,"*
    5. Matthew 27:28 – *"And they stripped him, and put on him a scarlet robe."*
    6. Leviticus 14:4-5 – *"Then shall the priest command to take for him that is to be cleansed two birds alive and clean, and cedar wood, and scarlet, and hyssop..."*

    7. Blood (red)

        a. Revelation 1:5 – *"And from Jesus Christ, who is the faithful witness...Unto him that loved us, and washed us from our sins in his own blood,"*
        b. Revelation 7:14 – *"...and made them white in the blood of the Lamb."*
        c. Hebrews 9:22 – *"And almost all things are by the law purged with blood; and without shedding of blood is no remission."*
        d. Exodus 12:5-7 – *"Your lamb shall be without blemish...And they shall take of the blood, and strike it on*

the two side posts and on the upper door post of the houses, wherein they shall eat it."

    e.   Exodus 12:23 – *"For the LORD will pass through to smite the Egyptians; and when he seeth the blood upon the lintel, and on the two side posts, the LORD will pass over the door, and will not suffer the destroyer to come in unto your houses to smite you."*

G. **Purple** – Royalty, majesty, wealth

    1.   Dictionary definition – any color intermediate between red and blue; symbol of imperial, royal or other high rank

    2.   Other facts

        a.   Canaan (land of our inheritance) means land of purple.
        b.   In Bible times, purple dye was expensive and was worn only by those of high rank.

    3.   Judges 8:26 – *"And the weight of the golden earrings that he requested was a thousand and seven hundred shekels of gold; beside ornaments, and collars, and purple raiment that was on the kings of Midian, and beside the chains that were about their camels' necks."*

    4.   Luke 16:19 – *"There was a certain rich man, which was clothed in purple and fine linen, and fared sumptuously every day:"*

    5.   Esther 8:15 – *"And Mordecai went out from the presence of the king in royal apparel of blue and white, and with a great crown of gold, and with a garment of fine linen and purple..."*

    6.   Song of Solomon 7:5 – *"Thine head upon thee is like Carmel, and the hair of thine head like purple; the king is held in the galleries."*

    7.   Song of Solomon 3:9-10 – *"King Solomon made himself a chariot of the wood of Lebanon. He made the pillars thereof of silver, the bottom thereof of gold, the covering of it of purple..."*

    8.   Proverbs 31:22, 25 – *"She maketh herself coverings of tapestry; her clothing is silk and purple...Strength and honour are her clothing..."*

    9.   John 19:2, 5 – *"And the soldiers platted a crown of thorns, and put it on his head, and they put on him a purple robe...Then came Jesus forth, wearing the crown of thorns, and the purple robe. And Pilate saith unto them, Behold the man!"*

H. **Black** – Judgment, darkness, famine, sin or that which is unredeemed in us

1. Hebrew definition – dusky, to be dim or dark in color; ashy dark colored
2. Dictionary definition – lacking hue or brightness, absorbing light without reflecting any of the rays composing it

3. Scriptures for judgment

   a. Jude 13 – "*Raging waves of the sea, foaming out their own shame; wandering stars, to whom is reserved the blackness of darkness for ever.*"
   b. Jeremiah 4:28 – "*For this shall the earth mourn, and the heavens above be black: because I have spoken it, I have purposed it, and will not repent...*"
   c. Jeremiah 14:2 – "*Judah mourneth, and the gates thereof languish; they are black unto the ground; and the cry of Jerusalem is gone up.*"
   d. Zechariah 6:2, 6 – "*In the first chariot were red horses; and in the second chariot black horses...The black horses which are therein go forth into the north country...*"
   e. Revelation 6:5, 12 – "*And when he had opened the third seal, I heard the third beast say, Come and see. And I beheld, and lo a black horse; and he that sat on him had a pair of balances in his hand...And I beheld when he had opened the sixth seal, and, lo, there was a great earthquake; and the sun became black as sackcloth of hair, and the moon became as blood;*"
   f. Nahum 2:10 – "*She is empty, and void, and waste: and the heart melteth, and the knees smite together, and much pain is in all loins, and the faces of them all gather blackness.*"
   g. Isaiah 50:3 – "*I clothe the heavens with blackness, and I make sackcloth their covering.*"
   h. Joel 2:6 – "*Before their face the people shall be much pained: all faces shall gather blackness.*"

4. Scriptures for darkness or total deception

   a. Proverbs 7:9 – "*In the twilight, in the evening, in the black and dark night:*"

b. Jude 8-13 – *"Likewise also these filthy dreamers defile the flesh, despise dominion, and speak evil of dignities...to whom is reserved the blackness of darkness for ever."*

5. Scripture for sin or that which is unredeemed in us

    a. Song of Solomon 1:5-6 – *"I am black, but comely, O ye daughters of Jerusalem, as the tents of Kedar, as the curtains of Solomon. Look not upon me, because I am black, because the sun hath looked upon me..."*

6. Scriptures for famine

    a. Revelation 6:5-6 – *"And when he had opened the third seal, I heard the third beast say, Come and see. And I beheld, and lo a black horse; and he that sat on him had a pair of balances in his hand. And I heard a voice in the midst of the four beasts say, A measure of wheat for a penny, and three measures of barley for a penny..."*

    b. Lamentations 5:10 – *"Our skin was black like an oven because of the terrible famine."*

    c. Jeremiah 14:2 – *"Judah mourneth, and the gates thereof languish; they are black unto the ground; and the cry of Jerusalem is gone up."*

    d. Lamentations 4:8 – *"Their visage is blacker than a coal; they are not known in the streets: their skin cleaveth to their bones; it is withered, it is become like a stick."*

I. **White** – Purity, holiness, righteousness

1. Dictionary definition – the color of pure snow; reflecting nearly all the rays of sunlight

2. Scriptures for purity

    a. Daniel 12:10 – *"Many shall be purified, and made white, and tried..."*

    b. Ecclesiastes 9:8 – *"Let thy garments be always white; and let thy head lack no ointment."*

    c. Isaiah 1:18 – *"Come now, and let us reason together, saith the LORD: though your sins be as scarlet, they shall be as white as snow..."*

    d. Revelation 7:13-14 – *"...What are these which are arrayed in white robes? and whence came they?...These* are they which came out of great tribulation, and have washed their robes, and made them white in the blood of the Lamb."

e. Psalms 51:7 – *"Purge me with hyssop, and I shall be clean: wash me, and I shall be whiter than snow."*

3. Scriptures for holiness

a. Matthew 17:2 – *"And was transfigured before them: and his face did shine as the sun, and his raiment was white as the light."*

b. Daniel 7:9 – *"I beheld till the thrones were cast down, and the Ancient of days did sit, whose garment was white as snow..."*

c. Song of Solomon 5:10 – *"My beloved is white and ruddy, the chiefest among ten thousand."*

d. Revelation 1:14 – *"His head and his hairs were white like wool, as white as snow; and his eyes were as a flame of fire;"*

e. Revelation 20:11 – *"And I saw a great white throne, and him that sat on it, from whose face the earth and the heaven fled away..."*

4. Scriptures for righteousness

a. Revelation 19:8 – *"And to her was granted that she should be arrayed in fine linen, clean and white: for the fine linen is the righteousness of saints."*

b. Revelation 19:14 – *"And the armies which were in heaven followed him upon white horses, clothed in fine linen, white and clean."*

c. Revelation 6:11 – *"And white robes were given unto every one of them..."*

d. John 20:12 – *"And seeth two angels in white sitting, the one at the head, and the other at the feet, where the body of Jesus had lain."*

e. Acts 1:10 – *"And while they looked stedfastly toward heaven as he went up, behold, two men stood by them in white apparel;"*

J. **Yellow** – Sickness, sin, glory and the divine nature (Gold)

1. Hebrew definition – golden, to glitter, sallow color of sick skin

2. Leviticus 13:30, 32, 36, 49 – *"Then the priest shall see the plague: and behold, if it be in sight deeper than the skin; and there be in it a yellow thin hair; then the priest shall pronounce him unclean: it is a dry scall, even a leprosy upon the head or beard..."*

3. Psalms 68:13 – *"Though ye have lien among the pots, yet shall ye be as the wings of a dove covered with silver, and her feathers with yellow gold."*

4. **Gold** – God's divine nature or character

   a. Revelation 1:13 – *"And in the midst of the seven candlesticks one like unto the Son of man, clothed with a garment down to the foot, and girt about the paps with a golden girdle."*

   b. Revelation 8:3 – *"And another angel came and stood at the altar, having a golden censer; and there was given unto him much incense, that he should offer it with the prayers of all saints upon the golden altar which was before the throne."*

   c. Exodus 28:34 – *"A golden bell and a pomegranate, a golden bell and a pomegranate, upon the hem of the robe round about."*

   d. Revelation 21:21 – *"And the twelve gates were twelve pearls; every several gate was of one pearl: and the street of the city was pure gold, as it were transparent glass."*

   e. Revelation 3:18 – *"I counsel thee to buy of me gold tried in the fire, that thou mayest be rich..."*

   f. Song of Solomon 5:11, 14-15 – *"His head is as the most fine gold, his locks are bushy, and black as a raven..."*

   g. Psalms 45:9, 13 – *"Kings' daughters were among thy honourable women: upon thy right hand did stand the queen in gold of Ophir...The king's daughter is all glorious within: her clothing is of wrought gold."*

   h. Exodus 25:11-39

   i. I Peter 1:7 – *"That the trial of your faith, being much more precious than of gold that perisheth, though it be tried with fire, might be found unto praise and honour and glory at the appearing of Jesus Christ:"*

K. **Amber** – The glow of God, the glory of God, the brilliance of His presence, God's fire, the brightness of God.

    1.   Hebrew word, *Chashmal* – bronze or polished spectrum metal; it is important to note this word is of uncertain derivation.

    2.   Amber is a brilliant glowing yellow

    3.   Ezekiel 1:4 – "*And I looked, and, behold, a whirlwind came out of the north, a great cloud, and a fire infolding itself, and a brightness was about it, and out of the midst thereof as the colour of amber, out of the midst of the fire.*" – It appears amber is the color of fire. Other translations:

"*...out of the midst...a glowing metal...*"
"*...in the midst of the fire...a gleaming bronze...*"

Ezekiel's visions concerning the color amber are all related specifically to the glory of God. It is the color of the glory. Also, Ezekiel's vision as related to the color amber relates more directly to the fire of God. However, it must be said that the fire of God is tied very heavily to the glory of God to the point where it is hard to discern much difference between the two.

    4.   Ezekiel 1:27 – "*And I saw as the colour of amber, as the appearance of fire round about within it...I saw as it were the appearance of fire, and it had brightness round about.*"

    5.   Ezekiel 8:2 – "*Then I beheld, and lo a likeness as the appearance of fire...as the appearance of brightness, as the colour of amber.*"

L. **Vermilion** – A false covering

    1.   Hebrew word, *Shasher* – red ochre (from its piercing color); It is a dyed red paint probably an oxide of iron

    2.   Jeremiah 22:14 – "*That saith, I will build me a wide house and large chambers, and cutteth him out windows; and it is cieled with cedar, and painted with vermilion.*"

    3.   Ezekiel 23:14 – "*And that she increased her whoredoms: for when she saw men pourtrayed upon the wall, the images of the Chaldeans pourtrayed with vermilion,*"

M. **Pale** – Death, hell, shame

    1.   The Hebrew word means – to blanch as with shame

2. The Greek word means – greenish, pale; It is the color of greenish grey, the color of a corpse.
3. Isaiah 29:22 – *"Therefore thus saith the LORD, who redeemed Abraham, concerning the house of Jacob, Jacob shall not now be ashamed, neither shall his face now wax pale."*
4. Revelation 6:8 – *"And I looked, and behold a pale horse: and his name that sat on him was Death, and Hell followed with him. And power was given unto them over the fourth part of the earth, to kill with sword, and with hunger, and with death, and with the beasts of the earth."*

N. **Bay** – Spirits wandering over creation in the last days

1. The Hebrew word means – a strong color (red)
2. It was the fourth horse – four is the number of creation
3. Zechariah 6:3, 7 – *"...in the fourth chariot grisled and bay horses...And the bay went forth, and sought to go that they might walk to and fro through the earth: and he said, Get you hence, walk to and fro through the earth. So they walked to and fro through the earth."*

O. **Grisled** – Judgment on creation

1. The Hebrew word means spotted with hail, white spots
2. It was the fourth chariot – four is the number of creation
3. Genesis 31:10, 12 – *"And it came to pass at the time that the cattle conceived, that I lifted up mine eyes, and saw in a dream, and, behold, the rams which leaped upon the cattle were ringstraked, speckled, and grisled...And he said, Lift up now thine eyes, and see, all the rams which leap upon the cattle are ringstraked, speckled, and grisled: for I have seen all that Laban doeth unto thee."*
4. Zechariah 6:3 – *"And in the third chariot white horses; and in the fourth chariot grisled and bay horses...and the grisled go forth toward the south country."*

III. The Rainbow

As we study this beautiful truth, I pray that your heart, as mine has been, will be overwhelmed with joy!

A. What is it?

1. Two things required for a rainbow – sun and water

92

2. It is an arch of colors in the sky caused by light passing through moisture in the air. It happens when the sun's rays are refracted through rain at different angles and so producing different prismatic colors.
3. The most important reference in Scripture to the rainbow is found in Genesis 9, the story of Noah after the flood of judgment.

4. Colors found in the rainbow are:

    a. Red – suffering, sacrifice, blood
    b. Orange – the divine nature of God
    c. Yellow – the glory of God
    d. Green – life, prosperity
    e. Blue – all things heavenly
    f. Violet – royalty, honor (purple)

The rainbow represents (especially in its first Biblical reference) and serves as a sign of God's covenant with Noah and the human race. This covenant was a promise by God to the world that it would never again be destroyed by a flood. The rain clouds and the rainbow were never again to be regarded by man as a threat of ultimate judgment, but as an unchanging indicator of God's mercy. All the references found in Scripture concerning the rainbow symbolize God's mercy over judgment. It is also a sign of the glorious presence of God. The rainbow is a symbol of God's faithfulness and mercy. It is a symbol of hope and God's bright emblem to the world of mercy and love. Remember this is all the more true as a symbol because it was reflected from the storm of judgment itself.

B. The Scriptures concerning the rainbow

1. Genesis 6:11-22, 7:4-7, 11, 12, 16-24, 8:1-13, 20-22, 9:9-17
2. Ezekiel 1:25-28
3. Isaiah 54:1-10
4. Matthew 24:27-39
5. Revelation 4:1-5
6. Revelation 10:1-11

Chapter 12
Symbolism Of Directions

I.   Directions Are Important To God

    A.   God gives direction for our lives. God wants us to be going somewhere.

        1.   I Corinthians 9:26 – *"I therefore so run, not as uncertainly; so fight I, not as one that beateth the air:"*
        2.   Psalms 37:23 – *"The steps of a good man are ordered by the LORD..."*
        3.   Acts 2:40 – *"...Save yourselves from this untoward generation."*
        3.   II Kings 7:3 – *"...Why sit we here until we die?"*
        4.   Deuteronomy 2:3 – *"Ye have compassed this mountain long enough: turn you northward."*
        5.   Psalms 107:4 – *"They wandered in the wilderness in a solitary way; they found no city to dwell in."*
        6.   Genesis 16:7-9 – *"And the angel of the LORD found her by a fountain of water in the wilderness, by the fountain in the way to Shur. And he said, Hagar, Sarai's maid, whence camest thou? and whither wilt thou go? And she said, I flee from the face of my mistress Sarai. And the angel of the LORD said unto her, Return to thy mistress, and submit thyself under her hands."*

God knows where we are coming from and where we are going. For many people, they need to know and deal with first where they came from before they can know where they are going.

    B.   Direction is not in man

        1.   Jeremiah 10:23 – *"O LORD, I know that the way of man is not in himself: it is not in man that walketh to direct his steps."*
        2.   Luke 6:39 – *"And he spake a parable unto them, Can the blind lead the blind? Shall they not both fall into the ditch?"*

    C.   Where does God want us to be going?

        1.   Philippians 3:14 – *"I press toward the mark for the prize of the high calling of God in Christ Jesus."*
        2.   Hebrews 6:1 – *"...let us go on unto perfection..."*
        3.   Song of Solomon 2:10 – *"My beloved spake, and said unto me, Rise up, my love, my fair one, and come away."*

4. Revelation 4:1 – *"After this I looked, and, behold, a door was opened in heaven: and the first voice which I heard was as it were of a trumpet talking with me; which said, Come up hither..."*
5. Matthew 26:36-46 – *"...Rise, let us be going..."*
6. Hebrews 13:13 – *"Let us go forth therefore unto him without the camp, bearing his reproach."*

II. Symbolic Directions In Scripture

A. **East** – Coming of the Lord; Place of God's glory

1. Numbers 3:38 – *"But those that encamp before the tabernacle toward the east, even before the tabernacle of the congregation eastward, shall be Moses, and Aaron and his sons, keeping the charge of the sanctuary for the charge of the children of Israel..."*
2. Matthew 2:2 – *"Saying, Where is he that is born King of the Jews? for we have seen his star in the east, and are come to worship him."*
3. Matthew 24:27 – *"For as the lightning cometh out of the east, and shineth even unto the west; so shall also the coming of the Son of man be."*
4. Revelation 7:2 – *"And I saw another angel ascending from the east, having the seal of the living God..."*
5. Ezekiel 43:1-2 – *"Afterward he brought me to the gate, even the gate that looketh toward the east: And, behold, the glory of the God of Israel came from the way of the east..."*
6. Genesis 3:24 – *"So he drove out the man; and he placed at the east of the garden of Eden Cherubims, and a flaming sword which turned every way, to keep the way of the tree of life."*

A. **North** – Judgment; Place of God's Throne

1. Judgment

   a. Jeremiah 50:3 – *"For out of the north there cometh up a nation against her, which shall make her land desolate..."*
   b. Jeremiah 50:9, 41 – *"...I will raise and cause to come up against Babylon an assembly of great nations from the north country..."*
   c. Jeremiah 4:6 – *"Set up the standard toward Zion: retire, stay not: for I will bring evil from the north, and a great destruction."*

    d.   Jeremiah 6:22 – *"Thus saith the LORD, Behold, a people cometh from the north country, and a great nation shall be raised from the sides of the earth."*

    e.   Jeremiah 6:1 – *"O ye children of Benjamin, gather yourselves to flee out of the midst of Jerusalem...for evil appeareth out of the north, and great destruction."*

    f.   Job 26:7 – *"He stretcheth out the north over the empty place, and hangeth the earth upon nothing."*

    g.   Isaiah 14:31 – *"Howl, O gate; cry, O city; thou, whole Palestina, art dissolved: for there shall come from the north a smoke..."*

2.   Place of God's Throne

    a.   Isaiah 14:12-13 – *"How art thou fallen from heaven, O Lucifer, son of the morning! how art thou cut down to the ground, which didst weaken the nations! For thou hast said in thine heart, I will ascend into heaven, I will exalt my throne above the stars of God: I will sit also upon the mount of the congregation, in the sides of the north:"*

    b.   Psalms 75:6-7 – *"For promotion cometh neither from the east, nor from the west, nor from the south. But God is the judge: he putteth down one, and setteth up another."*

    c.   Psalms 48:2 – *"Beautiful for situation, the joy of the whole earth, is mount Zion, on the sides of the north, the city of the great King."*

C.   **South** – Blessing; Refreshing; Prosperity

1.   Numbers 13:17-18, 27 – *"...Moses sent them to spy out the land of Canaan, and said unto them, Get you up this way southward, and go up into the mountain: And see the land, what it is...And they told him, and said, We came unto the land whither thou sentest us, and surely it floweth with milk and honey; and this is the fruit of it."*

2.   Luke 12:55 – *"And when ye see the south wind blow, ye say, There will be heat; and it cometh to pass."*

3.   Psalms 126:4 – *"Turn again our captivity, O LORD, as the streams in the south."*

4.   Job 37:17 – *"How thy garments are warm, when he quieteth the earth by the south wind?"*

5.   Song of Solomon 4:16 – *"Awake, O north wind; and come, thou south; blow upon my garden, that the spices thereof may flow*

out. Let my beloved come into his garden, and eat his pleasant fruits."

D. **West** – Darkness; Backsliding (i.e. moving away from the Lord)

1. Psalms 104:19-23 – "*He appointed the moon for seasons: the sun knoweth his going down. Thou makest darkness, and it is night: wherein all the beasts of the forest do creep forth. The young lions roar after their prey, and seek their meat from God. The sun ariseth, they gather themselves together, and lay them down in their dens. Man goeth forth unto his work and to his labour until the evening.*"
2. Psalms 103:12 – "*As far as the east is from the west, so far hath he removed our transgressions from us.*"
3. Matthew 24:27 – "*For as the lightning cometh out of the east, and shineth even unto the west; so shall also the coming of the Son of man be.*"

E. **Up** – Ascending in God

1. Isaiah 37:31 – "*And the remnant that is escaped of the house of Judah shall again take root downward, and bear fruit upward:*"
2. Genesis 13:1 – "*And Abram went up out of Egypt...*"
3. Revelation 12:5 – "*And she brought forth a man child, who was to rule all nations with a rod of iron: and her child was caught up unto God, and to his throne.*"

F. **Down** – Humility (i.e. abasing oneself); Spiritual decline; Judgment

1. Humility (i.e. abasing oneself)

   a. Psalms 116:6 – "*The LORD preserveth the simple: I was brought low, and he helped me.*"
   b. Revelation 5:8 – "*And when he had taken the book, the four beasts and four and twenty elders fell down before the Lamb, having every one of them harps, and golden vials full of odours, which are the prayers of saints.*"
   c. I John 3:16 – "*Hereby perceive we the love of God, because he laid down his life for us: and we ought to lay down our lives for the brethren.*"

2. Spiritual decline

        a.   Luke 10:30-37 – *"And Jesus answering said, A certain man went down from Jerusalem to Jericho, and fell among thieves, which stripped him of his raiment, and wounded him, and departed, leaving him half dead..."*

        b.   Job 33:24 – *"Then he is gracious unto him, and saith, Deliver him from going down to the pit: I have found a ransom."*

3.   Judgment

        a.   Isaiah 14:14-15 – *"I will ascend above the heights of the clouds; I will be like the most High. Yet thou shalt be brought down to hell, to the sides of the pit."*

        b.   Luke 10:15 – *"And thou, Capernaum, which art exalted to heaven, shalt be thrust down to hell."*

        c.   II Peter 2:4 – *"For if God spared not the angels that sinned, but cast them down to hell, and delivered them into chains of darkness, to be reserved unto judgment;"*

G.   **Forward** – Growth; Vision; Direction

1.   Exodus 14:15 – *"And the LORD said unto Moses, Wherefore criest thou unto me? speak unto the children of Israel, that they go forward:"*

2.   Ezekiel 1:12 – *"And they went every one straight forward: whither the spirit was to go, they went; and they turned not when they went."*

3.   III John 6 – *"Which have borne witness of thy charity before the church: whom if thou bring forward on their journey after a godly sort, thou shalt do well:"*

H.   **Back** – Backsliding

1.   Hebrews 10:38-39 – *"Now the just shall live by faith: but if any man draw back, my soul shall have no pleasure in him. But we are not of them who draw back unto perdition; but of them that believe to the saving of the soul."*

2.   Proverbs 14:14 – *"The backslider in heart shall be filled with his own ways..."*

3.   Lamentations 1:8 – *"Jerusalem hath grievously sinned; therefore she is removed: all that honoured her despise her, because they have seen her nakedness: yea, she sigheth, and turneth backward."*

I.   **Straight** – Spiritual purity; Having direction; Going on with God

1. Hebrews 12:13 – *"And make straight paths for your feet, lest that which is lame be turned out of the way; but let it rather be healed."*
2. Ezekiel 1:9 – *"Their wings were joined one to another; they turned not when they went; they went every one straight forward."*
3. Ecclesiastes 1:15 – *"That which is crooked cannot be made straight..."*
4. Ecclesiastes 7:13 – *"Consider the work of God: for who can make that straight, which he hath made crooked?"*
5. Isaiah 45:2 – *"I will go before thee, and make the crooked places straight: I will break in pieces the gates of brass, and cut in sunder the bars of iron:"*

J.   **Right** – Blessed; Special; Chosen; Strength

1. Genesis 48:8-20
2. Psalms 98:1 – *"O sing unto the LORD a new song; for he hath done marvelous things: his right hand, and his holy arm, hath gotten him the victory."*
3. Psalms 118:15-16 – *"The voice of rejoicing and salvation is in the tabernacles of the righteous: the right hand of the LORD doeth valiantly. The right hand of the LORD is exalted: the right hand of the LORD doeth valiantly."*
4. Genesis 35:16-18 – *"...but his father called him Benjamin (son of my right hand)."*
5. Psalms 16:11 – *"Thou wilt shew me the path of life: in thy presence is fulness of joy; at thy right hand there are pleasures for evermore."*
6. Song of Solomon 2:6 – *"...and his right hand doth embrace me."*

K.   **Left** – Judgment

1. Song of Solomon 2:6 – *"His left hand is under my head..."*
2. Matthew 25:33 – *"...he shall set the sheep on his right hand, but the goats on the left."*
3. Ecclesiastes 10:2 – *"...a fool's heart at his left."*
4. Job 23:9 – *"On the left hand, where he doth work, but I cannot behold him..."*

Chapter 13
Biblical Numerics

The study of numbers in the Scriptures is both enlightening and deep as well as fun. Once you understand that most numbers have not only a numerical value as well as a revelation behind them, it will change your Bible study forever. Some portions of Scripture could never fully be understood, that is, in their deepest revelation without this key to Bible interpretation. This study, along with an understanding of the colors, names, objects, man-made and natural, will add great meaning and depth to any passage of scripture. This chapter on Bible numbers has been carefully researched and prepared to aid every Bible student and seeker of God in their pursuit of the Lord, and their understanding of His great ways. I have compared this book with others to make sure I was somewhat on a similar path. However, there are numbers here that will be found in no other publication on this subject.

I.   The Significance Of Numbers

    A.   The Bible reveals God to be a God of numbers

        1.   Psalm 147:4 – *"He telleth the number of the stars; he calleth them all by their names."* God knows the exact number of stars in the infinite space.

        2.   Luke 12:6-7 – *"⁶Are not five sparrows sold for two farthings, and not one of them is forgotten before God? ⁷But even the very hairs of your head are all numbered. Fear not therefore: ye are of more value than many sparrows."* God knows the number of hairs on the head of every human being that has ever lived. Does that seem like a trivial thing to you? He even counts and knows the number of birds there are.

        3.   Daniel 5:26 – *"This is the interpretation of the thing: MENE; God hath numbered thy kingdom, and finished it."* God knows the exact amount of time a kingdom, nation, or dynasty will exist.

        4.   Job 14:5,10 – *"⁵Seeing his days are determined, the number of his months are with thee, thou hast appointed his bounds that he cannot pass... ¹⁰But man dieth, and wasteth away: yea, man giveth up the ghost, and where is he?"* God knows the number of months a man will live; he has numbered his steps. God has given everything an exact, appointed time.

        5.   Isaiah 40:12 – *"Who hath measured the waters in the hollow of his hand, and meted out heaven with the span, and*

comprehended the dust of the earth in a measure, and weighed the mountains in scales, and the hills in a balance?"

6. Exodus 27:1, 9, 18 – *"¹And thou shalt make an altar of shittim wood, five cubits long, and five cubits broad; the altar shall be foursquare: and the height thereof shall be three cubits...⁹And thou shalt make the court of the tabernacle: for the south side southward there shall be hangings for the court of fine twined linen of an hundred cubits long for one side...¹⁸The length of the court shall be an hundred cubits, and the breadth fifty every where, and the height five cubits of fine twined linen, and their sockets of brass."*

God is very specific about how long, short, wide, or deep things are to be. The Tabernacle certainly brings this out. He gives exact dimensions. This is just one example of a multitude, where the Lord gives specific directions and dimensions.

a. Exodus 30:1-2 – *"¹And thou shalt make an altar to burn incense upon: of shittim wood shalt thou make it. ²A cubit shall be the length thereof, and a cubit the breadth thereof; foursquare shall it be: and two cubits shall be the height thereof: the horns thereof shall be of the same."*

B. As we search the scriptures, we see that every number has a specific meaning. We understand this as we look at the number throughout the Word of God and compare it with examples of when a certain thing happened a certain number of times. Then, we can come to a conclusion about what they mean as found in the whole Bible.

1. In other words, we see the number seven related to perfection after we do a word study on it.
2. We can also determine it means this by different examples in the scriptures where something happened seven times.

3. This is also arrived at by finding a word seven times in one passage. Or finding a truth or revelation seven times in one passage.

C. Every word in the Bible, Hebrew, and Greek, has a certain number arrived at by counting the letters in each word. God specifically gave each word a certain number (letters) so it would mean a certain thing. Every letter has a number. A word can then be numbered when you count up the total number of the letters.

1. He also allowed that word to be placed in the Bible a certain amount of times.
2. In the Hebrew alphabet, every letter has a corresponding number. To determine the number of a word, you count the letters
3. It is the same in the Greek alphabet, every letter has a corresponding number.

D. God's law is perfect. He does not use numbers by chance, but by design

II. Basic Principles How To Properly Interpret The Meaning Of Numbers

If we will follow certain proper Biblical principles of interpretation, we will never go into error, or extremes, or find ourselves out of balance.

A. All the numbers in the Bible have spiritual significance. A certain number will be our basic foundation.
B. Multitudes of these numbers, or doubling and tripling, carry basically the same meaning as the original, only the meaning is intensified.
C. The first use of a number, as found in scripture, will usually give it's spiritual meaning. This principle of interpretation is called "The law of first reference."
D. As we search out numbers and their meanings, there should be a consistent definition throughout the Word. As we finish looking at all of the scriptures related to a certain number, we should be able to come away with a general consensus of what that number means by seeing throughout the Word a basic definition.
E. We must remember that a number in a certain passage of scripture may not carry any spiritual significance at all. We must always read the Word in context to ascertain this.
F. Never force a scripture to say something you want it to say. God's Word can defend Itself. Error starts when we stretch the Word.
G. Don't go beyond the realm of understanding and balance. You can do this by trying to string numbers together to say what you want them to say. One example of error is using someone's natural address to give spiritual significance. We need to stay in the Scriptures! (Proverbs 11:1) If you need to keep adding, subtracting, multiplying or dividing to achieve a certain

definition, leave it alone, you are trying to reason it out with a carnal mind. The Bible is spiritually discerned, not reasoned out (I Cor. 2:12-15).

H. The spiritual significance of a number will not always be stated plainly. It may be hidden or concealed, so we must meditate on the passage and allow the Holy Ghost to witness something to us. Another way to bring out true meaning is to compare other passages.

I. We must remember as we are searching out the meaning of numbers that we will often find godly and satanic, good and evil, true and false aspects to the numbers.

J. What the Scriptures say about how to search and rightly divide:

1. Acts 17:11 – *"These were more noble than those in Thessalonica, in that they received the word with all readiness of mind, and searched the scriptures daily, whether those things were so."* We are to search

   a. Proverbs 25:2 – *"It is the glory of God to conceal a thing: but the honour of kings is to search out a matter."*

   b. Psalms 111:2 – *"The works of the Lord are great, sought out of all them that have pleasure therein."*

   c. Psalms 119:94 – *"I am thine, save me; for I have sought thy precepts."*

   d. Proverbs 2:1-5 – *"¹My son, if thou wilt receive my words, and hide my commandments with thee; ²So that thou incline thine ear unto wisdom, and apply thine heart to understanding; ³Yea, if thou criest after knowledge, and liftest up thy voice for understanding; ⁴If thou seekest her as silver, and searchest for her as for hid treasures; ⁵Then shalt thou understand the fear of the Lord, and find the knowledge of God."*

2. II Timothy 2:15 – *"Study to shew thyself approved unto God, a workman that needeth not to be ashamed, rightly dividing the word of truth."* We have to rightly divide the Word of God

3. I Thessalonians 5:21 – *"Prove all things; hold fast that which is good."* Test everything

   a. I John 4:1 – *"Beloved, believe not every spirit, but try the spirits whether they are of God: because many false prophets are gone out into the world."*

      b.   Job 34:2-4 – *"²Hear my words, O ye wise men; and give ear unto me, ye that have knowledge. ³For the ear trieth words, as the mouth tasteth meat. ⁴Let us choose to us judgment: let us know among ourselves what is good."*

    4.   I Corinthians 2:13 – *"Which things also we speak, not in the words which man's wisdom teacheth, but which the Holy Ghost teacheth; comparing spiritual things with spiritual."*

III. Biblical Numbers and Their Meaning

One, 1

The number one represents **unity, God who is the beginning, or that which was first**

    1.   Unity – The word unity comes from the Latin word *unus* which means one.

        a.   Deuteronomy 6:4 – *"Hear, O Israel: The Lord our God is one Lord:"*
            This is a compound unity (Hebrew: *Echad*). The three-fold God is one (compound unity) Lord.
        b.   John 17:20-22 – *"²⁰Neither pray I for these alone, but for them also which shall believe on me through their word; ²¹That they all may be one; as thou, Father, art in me, and I in thee, that they also may be one in us: that the world may believe that thou hast sent me..."*
        c.   Acts 4:32 – *"And the multitude of them that believed were of one heart and of one soul: neither said any of them that ought of the things which he possessed was his own; but they had all things common."*
        d.   John 10:30 – *"I and my Father are one."*
        e.   Zechariah 14:9 – *"And the Lord shall be king over all the earth: in that day shall there be one Lord, and his name one."*
        f.   I Corinthians 12:12 – *"For as the body is one, and hath many members, and all the members of that one body, being many, are one body: so also is Christ."*
        g.   Genesis 11:6 – *"And the Lord said, Behold, the people is one, and they have all one language; and this they begin to do: and now nothing will be restrained from them, which they have imagined to do."*
        h.   I Peter 3:8 – *"Finally, be ye all of one mind, having compassion one of another, love as brethren, be pitiful, be courteous:"*

    i.   Ephesians 1:10 – *"That in the dispensation of the fulness of times he might gather together in one all things in Christ, both which are in heaven, and which are on earth; even in him:"*

    j.   Ephesians 4:4-6 – *"⁴There is one body, and one Spirit, even as ye are called in one hope of your calling; ⁵One Lord, one faith, one baptism, ⁶One God and Father of all, who is above all, and through all, and in you all."*

    k.   I John 5:7 – *"For there are three that bear record in heaven, the Father, the Word, and the Holy Ghost: and these three are one."*

2.   God – The number one, as we've seen so many times, refers to the unity of God. He is first, as is the number one.

    a.   Genesis 1:1 – *"In the beginning God created the Heaven and the earth."*

    b.   John 1:1-3 – *"¹In the beginning was the Word, and the Word was with God, and the Word was God. ²The same was in the beginning with God. ³All things were made by him; and without him was not any thing made that was made."*

    c.   Revelation 1:11 – *"Saying, I am Alpha and Omega, the first and the last: and, What thou seest, write in a book, and send it unto the seven churches which are in Asia; unto Ephesus, and unto Smyrna, and unto Pergamos, and unto Thyatira, and unto Sardis, and unto Philadelphia, and unto Laodicea."*

    d.   Isaiah 41:4 – *"Who hath wrought and done it, calling the generations from the beginning? I the Lord, the first, and with the last; I am he."*

    e.   Isaiah 44:6 – *"Thus saith the Lord the King of Israel, and his redeemer the Lord of hosts; I am the first, and I am the last; and beside me there is no God."*

    f.   Isaiah 48:12 – *"Hearken unto me, O Jacob and Israel, my called; I am he; I am the first, I also am the last."*

    g.   Matthew 6:33 – *"But seek ye first the kingdom of God, and his righteousness; and all these things shall be added unto you."*

Two, 2

The number two is the number of **witness and division or separation**

1.   Witness

a. Deuteronomy 19:15 – *"One witness shall not rise up against a man for any iniquity, or for any sin, in any sin that he sinneth: at the mouth of two witnesses, or at the mouth of three witnesses, shall the matter be established."*

b. John 8:17 – *"It is also written in your law, that the testimony of two men is true."*

c. I Timothy 5:19 – *"Against an elder receive not an accusation, but before two or three witnesses."*

d. Hebrews 10:28 – *"He that despised Moses' law died without mercy under two or three witnesses:"*

e. Matthew 18:16 – *"But if he will not hear thee, then take with thee one or two more, that in the mouth of two or three witnesses every word may be established."*

f. Genesis 41:32 – *"And for that the dream was doubled unto Pharaoh twice; it is because the thing is established by God, and God will shortly bring it to pass."*

g. Revelations 11:3 – *"And I will give power unto my two witnesses, and they shall prophesy a thousand two hundred and threescore days, clothed in sackcloth."*

h. Luke 10:1 – *"After these things the Lord appointed other seventy also, and sent them two and two before his face into every city and place, whither he himself would come."*

i. II Corinthians 13:1 – It is the number of confirmation.

2. Division or Separation – Two can be divided into separate parts.

    a. Genesis 1:16-18 – God separating night from day in creation

    b. Matthew 24:40-41 – *"⁴⁰Then shall two be in the field; the one shall be taken, and the other left. ⁴¹Two women shall be grinding at the mill; the one shall be taken, and the other left."*

    c. Exodus 8:23 – *"And I will put a division between my people and thy people: to morrow shall this sign be."* Two peoples

    d. Ezekiel 37:21-22 – *"²¹And say unto them, Thus saith the Lord God; Behold, I will take the children of Israel from among the heathen, whither they be gone, and will gather them on every side, and bring them into their own land: ²²And I will make them one nation in the land upon the mountains of Israel; and one king shall be king to them* all: and they shall be no more two nations, neither shall they be divided into two kingdoms any more at all:"

e. Mark 6:41 – "And when he had taken the five loaves and the two fishes, he looked up to heaven, and blessed, and brake the loaves, and gave them to his disciples to set before them; and the two fishes divided he among them all."

f. Two Men – Divided

   1) Jacob – Esau
   2) Isaac – Ishmael
   3) Abraham – Lot (Genesis 13:5-14)
   4) Paul – Barnabas (Acts 15:36-41)

Three, 3   The number three speaks of *Godhead and Resurrection*

1. Godhead

   a. I John 5:6-7 – "*6This is he that came by water and blood, even Jesus Christ; not by water only, but by water and blood. And it is the Spirit that beareth witness, because the Spirit is truth. 7For there are three that bear record in heaven, the Father, the Word, and the Holy Ghost: and these three are one.*"
   b. Matthew 28:19 – "*Go ye therefore, and teach all nations, baptizing them in the name of the Father, and of the Son, and of the Holy Ghost:*"
   c. II Corinthians 13:14 – "*The grace of the Lord Jesus Christ, and the love of God, and the communion of the Holy Ghost, be with you all. Amen.*"

2. Resurrection

   a. Matthew 12:40 – "*For as Jonas was three days and three nights in the whale's belly; so shall the Son of man be three days and three nights in the heart of the earth.*"
   b. Hosea 6:2 – "*After two days will he revive us: in the third day he will raise us up, and we shall live in his sight.*"
   c. John 2:19-21 – "*19Jesus answered and said unto them, Destroy this temple, and in three days I will raise it up. 20Then said the Jews, Forty and six years was this temple in building, and wilt thou rear it up in three days? 21But he spake of the temple of his body.*"

    d.   Jesus raised three from the dead

        1)   Luke 7:15 – *"And he that was dead sat up, and began to speak. And he delivered him to his mother."* – Widow's son
        2)   Luke 8:41-55 – Daughter of Jairus
        3)   John 11:43-44 – *"[43]And when he thus had spoken, he cried with a loud voice, Lazarus, come forth. [44]And he that was dead came forth, bound hand and foot with graveclothes: and his face was bound about with a napkin. Jesus saith unto them, Loose him, and let him go."* – Lazarus

    e.   Three dead raised in Old Testament

        1)   II Kings 17:21-22 – *"[21]For he rent Israel from the house of David; and they made Jeroboam the son of Nebat king: and Jeroboam drave Israel from following the Lord, and made them sin a great sin. [22]For the children of Israel walked in all the sins of Jeroboam which he did; they departed not from them;"* – Child
        2)   II Kings 4:16-36
        3)   II Kings 13:21 – *"And it came to pass, as they were burying a man, that, behold, they spied a band of men; and they cast the man into the sepulchre of Elisha: and when the man was let down, and touched the bones of Elisha, he revived, and stood up on his feet."*

Four, 4

The number four represents *that which is created; it speaks of total dependence on the creator.* It could also speak of *man in his lost state.*

    1.   That Which is Created – We have seen that three signifies the Godhead. The number four is made up of three and one; that which follows three follows the Godhead, speaking of His creative works. (Romans 1:17) Creation is the next thing after the Godhead.

        a.   Elements – Earth, air, fire, water
        b.   Isaiah 11:12 – *"And he shall set up an ensign for the nations, and shall assemble the outcasts of Israel, and*

gather together the dispersed of Judah from the four corners of the earth." Four corners of the earth: east, west, north, south

c. Divisions of the day – Mark 13:35 – "*Watch ye therefore: for ye know not when the master of the house cometh, at even, or at midnight, or at the cockcrowing, or in the morning:*" Morning, noon, evening, night

d. Seasons – Winter, spring, summer, fall

e. Genesis 1:14-19 – The end of the fourth day saw the material creation finished. All that was left was the furnishing of created beings in the earth.

f. Genesis 2:10-14 – Four rivers

g. Human Race (man) – Genesis 10:5 – "*By these were the isles of the Gentiles divided in their lands; every one after his tongue, after their families, in their nations.*" Nations, families, tongues, lands

h. Created Beings – 1 Corinthians 15:39 – "*All flesh is not the same flesh: but there is one kind of flesh of men, another flesh of beasts, another of fishes, and another of birds.*" Men, beasts, fishes, birds

i. Four Winds – Jeremiah 49:36

j. Four Living Creatures – Ezekiel 1:4-9

Five, 5   The number five represents **grace and redemption, and spiritual ministry**. The natural created man in a lost state stands in need of grace (4). That is why the next number stands for grace (5).

1. Grace

   a. Five wounds of Jesus on the cross: hands (nails), Feet (nails), Side (pierced), Brow (thrones), Back (beaten)

   b. The fifth time each of these names appears in Scripture, it is related to grace.

      1) Noah – Genesis 6:8 – "*But Noah found grace in the eyes of the Lord.*"

      2) Ruth – Ruth 2:2 – "*And Ruth the Moabitess said unto Naomi, Let me now go to the field, and glean ears of corn after him in whose sight I shall find grace. And she said unto her, Go, my daughter.*"

      3) David – I Samuel 16:22 – "*And Saul sent to Jesse, saying, Let David, I pray thee, stand before me; for he hath found favour in my sight.*"

     c.   Brazen Altar – Five cubits long; the Brazen Altar speaks of our redemption, His grace, and His substitution sacrifice.

     d.   Five Offerings in Old Testament: Burnt, Meal, Peace, Sin, Trespass. All of this speaks of Jesus' sacrifice for us, His grace and favor on our behalf.

     e.   Five animals used in offerings. Jesus is represented here in type by all of these animals: bullock, sheep, goat, turtledove, pigeon

     f.   Luke 15:20-23 – Parable of the prodigal son

         1)   The Father's five gracious responses to his return: saw him, had compassion, ran, hugged him, kissed him

         2)   The prodigal son received five things: robe, ring, shoes, fatted calf, party (made merry)

2.   Spiritual Ministry

     a.   Ephesians 4:11 – *"And he gave some, apostles; and some, prophets; and some, evangelists; and some, pastors and teachers;"*

     b.   I Samuel 17:40 – *"And he took his staff in his hand, and chose him five smooth stones out of the brook, and put them in a shepherd's bag which he had, even in a scrip; and his sling was in his hand: and he drew near to the Philistine."*

     c.   Matthew 14:15-21

     d.   Matthew 25:14-16

Six, 6   This is the number of *man and his limitations, and satan.*

1.   Man – Six falls short of seven (perfection) thus signifying man in his imperfect, limited state.

     a.   Revelation 13:18 – *"Here is wisdom. Let him that hath understanding count the number of the beast: for it is the number of a man; and his number is Six hundred threescore and six."* Here we see that six (in triplicate) is spoken of as the number of man. In this case, the antichrist.

     b.   Exodus 20:9 – *"Six days shalt thou labour, and do all thy work:"* – Six is the number of man's labor apart from God's rest. Man will not rest until the seventh day. He is still laboring in an imperfect state.

     c.   Genesis 1:26-31 – Man was created on the sixth day.

d. Six is man in his imperfect state:

1) Hebrew slaves had to serve six years before receiving freedom.
2) The kingdoms of this world will last 600 years.
3) Moses waited six days on the mountain before God revealed Himself to him. Exodus 24:15-18
4) Genesis 4:15-24 – Cain's descendants are given only as far as the sixth generation.
5) Twelve is the number of governmental perfection and order; six is only half of that.
6) Exodus 20:13 – *"Thou shalt not kill"* The sixth commandment deals with murder.

e. Daniel 3:1-30 - Revelations 13:13-18 – The image was six cubits broad and six cubits high.

2. satan and His Influence

a. Genesis 1:24 –The serpent was created on the sixth day.
b. Jesus was accused six times of having a devil: Mark 3:22, John 10:20, John 7:20, John 8:48, John 8:52, Luke 11:15
c. The sixth commandment was murder; Jesus said satan (6) was a murderer (6) from the beginning: Exodus 20:13, John 8:44
d. Matthew 4:1-13 – The devil is spoken of six times in this passage. (tempter, satan)
e. satan has six proper names: beelzebub (Matthew 10:22-25, Mark 3:22), devil (This name is used 60 times in the New Testament), dragon (Psalms 91:13, Revelation 12:3-4, 7-9, 13,16-17), lucifer (Isaiah 14:12), prince – ruler of darkness (John 12:31, John 14:30, II Corinthians 4:3-4), satan (Luke 10:18, Romans 16:20)
f. Satan appears in six types: serpent, adversary, belial, leviathan, star, wormwood

Seven, 7   This number means *perfection, completeness, rest.* The *Hebrew* word for seven means to be *full, satisfied, to have enough.*

1. Completeness

a.   Revelation 10:7 – *"But in the days of the voice of the seventh angel, when he shall begin to sound, the mystery of God should be finished, as he hath declared to his servants the prophets."*

b.   Leviticus 23:15 – *"And ye shall count unto you from the morrow after the sabbath, from the day that ye brought the sheaf of the wave offering; seven sabbaths shall be complete:"*

c.   John 19:30 – *"When Jesus therefore had received the vinegar, he said, It is finished: and he bowed his head, and gave up the ghost."* This is the seventh time Jesus spoke from the cross. Notice it's connection with the word "finished."

d.   The word seven is found 49 times in the book of Revelation. (seven times seven equals 49)

e.   Genesis 2:1-2 – Seven creating days. On the seventh day, God completed the work.

f.   Seven Spirits of God – All of these basically speak of the seven-fold aspects of the Spirit of God (Rev. 3:1, Isaiah 11:2).

g.   Seven Churches – Seven Church Ages (Revelation 1:19-20) – Most scholars believe these seven churches represent the seven dispensations of the church.

h.   Proverbs 6:16-19 – Seven things God hates. This is His complete number.

i.   Joshua 6:1-6 – On the seventh day, Jericho fell. They had marched around it for six days previous. Seven signified completion.

j.   Proverbs 9:1 – *"Wisdom hath builded her house, she hath hewn out her seven pillars:"* Wisdom also has a seven-fold aspect which all combined together makes it complete.

k.   Matthew 18:21-22 – *"21Then came Peter to him, and said, Lord, how oft shall my brother sin against me, and I forgive him? till seven times? 22Jesus saith unto him, I say not unto thee, Until seven times: but, Until seventy times seven."* Seventy times seven. This is completeness multiplied; in other words, we never stop forgiving.

l.   2 Kings 4:32-36 – The son of the Shunammite woman is raised up. The process is completed only after he sneezed seven times.

m.   Seven Seals of Judgment (Revelation 5:1, 8:1)

n.   Leviticus 16:14 – The blood sprinkled on the mercy seat seven times thus signifying that the blood's work was complete.

o.   II Kings 5:10-14

p.   I Kings 6:38

2.   Perfection

a. Hebrews 6:1-3 – The six principles that make up our foundation are listed here. Then we see "going on to perfection." The seventh and final thing will be our perfection.

b. Jude 14 (Genesis 5:18-24 – Hebrews 11:5) – Enoch, the seventh was taken or translated that he should not see death. I believe he was perfected. He reached completion, maturity, and fullness.

c. I Chronicles 2:15 – *"Ozem the sixth, David the seventh:"* – David, Jesse's seventh son, was God's choice. He was a type of that overcoming, worshipping army that will fulfill the will of God in their generation (perfection) as David did.

d. Psalms 12:6 – *"The words of the Lord are pure words: as silver tried in a furnace of earth, purified seven times."* The Word of God has been purified (perfected) seven times.

e. Proverbs 24:16 – *"For a just man falleth seven times, and riseth up again: but the wicked shall fall into mischief."* A just man may fall seven times, but eventually he won't fall anymore (Job 5:19).

f. Exodus 21:2 – *"If thou buy an Hebrew servant, six years he shall serve: and in the seventh he shall go out free for nothing."* – Slaves released

g. Deuteronomy 15:1-3 – those in debt released.

These Scriptures and this principle, God Himself instituted, speak to us of that perfect day that has come. We have served, but now we are released. We have labored and been in debt, but now we are released from every debt. Seven here relates to our perfect deliverance.

Eight, 8   This number represents a *new beginning*.

1. I Peter 3:20 – *"Which sometime were disobedient, when once the longsuffering of God waited in the days of Noah, while the ark was a preparing, wherein few, that is, eight souls were saved by water."* There were eight people in Noah's ark specifically there for the purpose of replenishing and bringing a new beginning to the earth.

2. II Peter 8-13 – At the end of the seven days (1000 years per day – 7000 years) on the eighth day, new heavens and a new earth will come forth.

3. The numerical value of Jesus' name is 888. Thus, Jesus signifies a new beginning for us.

4. John 20:26-28 – *"After eight days..."* Thomas definitely experienced a new beginning here.
5. Genesis 17:9-12 – This is the token of the covenant with God. Circumcision was the beginning of their walk with God. In the spirit, we enter into a new beginning with God as our old flesh nature is cut off and our heart is circumcised (Romans 6:6-14, Romans 2:29, Philippians 3:3, Colossians 3:11, Galatians 6:14)
6. Matthew 28:1-6 – Jesus was raised on the first day of the week or the eighth day.
7. The miracles of Elijah were eight in number. This signified a new beginning brought about by the supernatural blessing (I Kings 17:1, 8-23, 18:36-45, II Kings 1:10, 12, 2:8)
8. Leviticus 23:33-36 – The last day of the Feast of Tabernacles was the eighth day. It was to be a special time of worship and offering unto the Lord. Jesus chose this day to speak of the coming of the Holy Spirit which would bring water from Heaven. What a new beginning occurs when that precious latter rain comes into our soul (Numbers 29:35-40, John 7:37-39)!

Nine, 9   The number nine represents *finality*.

1. Galatians 5:22-23 – There are nine fruits of the Spirit.
2. I Corinthians 12:8-11 – There are nine gifts of the Spirit.
3. Matthew 5:3-11 – There are nine beatitudes. They begin with these two words: *"Blessed are...."*
4. The word "Amen" has a numerical value of 99. It speaks to us of finality.
5. Matthew 27:45-50 –It was in the ninth hour of the day that Jesus died.
6. Women carry their babies for nine months.
7. It is the last of the single digits, signaling the end.
8. Haggai 1:11 – God called for a nine-fold judgment here. It covers just about everything on earth.

Ten, 10   The number ten represents *law, government, and a completed cycle*

1. Law

    a. Exodus 34:28 – Ten commandments
    b. Genesis 1 – Ten "God said" signifying His Word.
    c. Tithes – Leviticus 27:32 – This represents the whole of what man was to give to God. It was God's commandment.
    d. There are ten parables in the gospel of Matthew.

2. A Completed Cycle

    a. Noah completed the antediluvian age in the tenth generation.
    b. Deuteronomy 23:3-5 – The tenth generation completed and represented the whole existence of a family or nation.
    c. Matthew 25:1 – *"Then shall the kingdom of heaven be likened unto ten virgins, which took their lamps, and went forth to meet the bridegroom."*

3. Government

    a. Daniel 2 – ten toes
    b. Daniel 7 – ten horns
    c. Revelation 12:3 – ten horns

Eleven, 11   The number eleven represents *disorder, disorganization, and confusion.*

1. It is one beyond ten (God's law) and one short of twelve (divine government).
2. At the eleventh hour he finds these standing in confusion and disorder.
3. Genesis 11:1-9 – The eleventh chapter of the Bible tells the story of Babel, when God brought confusion and disorder to the people.
4. Acts 1:15-26 – There were only 11 apostles. They needed one more for proper government. Without the twelfth, there would be confusion.
5. Jeremiah 39:2 – In the eleventh year of Zedekiah, the King of Judah, "the city was broken up", brought to ruin, disorder and confusion.
6. Isaiah 53:8 – Jesus was 33 when he was crucified (3 x 11) – the Godhead was in disorder.
7. John 6:70 – *"Jesus answered them, Have not I chosen you twelve, and one of you is a devil?"* (12 – 1 = 11)

Twelve, 12   The number twelve represents *divine order, government, and governmental perfection.*

1. Jesus chose exactly twelve disciples. This was the divine number for Apostolic government (Matthew 10:1-5, Matthew 19:28).
2. There were twelve tribes in Israel, the extent of God's government in the earth at that time. Also, there will be twelve

tribes who will be sealed, the sum of God's number of perfection (Genesis 35:22, Revelation 2:7-8).

3. I Kings 4:7 – Solomon had twelve stewards who saw to his household. They had his authority, representing the government of Solomon's house.

4. Revelation 12:1 – *"And there appeared a great wonder in heaven; a woman clothed with the sun, and the moon under her feet, and upon her head a crown of twelve stars:"* This woman represents the church (spiritual, not Israel). Notice her government included twelve stars. (Revelation 1:20 – the messengers or pastors of God's churches.)

5. Exodus 28:15-21 – These are the twelve stones representing the twelve tribes of Israel that the priest would wear in the Presence of God. They represented the place of God's government in the earth.

6. Acts 7:8 – There were twelve patriarchs. These would later become the twelve tribes of Israel. They were God's people.

7. John 11:9 – *"Jesus answered, Are there not twelve hours in the day? If any man walk in the day, he stumbleth not, because he seeth the light of this world."* Twelve hours of the day, twelve hours of the night: God's order in the natural world.

8. Joshua 4:1-9, 19-24 – Twelve men and twelve stones: God's order of remembering the miraculous crossing of the Jordan into the land.

9. Book of Revelation – Showing twelve as the number of divine order, divine government.

   a. Revelation 21:12-21
   b. Revelation 22:2 – *"In the midst of the street of it, and on either side of the river, was there the tree of life, which bare twelve manner of fruits, and yielded her fruit every month: and the leaves of the tree were for the healing of the nations."* This is God's divine order in the New Jerusalem:

      1) Twelve gates – Revelation 21:12
      2) Twelve Angels – Revelation 21:12
      3) Twelve foundations – Revelation 21:14
      4) Names of the twelve Apostles – Revelation 21:14
      5) Twelve gates – Revelation 21:21
      6) Twelve pearls – Revelation 21:21
      7) Twelve thousand furlongs – Revelation 21:10
      8) Twelve Stones – Revelation 21:19-21
      9) Twelve thousand sealed for each tribe – Rev. 7:4-8
      10) Twelve fruits – Revelation 22:2

10. Matthew 26:53 – *"Thinkest thou that I cannot now pray to my Father, and he shall presently give me more than twelve legions of angels?"* Twelve legions of angels, denoting the perfection of angelic powers.
11. Leviticus 24:5-9 – Twelve loaves of shewbread. This is the divine order or number. There was one loaf for each tribe; all were represented before God.
12. Luke 2:42 – Jesus was 12 years old when he first appeared before people.
13. There are twelve months in a year.

Thirteen, 13

The number thirteen represents *rebellion, backsliding, sin or depravity*.

1. Genesis 14:4 – *"Twelve years they served Chedorlaomer, and in the thirteenth year they rebelled."* – In the thirteenth year they rebelled.
2. Mark 7:21-23 – There are thirteen evil things coming out of the heart of man that will defile him.
3. Genesis 10:6-10 – Nimrod was the thirteenth generation from Adam through Ham. Nimrod's kingdom was Babel of Babylon. He builds the tower of Babel, a symbol of total rebellion against God.
4. Dragon (devil) found 13 times in Revelation (Revelation 12:3, 4, 7, 7, 9, 13, 16, 17, 13:2, 4, 11, 16:13, 20:2). The devil is the greatest symbol of rebellion.
5. Gen. 17:25 – Ishmael was 13 years old when he was circumcised. He was the son of the bondwoman, the son of the flesh.
6. The words *"ye say"* are found 13 times in the book of Malachi in relation to Israel's rebellion (Malachi 1:2, 6, 7, 7, 12, 13, 2:14, 17, 17 3:7, 8, 13, 14)
7. Jeremiah 1:2 – Jeremiah was called in the 13th year to prophesy against rebellious Jews.

Fourteen, 14

This number represents a *multiple of seven or a doubling of perfection.*

1. Exodus 12:5-8 – The lamb (typified in Jesus) had to be kept 14 days to make sure it was perfect. The lamb was slain on Passover.
2. Numbers 9:5 – *"And they kept the passover on the fourteenth day of the first month at even in the wilderness of Sinai..."* Passover was on the fourteenth day.

Fifteen, 15 The number fifteen is the number for *rest* and for *3 (Godhead) x 5 (grace) or acts brought about by the energy of His grace.*

1. Rest

    a. Psalms 120–134 – These are the 15 songs of degrees in Psalms. They speak of our journey, our ascent by degrees into His rest.
    b. Leviticus 23:4-7, 34-25 (Esther 9:18) – These were during the feast days. On the 15th they were to do no work.

2. Acts of Grace (The Godhead involved in Grace.)

    a. Genesis 7:20 – *"Fifteen cubits upward did the waters prevail..."* Noah's ark was borne by the flood 15 cubits upward.
    b. II Kings 20:6 – Hezekiah had fifteen years added to his life by God's act of grace.

Sixteen, 16 The number sixteen seems to represent *fullness*.

1. II Chronicles 29:17 – Made an end of cleansing the temple on the sixteenth day; sanctification was complete.
2. I Corinthians 13:4-8 – Here are 16 adjectives describing love. This is love in its fullness.
3. Eight is the number of new beginning; double that and you have fullness.
4. Four is the number of that which is created. 4 + 4 is creation at its height or fullness.

Seventeen, 17 The number seventeen represents *Spiritual Order or the perfection of spiritual order.*

1. Romans 8:35-39 – This is a list of the 17 things that cannot separate us from Christ (tribulation, distress, persecution, famine, nakedness, peril, sword, death, life, angels, principalities, things present, things to come, powers, height, depth, any creature). This lets us know the spiritual and eternal perfection and order of our standing Jesus.

2. Hebrews 12:18-24 – Here the Old and New Testament are contrasted as they relate to our approaching unto God. The

combination of these equals 17 and represents spiritual order in the whole of the Bible.

    a.   Ye are not come: to the mount that might be touched, that burned with fire, blackness, darkness, tempest, sound of trumpet, voice of words (7)

    b.   Ye are come: to Mt. Zion, city of the Living God, heavenly Jerusalem, company of angels, general assembly, church of the firstborn, God the Judge of all, spirits of just men made perfect, Jesus, the mediator of the new covenant, blood of sprinkling (10)

3. Ten is the number of the Law. Seven is the number of perfection, henceforth, spiritual order.
4. Genesis 37:2 – Joseph at the age of 17 was feeding the flock and overseeing his brethren. He was doubly loved.
5. Genesis 7:11-12 – On the seventeenth day of the month in God's order and timing, the windows of heaven opened and rain fell for forty days and nights.
6. I John 5:5 – Seventeen Greek words are found here. This is an obvious statement of spiritual order.

Eighteen, 18

The number eighteen represents *bondage or binding*.

1. Luke 13:10-16 – "...*there was a woman which had a spirit of infirmity eighteen years, and was bowed together, and could in no wise lift up herself...*" She was bound 18 years.
2. Judges 3:12-14 – Israel in bondage to Moab 18 years.
3. Judges 10:6-8 – Israel once again in bondage to another nation 18 years.
4. Revelation 20:2 – In this verse there are 18 Greek words, then satan is bound.
5. Acts 21:13 – "*Then Paul answered, What mean ye to weep and to break mine heart? for I am ready not to be bound only, but also to die at Jerusalem for the name of the Lord Jesus.*" Once again there are 18 Greek words in this verse.

Nineteen, 19

The number nineteen represents *divine order in judgment*.

1. Jeremiah 52:12-15 – This was God's judgment; he had already told them to surrender.
2. II Kings 25:8-10

Twenty, 20   The number twenty represents *expectancy*.

1. Exodus 27:9-11 – The south and north sides of the court of the Tabernacle had 20 pillars made of brass (judgment) with 20 silver hooks. Each pillar was filleted with silver (redemption). The brass pillars (those in judgment) are waiting to be <u>filled</u> with silver (God's redemption).
2. Revelation 20:6 - *"Blessed and holy is he that hath part in the first resurrection. On such the second death hath no power..."* This statement has 20 Greek words. This is our greatest expectancy, isn't it? To be part of the first resurrection.
3. It seems, rather than being the double of ten (law), the significance of twenty is found in the fact that it is *short of twenty-one* which would be three fold seven. 3 (Godhead) x 7 (perfection) is Godly Perfection. Twenty, falling one short, seems to indicate a waiting for, or an expectancy.
4. Genesis 31:38-42 – Jacob waited twenty years to obtain possession of his wives and property.
5. I Samuel 7:1-2 – Twenty years Israel waited for the Ark as it rested at Kirjathjearim.

Twenty One, 21   As far as we can determine, this number represents *divine perfection*. Three is the number for the Godhead, seven is the number for perfection, and therefore twenty one represents divine perfection.

Twenty Two, 22   This number is double the number eleven (disorder, confusion, disorganization). So, it means *double confusion, and disorder.*

1. Two of Israel's worst kings ruled for 22 years each.

   a. Jeroboam – I Kings 14:20 – *"And the days which Jeroboam reigned were two and twenty years..."*
   b. Ahab – I Kings 16:29 – *"...Ahab the son of Omri reigned over Israel in Samaria twenty and two years."*

Twenty Three, 23   The number twenty three represents *death*.

1. The words death, die, dead, dieth are found 23 times in the book of Hebrews.

2. Revelation 11:7 – *"And when they shall have finished their testimony, the beast that ascendeth out of the bottomless pit shall make war against them, and shall overcome them, and kill them."* This statement has 23 Greek words. Notice its connection with death.
3. Romans 1:28-32 – Paul lists 23 things here that are worthy of death.

Twenty Four, 24

This number represents the ***priesthood and heavenly government.***

1. Priesthood

    a. I Chronicles 24:1-20 – Here the 24 divisions of the priesthood are found.
    b. There are 24 hours in a day, and a priest is to be ready to intercede every hour.
    c. Joshua 4:2-7 – Twelve men took twelve stones from where the priests were standing as a memorial of their deliverance to their children.

2. Heavenly Government, Revelation 4:4-10 – Here we see 24 elders around the Throne. Also, the 4 beasts had 6 wings each (24)

Twenty Five, 25

The number twenty five represents ***grace intensified.***

1. Five is the number for grace; the only way to reach 25 is to multiply five times five; Grace multiplied.
2. Jeremiah 52:31-33 – King Jehaiachin of Judah was pardoned by the King of Babylon on the 25th day of the month.

Twenty Six, 26

The number twenty six represents ***rebellion intensified.***

1. 13 + 13 = 26

Twenty Seven, 27

The number twenty seven represents ***finality (9) of what God (3) is going to do in the earth. It is the summation of all that God will do.***

Twenty Eight, 28

The number twenty eight is the number of ***eternal life.***

1. The twenty eighth time Noah's name is found is in Genesis 8:15 *"And God spake unto Noah saying, Go forth of the ark, them and thy wife, and thy sons, and thy sons' wives with thee."* This is a picture of the church being caught up out of judgment and then entering into eternal life.
2. 4 x 7 or creation times perfection = eternal life.

Twenty Nine, 29

The number twenty nine is the number for *departure*.

1. Genesis 8:18-19 – The twenty ninth time the name of Noah is found is when he and his family came forth from the ark.
2. The twenty ninth time the name Abraham occurs is in Genesis 14:12 (*"And they took Lot, Abram's brother's son, who dwelt in Sodom, and his goods, and departed."*) when the kings overtook the kings of Sodom and Gomorrah and they took Lot with his goods and departed.
3. The twenty ninth time the name Isaac occurs is when he left Lahari Roi and went unto Abimelech in Gerar (Genesis 25:11, 26:1)
4. The twenty ninth time the name of Labon is found is when God told Jacob to leave Labon's place and return home.
5. Twenty + Nine or Expectancy + Finality = results in our departure.

Thirty, 30

The number thirty represents *maturity, prepared for ministry, authority to rule.*

1. Luke 3:23 – Jesus was thirty years of age when he began his public ministry.
2. Genesis 41:46 – Joseph was thirty years old when he began to rule alongside Pharaoh.
3. II Samuel 5:4 – David was thirty years old when he began to reign in Israel.
4. Numbers 4:1-3, 21-23, 29-30 – These priests began their ministry when they were thirty years old.
5. Thirty was the age of adulthood among the Jews at that time.
6. Remember that the Godhead (3) and the law (10) multiplied would mean a perfection of Divine Order.
7. Mark 4:8 – *"And other fell on good ground, and did yield fruit that sprang up and increased; and brought forth, some thirty, and some sixty, and some an hundred."* Thirty here signifies fruit has come

forth, maturity has already begun and it will continue to grow further.

Thirty One, 31
Thirty one is the number representing *offspring or seed*

1. Noah's name occurs the thirty first time when God said unto him, *"Be fruitful and multiply, and replenish the earth."* (Genesis 9:1)
2. Abram's name is mentioned the thirty first time when it speaks of his trained servants born in his house (Genesis 14:14)
3. The thirty first time Jacob's name occurs, God told him his seed would be as the dust of the earth. Genesis 28:13-16
4. The thirty first time the name Abraham occurs is where he prayed for the house of Abimelech, his wife, and maidservants so that they might bare children (Genesis 20:17-18)

Thirty Two, 32
Thirty Two is the number that represents *covenant.*

1. There are thirty two references in the book of Deuteronomy to the Abrahemic Covenant.
2. The thirty second time Noah's name is mentioned is when God makes a covenant with him (Genesis 9:8-9)

Thirty Three, 33
Thirty Three is the number that represents *promise.*

1. Abraham's name is found the thirty third time when Isaac the child of promise, was born (Genesis 21:1-2)
2. The thirty third time Jacob's name is found is when he promised God a tenth of all (Genesis 28:20-22)
3. Jesus was thirty three when he was crucified, the promised Messiah.

Thirty Four, 34
The number thirty four represents *birthing of a son.*

1. Genesis 11:16 – *"And Eber lived four plus thirty years and begat Peleg."*
2. The thirty fourth time Abraham's name is mentioned is in Genesis 21:3 – *"And Abraham called the name of his son that was born unto him..."*

3. 4 + 30 or Creation + Maturity, preparation for ministry = the new created son / the manifested son

Thirty Five, 35   The number thirty five represents *hope*.

1. 5 x 7 or grace times perfection = Hope
2. 5 + 30 or Grace + Maturity = Hope
3. 20 + 15 or Expectancy + Fullness = Hope

Thirty Six, 36   The number thirty six represents *enemy*.

1. Esther 7:6 – The thirty sixth time Haman occurs is when Esther called him the adversary and the enemy
2. The thirty sixth time David's name is found is in I Samuel 17:50 when he overcomes Goliath.
3. There are thirty six references to the beast in the book of Revelations.
4. 6 x 6 or man times satan = antichrist

Thirty Seven, 37   The number thirty seven represents the *Word of God.*

1. Bethlehem Judah is mentioned thirty seven times; House of Bread. Bread in Scripture is a type of the Word of God.
2. The Hebrew word for circumcise is *mul* which is mentioned thirty seven times.
3. The Hebrew word for uncircumcised is *ovel* which is mentioned thirty seven times. (Both Old and New Testaments)
4. The Golden Candle Stick is mentioned thirty seven times. Jesus the light of the world as well as the revealer of the Word of God.
5. The word 'glean' occurs thirty seven times. We glean the Word of God.

Thirty Eight, 38   The number thirty eight represents *slavery*.

1. John 5:5 –The man here was bound by an infirmity, thirty eight years.
2. I Kings 16:29 – "*And in the thirty and eighth year of Asa king of Judah began Ahab the son of Omri to reign over Israel...*" During Ahab's reign Israel came into slavery and idol worship.
3. Deuteronomy 2:14 – "*And the space in which we came from Kadesh-barnea, until we were come over the brook Zered, was thirty and eight years; until all the generation of the men of war*

were wasted out from among the host, as the Lord sware unto them." Unbelief caused the judgment of God upon Israel, they had become slaves to fear.

Thirty Nine, 39

The number thirty nine represents *disease.*

1. II Chronicles 16:12 – Asa was in his thirty ninth year of reigning when he became diseased in his feet.

Forty, 40

The number forty represents *trial, testing, probation, chastening.*

1. Trial or Testing

    a. Exodus 16:35 – The children of Israel had to eat manna for 40 years. They had to believe it would be there every morning.
    b. Deuteronomy 8:2 – Israel was proven, tested forty years in the wilderness.
    c. Numbers 13:25-33 – For forty days the spies sent out by Moses to gather information. They failed this test because they came back with a bad report.

    d. Jesus being tempted:

        1) Matthew 4:2 – *"And when he had fasted forty days and forty nights, he was afterward an hungred."*
        2) Mark 1:13 – *"And he was there in the wilderness forty days, tempted of Satan..."*
        3) Luke 4:2 – *"Being forty days tempted of the devil. And in those days he did eat nothing: and when they were ended, he afterward hungered."*

    e. I Kings 19:4-8 – Elijah going forty days without food.
    f. Ezekiel 4:6 – Ezekiel had to lie on the ground and prophesy against Jerusalem forty days.
    g. Exodus 24:15-18 – The children of Israel were tested the forty days Moses was on the mountain.
    h. II Corinthians 11:24 – *"Of the Jews five times received I forty stripes save one."* Paul was tested by being beaten with forty stripes.

2. Probation

a. Jonah 3:4 – Here Nineveh was given forty days to repent.
b. Acts 7:29-30 – Moses spent forty years in the land of Midian until the Lord appeared to him. He was learning that God, not Moses was the Deliver.

3. Chastening

a. Genesis 7:11-12 – God chastened the earth forty days and forty nights with a flood.
b. Deuteronomy 25:3 – A wicked man found guilty of something worthy of a beating, was beaten with forty stripes.

Forty One, 41   The number forty one represents *deception*.

1. There are forty one Greek words in II Corinthians 11:13-15 (false apostles, deceitful workers, satan an angel of light).

Forty Two, 42   The number forty two represents *antichrist*.

1. 6 x 7 or satan times fullness
2. Revelation 13:5 – The time of the beast's power was forty two months.
3. II Kings 2:23-25 – This is the forty two children who were the infidel children of God. They mocked the anointing. They had an antichrist spirit.
4. Revelation 12:14 – "*...where she is nourished for a time, and times, and half a time, from the face of the serpent.*" antichrists time

Forty Four, 44   The number forty four represents the *lake of fire*.

1. Revelation 20:15 – "*And whosoever was not found written in the book of life was cast into the lake of fire.*" There are eleven Greek words and forty four Greek letters in this verse. (Cast into lake of fire)
2. Revelation 19:20 – "*And the beast was taken, and with him the false prophet that wrought miracles before him, with which he deceived them that had received the mark of the beast, and them that worshipped his image. These both were cast alive into a lake of fire burning with brimstone.*" There are forty four Greek words here.

Forty Five, 45   The number forty five represents *inheritance*.

1. Joshua 14:14 – Caleb was given his inheritance forty five years after the promise was made.
2. Matthew 5:5 – *"Blessed are the meek: for they shall inherit the earth."* There are forty five Greek letters in this statement.

Forty Six, 46

The number forty six represents the **second death**.

1. 23 + 23 or death + death = second death

Forty Eight, 48

The number forty eight represents **dwelling place**.

1. Exodus 26:15-25 – There were forty eight boards in the wall of the Tabernacle: twenty on the south side, twenty on the north side and eight on the west end.
2. Joshua 21:41 – The Levites had forty eight cities to dwell in.

Fifty, 50

This number represents **Pentecost** and **Jubilee**.

1. Pentecost

   a. The very word Pentecost means fifty.
   b. Leviticus 23:15, Deuteronomy 16:9-12 –The Feast of Pentecost was held on the fiftieth day.
   c. Acts 2:1-4 – On the fiftieth day after His resurrection (on the day of Pentecost) Jesus gave the Holy Spirit to the church.

2. Jubilee

   a. Leviticus 25:8-10 – Israel had a "Year of Jubilee" every fifty years. During this year, all slaves were set free and returned to their families. Every man had his possessions returned to him.

Fifty Six, 56

This number represents **seeing into the heavenly realm.**

1. The phrase *"I saw"* occurs fifty six times in the Book of Revelations.
2. 7 x 8 or perfection times new beginnings = the new creation man seeing into perfection.

Sixty, 60

The number sixty represents **pride**.

1. Daniel 3:1 – The image Nebuchanezzar built was sixty cubits high. He did this in his pride.
2. 6 x 10 or man times law = human pride in keeping the law

Sixty Six, 66   The number sixty six represents *idol worship*.

1. Daniel 3:1 – Height of image sixty cubits breadth six cubits
2. Genesis 46:26-27 – All the souls that came with Jacob into Egypt were sixty six. Egypt caused Isaac to backslide.

Seventy, 70   This number represents *spiritual order*.

1. Luke 10:1,17 – *"¹After these things the Lord appointed other seventy also, and sent them two and two before his face into every city and place, whither he himself would come...¹⁷And the seventy returned again with joy, saying, Lord, even the devils are subject unto us through thy name."* Here the Lord sends out seventy disciples to the places he wanted them to go.
2. Numbers 11:16, 17, 24, 25 – These seventy elders of Israel were called to help Moses bring order. These elders later became the great tribunal, the Sanhedrin.
3. Daniel 9:24-27 – The seventy weeks of Daniel here seem to conclude with spiritual order.
4. Matthew 18:21-22 – *"²¹Then came Peter to him, and said, Lord, how oft shall my brother sin against me, and I forgive him? till seven times? ²²Jesus saith unto him, I say not unto thee, Until seven times: but, Until seventy times seven."* How often should we forgive? Seventy times seven. This is God's number of order.

Seventy Seven, 77   The number seventy seven represents *vengeance*.

1. Genesis 4:23-24 – Vengeance on Lamech seventy and seven fold
2. Judges 8:1-16 – Gideon takes vengeance on seventy seven elders of the city of Succoth.

Eighty, 80   The number eighty represents *a fulfilled life*.

1. II Samuel 19:32-38 – Barzillai is eighty years old
2. Psalms 90:10 – *"The days of our years are threescore years and ten; and if by reason of strength they be fourscore years, yet is their strength labour and sorrow; for it is soon cut off, and we fly away."* Eighty years the maximum

Ninety, 90

The number ninety represents *rebirth*.

Ninety Nine, 99

The number ninety nine represents *sealed*.

1. Genesis 17:1-11 – Abraham circumcised at ninety nine.
2. Ninety nine is the Greek numerical value of the word 'Amen'.

One Hundred, 100

The number one hundred represents *fruitfulness and the full measure (maturity).*

1. Full Measure (Maturity)

   a. Luke 15:4 – The shepherd had one hundred sheep, a full count from which one went astray.
   b. Mark 4:8 – One hundred fold fruit has been brought forth. This is full measure, full maturity.
   c. Genesis 21:5 – Abraham was one hundred years old when Isaac was born. He had reached a level of maturity where by he could receive God's promise.
   d. Genesis 26:12 – *"Then Isaac sowed in that land, and received in the same year an hundredfold: and the Lord blessed him."* Isaac received the full measure and was blessed of the Lord.
   e. Mark 10:30 – *"But he shall receive an hundredfold now in this time, houses, and brethren, and sisters, and mothers, and children, and lands, with persecutions; and in the world to come eternal life."*

One Hundred Twenty, 120

This number represents *the end of all flesh*.

1. Genesis 6:3 – *"And the Lord said, My spirit shall not always strive with man, for that he also is flesh: yet his days shall be an hundred and twenty years."* Man's days at one time were 120.
2. Deuteronomy 34:7 – Moses was one hundred twenty when he died.
3. This number is made up of three forties. 3 (Godhead) x 40 (testing, probation), thus the end of our time of probation and testing.

4. Acts 1:15 – One hundred twenty disciples awaiting the coming of the Holy Ghost, whose coming marked the end of our struggle in the flesh, giving us new life in the Spirit.
5. II Chronicles 5:11-14 – This represents the end of flesh in worship and God triumphing over by the Holy Ghost.

One Hundred Thirty, 130

This number represents the *appointed seed*.

1. Genesis 5:3 – Adam was one hundred thirty years old when Seth was born.
2. Seth's name in Hebrew means *appointed*.

One Hundred Forty Four, 144

This number represents *God's ultimate in creation: His Bride.*

1. Revelation 21:9-11, 17 – The wall of the city, Holy Jerusalem, was one hundred forty four cubits. This city is a type of the Bride, the Lamb's wife; that which He has been waiting for from the beginning.
2. Revelation 7:1-8 – These are the Jewish members of the Bride of Christ.
3. Revelation 14:1-5 – This is the true picture of the Bride. Here it defines their character.
4. 12 x 12 or divine order times divine order. I believe this would bring forth God's ultimate.

One Hundred fifty Three, 153

This number represents *renewal*.

1. John 21:11 – The disciples were fruitless trying to catch fish by themselves, but when the Lord appeared, they caught a multitude numbering one hundred fifty three. This speaks to us of revival that begins in His presence.

Two Hundred, 200

The number two hundred represents *insufficiency*.

1. John 6:7 – *"Philip answered him, Two hundred pennyworth of bread is not sufficient for them, that every one of them may take a little."*

2. Joshua 7:20-26 – Achan's two hundred shekels of silver were insufficient to save him from death.
3. II Samuel 14:25-26 – II Samuel 18:9-10 – Absalom's two hundred shekels weight of hair were insufficient to deliver him.
4. I Samuel 30:21 – *"And David came to the two hundred men, which were so faint that they could not follow David..."*

Three Hundred, 300

The number three hundred represents **a faithful remnant and deliverance**.

1. Faithful Remnant

   a. Judges 7:1-7
   b. Judges 8:4 – *"And Gideon came to Jordan, and passed over, he, and the three hundred men that were with him, faint, yet pursuing them."*
   c. Genesis 6:15 –The ark was three hundred cubits in length in which a faithful remnant found complete deliverance.

2. 3 x 100 – This defined means 3 (Godhead) times 100 (full count, faithfulness, maturity). This would give us the remnant, those who have matured and are compete in Him.

Three Hundred Ninety, 390

The number three hundred ninety represents **bearing iniquity**.

1. Ezekiel 4:5 – Ezekiel told he would bear the iniquity of Israel for three hundred ninety days.

Four Hundred, 400

The number four hundred represents **divine probation**.

1. Genesis 15:13-14 – Israel will serve four hundred years in slavery then be brought out.
2. Acts 7:6 – *"And God spake on this wise, That his seed should sojourn in a strange land; and that they should bring them into bondage, and entreat them evil four hundred years."*
3. 8 x 50 or new beginnings x jubilee = freedom

Four Hundred Eighty, 480

The number four hundred eighty represents the **building of the temple**.

1. I Kings 6:11 – Solomon began to build the house of the Lord four hundred eighty years after Israel came out of Egypt.

Six Hundred, 600

The number six hundred represents **warfare**.

1. Exodus 14:5-9 – Pharaoh took six hundred chosen chariots to try to destroy the children of Israel.
2. Judges 18:11 –Six hundred soldiers of the Tribe of Dan were sent to capture the city of Laish.
3. Judges 20:46-67 – Six hundred of the soldiers of Benjamin escaped slaughter.

Six Hundred Sixty Six, 666

The number six hundred sixty six represents **antichrist, satan**.

1. Revelation 13:17-18 – "*17And that no man might buy or sell, save he that had the mark, or the name of the beast, or the number of his name. 18Here is wisdom. Let him that hath understanding count the number of the beast: for it is the number of a man; and his number is Six hundred threescore and six.*" Six is the number both of man and satan. The antichrist (666) is a triplicate of satan and man: triplicate in human perfection, human wickedness, human pride, human rebellion, etc. Also, triplicate in satan's devices, rebellion, blasphemy, and wickedness.
2. I Samuel 17:4-7 – Goliath's description: Height – six cubits; spears head – six hundred shekels of iron; six pieces of armor; 666. Goliath is a type of the antichrist.
3. Daniel 3:1,7 – Nebuchadnezzar's image of gold was sixty cubits high, six cubits broad. Six instruments were used in worship – Another type of 666. Antichrist is a spirit just as much as it will be a real person.

Eight Hundred Eighty Eight, 888

Eight hundred eighty eight represents **Jesus**.

1. Jesus, the numbers of each letter of His Name adds up to 888

Nine Hundred Ninety Nine, 999

This number represents *God's wrath*.

1. Sodom, the numerical value of this word is nine hundred ninety nine.
2. Hebrews 3:11 – *"So I sware in my wrath, They shall not enter into my rest."* The numerical value of the phrase "my wrath" in this scripture is nine hundred ninety nine.

One Thousand, 1000

The number one thousand *represents perfect fruitfulness and rest.*

1. II Peter 3:8 – *"But, beloved, be not ignorant of this one thing, that one day is with the Lord as a thousand years, and a thousand years as one day."*
2. Millennial Reign is 1000 years.
3. Revelation 2:7 – *"He that hath an ear, let him hear what the Spirit saith unto the churches; To him that overcometh will I give to eat of the tree of life, which is in the midst of the paradise of God."*
4. Ezekiel 47:3-5

One Thousand Eighty One, 1081

The number one thousand eighty one represents *the abyss*.

1. The numerical value of the word abyss, the bottomless pit in the book of Revelation is 1081.

One Thousand Two Hundred Sixty, 1260

This number represents *tribulation*.

1. Revelations 12:6-14 – Last three and one half years of the tribulation.
2. Revelation 11:2 – *"But the court which is without the temple leave out, and measure it not; for it is given unto the Gentiles: and the holy city shall they tread under foot forty and two months."* Tribulation period forty-two months.
3. The beast's power was continued forty two months.
4. Time, Time, Time, ½ time.

One Hundred Forty Four Thousand, 144,000

The number one hundred forty four thousand represents *perfection of divine government.*

1. 12 x 12 x 1,000 = 144 or divine order times divine government times perfect fruitfulness and rest = perfection of God's government.

Chapter 14
Spiritual Definitions Of Objects

In this particular chapter, we will look alphabetically through the Scriptures at each object that has some spiritual meaning other than that which it naturally is. In some cases an object may mean nothing more than that which is written. Many objects however carry deep, revelational truth beyond their obvious meaning. Knowing what these objects represent in type will open to us a treasure house of understanding. We can apply these types or symbols and see deeper and greater truth in a passage of Scripture. It is true that sometimes people try to strain at certain objects or types and symbols and thus try to make the Word of God say something it isn't saying. I will not do this! Only when there is a witness of something truly deeper and has Scripture to back it up, will we apply this principle. Nor is it my desire to put too much emphasis on "knowledge" because the Bible does say *"knowledge puffeth up"* (I Corinthians 8:1). There is a great deal of difference between true Biblical knowledge that is supported by Scripture and someone trying to be super spiritual or as I like to call them "spooky". The Bible says, *"In the mouth of two or three witnesses shall every word be established"* (II Corinthians 13:1), *"rightly dividing the word of truth"* (II Timothy 2:15), *"comparing spiritual things with spiritual"* (I Corinthians 2:13).

Knowledge however is not something to be afraid of. In Proverbs 2:3 we are told to *"criest after knowledge, and liftest up thy voice for understanding"*; and *"By his knowledge the depths are broken up"* (Proverbs 3:20); also *"Wise men lay up knowledge"* (Proverbs 10:14); especially in Proverbs 22:20-21 where the Word declares *"Have not I written to thee excellent things in counsels and knowledge, That I might make thee know the certainty of the words of truth"*. The word excellent here means "threefold or weighty". So there are many passages with weighty, yes even threefold revelations in one verse. Peter says, *"Knowing this first, that no prophecy of the scripture is of any private interpretation"* (II Peter 1:20), meaning you cannot understand a passage alone. It must be compared and balanced with all other Scripture. Another translation reads, *"No Scripture is of its own private interpretation."* Every Scripture has a mate. In Isaiah 34:16 it says, *"Seek ye out of the book of the LORD, and read: no one of these shall fail, none shall want her mate: for my mouth it hath commanded, and his spirit it hath gathered them."*

So you see if one is to truly come to a place of understanding the Word, he or she cannot be just a cursory reader, but must go deeper like the Bereans in Acts 17:11, *"in that they received the word with all readiness of mind, and searched the scriptures daily, whether those things were so."*

This book has been written exclusively for the true disciple, the true student of the Word, to them as they look into the most wonderful book every written, the Bible. It is my desire to save others the countless hours and years of study that I have given to the Word of God (some 35 years now) of searching, seeking, studying, reading, and teaching the Scriptures daily for all these years, so that this generation can lead us on to perfection and to "*the knowledge of the Son of God*" (Ephesians 4:13). I ask the precious Holy Spirit, the Spirit of revelation to come upon us as we study. Amen!

Note also that in some of these objects I will refer to people's names that are a type or symbol, or that have spiritual significance beyond the definition of the name. Below are the objects as well as many key words, actions, animals, and names in Scripture listed in alphabetical order:

A

Aaron – ministry of the High Priest, Christ our High Priest, companion and fellow witness to

Aaron's rod – God's chosen priest, chosen priesthood, symbol of God's power and authority

Abaddon – satan, destruction, and of death, devil with authority, The Hebrew word for destruction is Abaddon; the Greek word is Apollyon

Abba – endearing term for God, daddy or papa

Abel – true sons of God, obedience, sons with revelation, Christ as shepherd, one who gives a righteous offering

Abiathar – disloyal priest, banished priesthood, carnal priesthood, forgotten priesthood

Abiding – waiting on the Lord, a place in God

Abigail – bride, virtuous woman, the true church

Abihu – carnal priest, proud, arrogant priest, priest destroyed for presumption and foolishness

Abishag – trying to revive past move of God, or Babylon and its human plans

Able – ability, God's divine enablement, God's grace, prepared, ready

Abomination – anything that offends God, disgusting, loathing, hateful things in the eyes of God or man

Abomination of desolation – idol or anything replacing God on the throne of our hearts

Abound – increase, growth, blessed abundantly

Abraham – man of faith, God the Father, Father ministry, Father of the faith, obedience, believer of God's promise

Abraham's bosom – Old Testament saints place of waiting in Hades, the place of the righteous death, waiting for the Messiah

Absalom – manipulative spirit, ambition, rebellion, spirit of antichrist, Babylon's choice

Abstain – refraining, fasting, staying away from evil of all kinds

Abundance – God's blessings, overflowing blessings, God's provision, more than enough

Acacia wood ("shittim wood" – KJV) – humanity, Jesus' humility

Acceptable – something God favors, something right or good.

Access – entrance to God, able to stand before God

Accomplish – completing a task, finished, an effort to please God, desired results

Accord – unity, fellowship, oneness

Accursed – something God has cursed, an abomination, unholy thing

Accuse – satan, false reporting, to find a reason to hurt someone

Achan – demon, sinful believer in your midst, trouble maker.

Achor – trouble, door of hope

Acquainted – knowing, desire for knowledge, understanding of something or someone

Acts – actions good or bad, what someone does

Adam – the old man, fallen nature, Christ the last Adam

Adamant – unyielding, firmness, hard

Add – growth in God, increase, desire for more, given

Adder (Asp) – satan, serpent, false teachers, poisonous doctrine or works

Adonijah – rebellion, ambition

Adoption – sonship, being made a member of God's family

Adorn – ornaments of religion, outward preparation of beauty

Adullam – place of refuge, hiding place, stronghold, place for oppressed people to go to God

Adultery – spiritual fornication, betrayal, violation of marriage vows, false doctrine that seduces

Adversary – satan, enemy of God and His people, accuser

Adversity – dealings of God, trouble, hardship

Advocate – Jesus our lawyer, defender, helper

Affections – desires of the flesh and soulish realm, concerned feelings for someone, true love and emotion

Afflictions (Afflict, Afflicted) – dealings of God, a sickness, trouble, persecution, part of our suffering in the Lord, testing or tests, things to overcome, hardships

Agag – king of flesh, wicked habit, or evil ways (Amalekite king).

Agate – characteristics of God, His nature in our hearts

Age – experience, wisdom, maturity

Ages – a prophetic time period in God

Agrippa – someone who lets a habit or person keep them from the Lord

Aha – showing contempt for the things of God and His people

Ahab – Babylon, weak husband, someone who's manipulated

Ai – sin, flesh, the world conquered by Jesus

Air – the heavenlies, fruitless endeavors

Alabaster box – worship, man's best given to God, symbol of Christ's sacrifice, a sacrifice of worship that costs something dear to us

Algum – pillars, humanity, strengthened by God, fragrant humanity, Christ's humanity

Alive – restoration, resurrection, life in Jesus

Alleluia – worship, heavenly worship

Almighty – all sufficient God, female characteristic of God (*El Shaddai*), ruler over all, complete authority and power

Almond – Christ's resurrection, fruitfulness, resurrection life, God's chosen

Alms – tithing, giving, offerings to God and His work, aid for the poor

Aloes – fragrance of the Lord, healing balm

Alpha – beginning, Jesus' everlasting life, Christ the first cause

Altar – Place of sacrifice, place of worship and incense, cross of Calvary, different levels of sacrifice, judgment and worship, place of death. There were altars of earth, stone, brass, and gold, each symbolizing a different sacrifice

Amalek – flesh, enemy of God

Ambassadors – witness for God, a governmental position, one who represents another

Amber – the glory of God, Jesus as the brightness of God's glory, glory of God in judgment

Amen – agreement (so be it), witness to the truth

Amethyst – a characteristic of God, royal priesthood

Ammon – mixture, compromise

Amorites – pride, evil giants (Nephilim), enemy of God and His people

Amos – good shepherd, burden bearer, symbol of Jesus our Shepherd

Anak – devilish giants (Nephilim), principalities, devils working through men

Anchor – hope, security, stability, something that roots us to Jesus

Ancient of days – the eternal God, throne of Christ, maturity, wisdom

Ancles (Ankles) – level of growth in God, our beginning walk with God

Angel – God's messenger, God's host sent to help His people, pastors, false messenger, our protectors

Angel of the Lord – Jesus appearing in the Old Testament, a supernatural, godly helper to us

Anger – Justified wrath, righteous indignation, also a work of the flesh, violent temper

Anguish – Emotional trauma, extreme sorrow, intense emotional distress

Anoint, Anointing, Anointed – consecration, God's presence, Holy Spirit, proof of God's call, set apart for God's service, empowered for God's work, God's supernatural ability given as a gift to accomplish His work

Ant – worker, wise, industrious, organized service, diligence, smallness but the ability to do great things

Apes – waste of riches, indulgence in foolishness, slothfulness, nothing to do with time or money, frivolousness, the beastly nature

Apostle – symbol of a Father ministry, one who plants churches, ministry confirmed by miracles, trustworthy leadership, a mature fruitful and proven ministry, one who has obvious spiritual sons, gift of the Spirit

Apothecary – Holy Spirit working in the lives of believers, a true worshipper preparing incense offered to God

Apparel – speaks of an outward show of our inward character, covering, false character hidden by clothing

Appear (Appearance, Appeared, Appeareth, Appearing) – Christ's coming, also a false showing of inner bad character, the glory of God revealed in the son's of God, God revealing inner working by the Holy Spirit Himself, coming before the Lord, the outward show of an inner working by the Holy Spirit

Apple – Jesus Christ, a symbol of someone dear to God, sweetness, the local church (apple tree)

Appoint, Appointed – a placement God gives, authority given, allotment, God chosen leadership or place, Jesus God's true appointed

Approved – God's pleasure, earned praised, to test or try, proven

Aprons – false religion covering of sin, man's attempt to hide his sin, a point of contact for God's anointing

Ararat – resting place in Jesus

Araunah – threshing, sacrifice

Archers – weapon used against people, people who like to slay with words

Aright – a good condition, something corrected

Arise – resurrection, going on with God, awaking out of sleep, shaking oneself from the flesh, the presence of God coming upon, answering the call of God, making a decision to do God's will

Ark – God's manifest presence, place of safety, humanity, Jesus Christ, vehicle for deliverance

Arm – God's saving power, authority, our works

Armed – trained sons of God, tools necessary to protect oneself

Armies – God's army in heaven and earth, spiritual powers evil or good

Armour – God's protection, divine protection in warfare

Armourbearer – servant, putting on Christ

Armoury – hidden riches, house of God's weapons

Arrow – swift and silent judgments, words, weapons of God's deliverance, evil words

Asa – 60-fold believer, one who loves and serves the Lord but yet in the end doesn't quite give himself completely and who dies knowing he could have done better

Asaph – chief singer, worshipper, father of worshippers

Ascend, Ascended, Ascending – worship going up before the Lord, rising into the heights of God's presence, Jesus' resurrection

Ash, Ashes – mourning, sacrifice, burnt offering, repentance

Ashamed – embarrassment, shame because of sin, not having done enough, falling short

Asher – happiness, joy of the Lord

Asleep – rest, resting in the Lord, slothfulness, death

Asp (Adder) – false teachers, satan, satan's lies

Ass – burden bearer, man's wild nature, God's chosen vessels, stubbornness, strength

Assemble, Assembled, Assemblies, Assembly – local churches, a gathering of God's people, to gather together

Assurance – confidence in God, peace, security, eternal salvation

Assyria – enemy, enemies of God's people, Babylon

Astray – to depart from the Lord, to sin, to be deceived

Athaliah – false religion

Athirst – desire and hunger for the Lord
Atonement – the Lord Jesus, redemption, God's anger satisfied, sin forgiven
Attain – reaching a place in God, a mark to press towards
Attend – Giving heed to, listening to
Aul – love slave, heart of a servant
Author – inventor of our salvation, the writer or planner
Authority – power, control, designated lead, or designated power
Availeth – something gained
Avenge, Avenger – justification, bring judgment for, enemy
Awake – rising out of sleep, resurrection, stirring oneself up
Aware – being alert, ready
Ax, Axe, Axes – judgment, warfare

B

Baal – false God, idol
Babel, Babylon – confusion, mixture, false church, religious system, old order rebellion, antichrist spirit
Babes – place of growth in God, beginning stage of work with God, immature believers
Baca – weeping, dealings of God
Back – turning away from someone, refusing to acknowledge
Backsliding – turning away from the Lord, not going on with God, going back to sinful ways
Badger – covering, Christ's humanity, God's protection
Bag – purse, weapon holder, an item God puts things in
Bake (Baked, Baken, Baker, Bakers, Baketh) – process of the Word becoming real in our lives, balanced message, Jesus the bread from heaven, revelation married to our situation
Balaam – false prophet, an hireling, ministers who love filthy lucre
Balance, Balances – an even weight, not over in any area, just judgment, fair, honest, a just weight, sound or balanced Scripturally
Bald, Baldness – weakness, humility, sorrow, no covering, shame
Balm – healing medicine, healing ministry, comfort
Band, Bands – a covenant, a group joined together for a common cause, shackle, bondage
Banished – extreme separation
Banks – limitation, perimeter
Banner – a standard, emblem, victory
Banquet – celebration, rejoicing

Baptism, Baptized – death to life, overflowing, to be immersed

Barabbas – man of the flesh, the other son, the old Adam

Barak – hero of the faith, submissive, abiding in his calling, acknowledging and supporting women ministry

Bare – burden bearer, giving birth, to have authority, to unveil, to yield, to witness to, nakedness

Barefoot – shame, no help in our walk with God, Preachers, unprepared

Barley – poverty, low reputation, Christ the bread from heaven, harvest, overcoming

Barn – storehouse

Barrel – container of blessing, the extent of man's resources

Barren – being unfruitful, unproductive, empty, human's desperate for a miracle, not bringing forth fruit

Bars – foundational material, strengthened house of God, judgment, barriers

Baruch – disciple, student of the Word, scribe

Barzillai – kindness, true companion

Base – to appear low or of bad reputation, looked upon as uncomely

Bases – a foundation

Bashan – a habitation of demons

Basket – divine protection, blessings

Bason – container of God

Bastard – a person without a father ministry, an illegitimate child, rebellion, bad reputation

Bath, Bathe, Baths – cleansing, purification, sanctification, baptisms

Bathsheba – adulterer redeemed, God can turn something bad into something fruitful or blessed

Battle – warfare of any type, resisting the enemy, we must let God fight for us, the good fight of faith

Bay – God's horses prepared, the wicked

Beacon – the church triumphant

Beam – support, strength, a character flaw, foundation, witnessing to something

Bear, Beareth, Bearest, Bearing – to carry or handle something, give birth, support, to give witness

Beard – maturity, full growth

Bears – evil men, God's judgment

Beast – worldly kingdom, evil spirits, flesh, Christ's sacrifice

Beat, Beaten – grind to powder, punish

Beauty, Beautiful – the bride, God's people, fair looking, something wonderful, the glory of God

Bed – a place of love, comfort, adultery, slothfulness, place attained to, resting in the Lord

Bee, Bees – judgment, enemies of God's people

Beersheba – a place of an oath, covenant

Befall, Befallen, Befalleth, Befell – something happening to us

Beg, Begging, Begged – being in want, unafraid to humble yourself

Begat – birthing someone or something

Beguile, Beguiling, Beguiled – seducing, deception, deluding

Behemoth – the Lord Jesus and the perfected sons of God (*Job 40:15-24*)

Bell – worship in the Most Holy Place, song of the Lord, our walk of worship

Belly – our innermost being, the human spirit, appetite, womb

Beloved – our bridegroom Jesus, one doubly loved, God's people

Bend – evil words, the wicked's tongue, bowing, submission

Benefit(s) – blessings of God

Benjamin – the doubly blessed one, sons of the right hand, manifest sons of God

Bent, Bending – wicked bowing before the just, God's people backsliding, the dealings of God, God's judgment

Beryl – some divine characteristics of God

Bethany – the dealings of God, Jesus' favorite place to visit personally, Bethany means house of figs and house of affliction

Bethel – the house of God, Bethel literally means house of God

Bethlehem – house of bread, the Word of God, Word in God's house, God's provision

Bethlehem-Judah – the house of bread and praise (literal Hebrew meaning), the place where true worship and a living Word are brought forth

Betray – disloyalty, turning on a friend or a family member, not standing with someone who expected it

Betroth, Betrothed – espousal, engagement, Jesus and His bride

Beulah – being married

Beware – to stand guard against, be wary of, be concerned

Bewitched – being deceived, tricked, seduced by a human, demon or false doctrine

Beyond the Jordan – entering into our full inheritance

Bezaleel – Apostle, master builder

Billows – the presence of God rolling over us

Bind, Bindeth, Binding – conquering, subduing someone, to yoke something, to heal, a sign of remembrance, to swear an oath, to gather, to take authority over someone or something

Bird(s) – sacrifice, demons, wandering from the Lord, living in heavenly places, wandering from your place

Birthright – our inheritance, sonship, double portion, the blessing

Bishop – overseer in the House of God, superintendent, place of authority in the church

Bit, Bits – something used to control our tongues

Bite, Biteth – demons attacking us or someone attacking another, words used to hurt

Bitter – bondage, misery, gall, resentful, harsh suffering, experiences necessary in our walk

Bitter herbs – Passover, suffering, the shame of the cross, bitter experiences to be reminded during Passover

Bitterness – bondage, misery, gall, resentful, harsh suffering, angry. Bitterness takes the word bitter to another level, where if you are bitter but repent or allow God to deal with you, freedom is assured, hence the term "bitter or better". We decide. But when someone is bitter and they won't make their heart right or allow the dealings of God to affect change in them, a root of bitterness begins to grow and it is like a cancer that will ultimately destroy that person

Black – death, darkness, famine, sin

Blame, Blamed – sin, shame, accusations against

Blameless – without accusation, free of shame and sin, pure

Blaspheme – cursing, denial of God, speak against, words of heresy, against God

Blasphemy of the Holy Ghost – attributing the works of God to the works of the devil. Contrary to what some believe, it is forgivable or else God speaks out of two sides of His mouth. He cannot say "all sin" can be forgiven and then say one can't be forgiven. The reason it is "unforgivable" is the person who does it is in such a bitter condition that he simply won't repent. Notice that in Mark's Gospel it says he is in <u>danger</u> of eternal damnation

Blemish – the stain of sin, an imperfection, a spot of sin, Jesus was our lamb without blemish

Bless – the Hebrew word for bless is *barak* which means to kneel, to bless God as an act of adoration. The same is true for God to man. It is a type then of God enriching someone, God showering someone with kindness, favour, etc. Also it is a type of worship for the believer, to kneel in body and in heart and with their mouth giving praise to God

Blessed – being highly favoured of God, enriched by God, worship of God

Blessing, Blessings – being highly favored of God, enriched with God's provision, worship toward God

Blind, Blindness – no vision (naturally or spiritually), lack of discernment, spiritual ignorance, darkness

Blood – life of all flesh, atonement, forgiveness, Christ's sacrifice

Blossom – fruitfulness, blooming

Blot – to rub out or erase, forgiveness, a stain or spot in our lives

Blue – all things heavenly

Blunt – dullness

Blush – embarrassment, man's image

Boards – individual members of the house of God

Boaz – kinsman redeemer, Jesus

Body – flesh of a person, many membered house of God, a local church

Bold, Boldly, Boldness – confidence, without fear and insecurities, unafraid, to speak or testify

Bond, Bondage – enslavement, captive, religious tradition, holy covenant

Bone(s) – flesh, body of Christ, individual members in the body

Book – a record of something, the Bible, a record God keeps, symbol of divine revelation

Booth(s) – temporary dwelling, house God inhabits

Born – being newly formed (naturally or spiritually)

Borne – carrying something, bearing something

Bosom – the heart of someone, intimacy, love, affection

Bottle(s) – a container (naturally or spiritually), spiritual life, source of supply

Bound – bondage, healing, captive, a union

Bounds – limits, area ordained of God, predetermined positions

Bow – God's covenant, kneeling, submissive in heart, weapon

Bowels – innermost being, compassion, human emotions

Bowl(s) – container of things holy

Bracelets – betrothal or seal, religious or fleshly, worldly ornaments

Bramble – curse, fruitlessness

Branch, Branches – Jesus, sons of God

Brass (Brazen) – judgment against sin, judgment over our idols, judgment over our sins, and over our walk with God; Jesus took our judgment on the cross. He became the wood overlaid with brass.

Brawling – contention, argumentative, fightings in the body or the world

Brazen altar – the cross, Christ's substitutionary sacrifice. It was made of brass (judgment) over wood (humanity – Jesus)

Brazen serpent – judgment on satan, Jesus on the cross defeating him

Breach – something broken, torn through, a break in a relationship (God and man) or (man to man); Jesus has healed our breach, now He wants us to do the same with others

Bread – the Word of God, a level of growth in the Word (milk, bread, meat, strong meat, hidden manna), staff of life, Jesus the true bread from heaven, provision, money, also unleavened or pure bread is sound doctrine

Breadth – width, how far, how wide God reaches to us

Break – something broken, a covenant, promise, oath, bondages, people, Jesus who breaks all our yokes and bondages

Breast – the heart

Breastplate – faith, love, judgment, righteousness, protection for the heart

Breasts – nourishment, El Shaddai, mother's milk, being weaned by men (teachers), deep devotion, love, heart

Breath – life, spirit, the Holy Spirit

Breeches – garments worn by priests, a covering to help us walk with God, to cover our nakedness

Brethren – brothers, God's people, the church, family, members of the body of Christ, a covenantal bond, Jesus our brother

Brick – Babylon's building blocks, flesh, works of men

Bride – married woman, the bride of Christ, what we are to run after and become, the prize of the high calling

Bridegroom – Jesus our husband

Bridle – restraint, taming of the tongue

Briers – thorns, hindrances to our walk, cares of this world, people who are our enemies

Bright, Brightness – the glory of God, shining with His light and glory

Brimstone – divine fire, God's judgment

Broad – wide, open, way of sin

Broken – to break something, a crushed heart, humility, covenant breached, area of a personality that is amiss, God destroying our bondages

Brook(s) – the place of God's provision

Brother, Brotherly, Brothers – a family member, fellow Christian, relationship, Jesus our brother

Brown – earth, warmth; Brown is the Hebrew word, *chuwm* which means to be warm, sunburnt. The Greek word is *therme* which means heat.

Bruise, Bruised, Bruises – a mark, hurts, cleansing, pains, deep wounds

Brute, Brutish – fleshly believers, bullies, a fool

Buckler(s) – God's protection, Jesus, strength

Bud, Budded, Buds – to blossom, bloom, come to life

Build – to make strong, to construct, to edify, to lay a foundation of the Scriptures in a believer's life

Builded – to construct, to join together

Builder, Builders, Built, Buildest, Buildeth – Jesus the cornerstone, God Himself, ministers, skilled men, teachers, five-fold ministry

Building(s) – the house of God, physical or spiritual structures, to edify

Bullock – Christ our sacrifice, servant hood, labor, strength

Bulls – demons, sacrifice, strength

Bulwarks – protection, God's protection for us, tower of strength

Bundle – a gathering of something, wrapped up

Burden(s) – something borne, carried, a weight, weight of the Word of God, a serious carrying a load for someone else, Jesus our burden bearer

Buried – death of the Adamic nature, blood and water Baptism, risen to new life

Burn, Burned, Burnt, Burning – to be angry, to give light, cleansing, judgment, on fire for God, everlasting light, the glory of God, sexual desire, the dealings of God

Burning bush – Jesus, Word of God on fire in our hearts

Burnt offering – Jesus our sacrifice, sacrifice for sin, consecration, voluntary sacrifice

Burst – overflowing of God's Spirit, yokes broken

Bushel – hiding the light and life of God within you

Business – God's work, general labor, that which causes a dream to come to pass

Busybodies – slothful, gossiping saints
Butter – riches of the Word of God
Buy, Buyeth, Buyest – paying the price, purchase something
Byword – outcast one who is made to look like a fool

C

Cabin – a cell, dungeon, prison house, bondage
Caesar – the world, worldly law, worldly government, ungodly authority
Cage – the religious system
Cain – natural man, self-willed, wicked slaying the righteous, spirit of antichrist, jealousy, demon possessed who departs from God's presence, uncaring about your brother
Cake(s) – living Word, unleavened Word, Jesus, believers unfinished in their walk, also the remnant, worshipping Babylon, defiled bread
Calamity, Calamities – ruin, evil, great adversity, misfortune, oppression, God's judgment
Calamus – the anointing oil, crushed, fragrance
Caldron(s) – God's people under attack, the dealings of God
Caleb – overcomer, willing to stand up to satan's giants, the remnant of dogs, endurance, Jesus the overcomer; His name in Hebrew is *Kaleb* which means forcible and comes from a root that means a dog, to attack
Calf – worship of an idol, celebration of joy, a willingness to work, found in the new creation man
Call – to cry out loud by men, God crying out loud to His people, God calling His people to service, men crying out to the Lord, identifying someone
Called – naming someone or something, the chosen people of God, God calling His people, those selected by God
Calleth, Calling – God's divine call to intimacy, calling or election of God to the ministry, our ministry
Calm – peace, storms of any kind stopped, peace after the storm
Calvary – the cross, salvation
Calves – sacrifice, offering, worship, growth in God
Camel(s) – burden bearer, service, not a beast to eat (no flesh), also carrying the Holy Spirit, an impediment to the will of God; The Hebrew word for camel, *gamal*, means – labor, burden bearer
Camp (s) – a gathering place, outside of religious order of things, number of people, an army

Camphire – the anointing, God covering and forgiving us; Camphire in Hebrew means – to cover or to coat, the root meaning to cover with bitumen; The word root of camphire is also translated in the King James Version as – appease, make atonement for, forgive, be merciful, pacify, pardon, reconcile

Cana – marriage of the bride and Jesus, beginning of miracles; Cana in the Greek means – place of reeds

Canaan (Canaanites) – our inheritance obtained through warfare, our enemies defeated; It is the land of our enemies; Canaan in Hebrew means – humiliated, merchant, or trader, and comes from a root that means – to bend the knee, humiliated, to vanquish

Candle – light, revelation, the spirit of man, Spirit of God, Word of God, life in God

Candlestick – light, revelation, the Holy Spirit, baptism of the Holy Spirit, gifts and fruits of the Holy Spirit, the local church, the two witnesses

Canker – false doctrine, impediments to our walk

Cankerworms – God's judgment

Captain (Captains) – ruler or leader, Jesus our Captain; Captain in Hebrew means – head person in any rank or class, ruler, chief, lord, governor; The Greek word means – to chief or leader

Captive (Captivity) – being in bondage, seduced by false doctrine, bound by Babylon or religion, prisoner; God will deliver us

Carbuncle – a characteristic of God's divine nature, worn by the High priest on his heart symbolizing God's nature is in us, also it is a type of prosperity or life; The Hebrew word for carbuncle means – a gem as flashing, and comes from a root meaning – lightning, a flashing sword; It is the color green

Carcass (Carcass) – dead bodies, God's people without true life

Care (Cares, Careful, Carefulness) – concern, worry, burden, worldly temptations, concerned loving help, concern over worldly things

Careless – uncaring people, slothfulness, not walking with the Lord

Carmel – confrontation, mind of Christ, the glory of God

Carnal (Carnally) – flesh, soulish mind, natural things

Carpenter – builders, masters of wood, Jesus, teachers in the body

Carried (Carriest, Carrieth) – to bear something, to take away, to take someone away against their will, to believe false doctrine

Carry (Carrying) – to bear a burden, to take something with you

Cart – man-made efforts, trying to control the anointing

Carved – engraved image either God or satan

Cassia – fragrance of the Lord, anointing oil, crushing, suffering; Cassia had to be crushed for the anointing oil

Cast – giving something away, to take something down, get rid of, depressed, to throw something, to give, to yield something to God

Castaway – being disqualified; The Greek word is *adokimos* which means – unapproved, rejected, worthless

Casteth (Casting) – to throw something, to remove something, to pat down, to give up, to kick something out, throwing stones or accusations at others

Castle – fortress

Catch – capturing something or someone

Caterpiller (Caterpillars) – destroying forces, demon spirits

Cattle – beast of burden, measure of wealth, beast

Caught –trapped, to grab something or someone, a catching away

Caul – liver, inner most being

Cause – to make something happen, reason for something, a holy reason

Cave – a hiding place, dealings of God, humility, burying place; The Hebrew root word for cave means – to be bare, to make naked

Cease (Ceased, Ceaseth, Ceasing) – stop, quitting, put an end to, death

Cedar (Cedars) – king of the trees, Jesus, strength, stability, sons of God, power, majesty, building with strength; The Hebrew root word for cedar means – to be firm

Censer – prayer, worship, and intercession

Centurion – authority, captain, great faith in a Gentile

Certainty – knowing something for sure

Chaff – that which is worthless, less worth, the wicked, false prophesies, false teachings

Chain (Chains) – bondage, punishment, symbol of honor, religious ornaments

Chamber (Chambers) – secret place, place of love, hiding place, the places within our soul

Champion – demon king, evil leader, victorious one, Jesus

Change (Changed) – not altering course, do not waffle, not double minded or double hearted, appointed season, altering your course, being double minded, not steadfast

Chapiter (Chapiters) – leadership in the house of God, crown, headship; a chapiter was the top of a pillar or column

Charge (Charged, Chargeable) – a solemn decree given to someone, an oath, a persons life or reputation, no payment

Chariot – place of honor, a vehicle, prophetic vehicle, human resources

Charity – agape love of God

Chaste – purity, to be clean, bride of Christ; the Greek word is *hagnos* which means – clean, innocent, modest, perfect, pure

Chasten (Chastened, Chastenest, Chasteneth, Chastening, Chastise, Chastised, Chastisement, Chastiseth) – dealings of God, discipline of the Lord, training God's sons, making disciples, punishment (naturally and spiritually), tutoring or mentoring; the Hebrew words for chasten, etc, are *yakach* – to be right, correct, to argue, to decide; the next is *yacar* – to chastise with blows or words, to instruct; the last Hebrew word is *muwcar* – to reproof, warning, instruction, restraint, discipline. The Greek words are *paideuo* – to train up a child, to educate, discipline by punishment; the next Greek word is *paideia* – tutorage, education or training, disciplinary correction, correction, to nurture. Most people think of these words in terms of terrible beatings. This is not our heavenly Father's way. Only in rare cases would someone be subject to severe discipline. It is really about educating, instructing, correcting, and teaching. It is about making disciples. God's chastening is done as a loving Father. We must see this as the true revelation of these words or be lost in natural thinking

Chebar – bondage to Babylon

Cheek (Cheeks) – suffering, testing, being smitten, persecution; it is also a type of reflecting the character of God as seen in our countenance; the Hebrew word for cheek is *lechiy* – to be soft, the jawbone; the Greek word is *siagon* – the jaw

Cheer (Cheerful, Cheerfulness) – happiness or merriment in spite of the circumstance, strengthened with God's Holy Spirit, just plain happiness that brings boldness; the Hebrew words are *yatab* – to be or make well, happy, successful, sound or right; *towb* – good in the widest sense, good or a good thing; *nuwb* – to make flourish, bring forth fruit; the Greek words are *tharseo* – to have courage, be of good cheer, and comes from a root – *tharsos* – boldness, courage; *euthumeo* – to cheer up, be cheerful, merry; *hilaros* – merry, hilarious, willing, and comes from a root – *hileos* – cheerful, attractive, gracious

Cheese – curdled milk, diminished Word of God

Chemosh – false god, idol, and abomination

Chenaanah – chief musician, planted worshipper, the song of the Lord; his name means "Jah has planted"

Cherethites – the sons of God, overcomers; this tribe was the personal body guard army of David

Cherish (Cherisheth) – to care deeply for, to nurture someone; the Hebrew word, *cakan* – to be familiar with, to minister to; the Greek word is *thalpo* – to warm, to brook, to foster

Cherub (Cherubims) – the remnant, those who guard God's glory, symbolic of overcomers who have attained unto a glorious place, deep worshippers who love and respect and are charged with guarding God's glory; the Hebrew word, *kruwb* – means an imaginary figure; These beings (and many scholars are in doubt who they really are) are believed by some to be a class of angels, others believe that they are redeemed men who have attained a place of greatness with the Lord

Chest – a box of hidden wealth, treasures

Chew (Chewed, Cheweth) – to meditate on God's Word

Chickens – mother hen, Jesus over His church

Chide – complaining, criticize

Chief (Chiefest) – captain, head, leader, Jesus our chief

Child – immaturity, little human being, not full grown, innocence, needing discipline and training

Children – a place of growth in God (babes, children, young men, men, aged), growing up but still immature

Choice – excellence, the best, God's appointed one

Choke (Choked) – to strangle, to stifle, and cut off, worldly things, cares of this world

Choose – to select, to pick out from among the rest, to make a heartfelt decision

Chose (Chosen) – selected, the remnant, God's called ones, to make a decision, God's choice; the Hebrew word is *bachar* – to try, select, appoint, selected; one Greek word is *eklegomai* – to select, to choose out from among; another Greek word is *eklektos* – to select a favorite

Christ – Jesus, anointed one, Messiah

Christian (Christians) – little anointed one, God's people

Church – God's people, called out ones, body of Christ

Cieled – hiding from God, veiling or covering something in a human or man-made way; one Hebrew word for cieled is *caphan* – to hide by covering; another is *chaphah* – to veil, to encase

Cinnamon – the anointing, false fragrance of the Lord, Babylon's fragrance, strange woman's deceptive fragrance

Circle – eternity, timeless, that which has no end

Circumcision – covenant relationship with God, a cutting away, cutting off the desires of the flesh, God's way to reproduce, not man made ideas

Circumspect (Circumspectly) – being aware, discerning, diligence.

Cistern – place where we drink from both naturally and spiritually, man made ways of drinking (spiritually) not God's way

Cities of Refuge – safety in Jesus, a place to turn to

City – a community encampment of people, town, and the people of God

City of David – the church, the city of God, the stronghold of Zion

Clap (Clapped) – to rejoice, to worship with the hands, persecution

Clave – to cut, God cutting, to cling to

Clay – earth, flesh, something to be molded in God's hands, Adamic nature

Clean (Cleanness) – not soiled, purity, innocence, walking uprightly, washed in the blood and in the Word

Cleanse (Cleansed, Cleanseth, Cleansing) – to wash oneself (naturally or spiritually), washed in the blood, made clean by the blood and the Word of God, to apply God's Word to your life, the process of sanctification, to make clean

Clear – transparency, guiltless, to see through, cleansing, right

Cleave (Cleaved, Cleaveth) – to hold fast to, to divide or separate

Cleft (Clefts) – the secret place, a hiding place; the Hebrew words for cleft and clefts are *chagav* – to take refuge, a rift in rocks; *neqarah* which comes from a root word meaning – to bore or penetrate, to dig; and *baqa* – to rend, break, or open

Clods – flesh, earth and dust, the Word of God ruined by being overwhelmed by our carnal desires

Cloke – a covering of some kind either good or bad, a garment

Closed – eyes shut to the truth, finished work, sealed up

Closet (Closets) – secret place, hiding place

Cloth – covering, a garment that speaks of your righteousness

Clothe (Clothed) – dressed with garments both naturally and spiritually, a covering of God or flesh, a covering of glory

Clothes (Clothing) – what you've attained to in God, our righteousness, the condition of a soul, a humbling of oneself, a covering for nakedness or sin, religious garments

Cloud (Clouds, Cloudy) – the glory of God, His manifest presence, the heavens, God's people, false believers

Cloven (Clovenfooted) – rightly dividing the Word, revelation of the Holy Spirit, that which was unclean

Cluster (Clusters) – new wine, gathering of Spirit-filled believers, provision

Coal (Coals) – kindling a fire, burning desire, intense cleansing, judgment

Coat (Coats) – the covering of the Lord, seasons of growth in God

Coat of many colors – favor, sonship, chosen ones, a covering from the Lord filled with all the aspects of His divine nature

Cock – resurrection, alarm, the coming of the dawn

Cockatrice – demons, snake

Cold – seasons of God, lack of zeal for the Lord, left your first love

Colors (Colours) – characteristics of the divine nature, many facets of God's glory

Colt – sons of God bearing the image of Jesus at His coming, though man is born wild as he is tied by the Holy Spirit he will learn to carry Jesus, not controlled by man or religion

Comeliness (Comely) – the beauty of the Lord upon a person, natural beauty

Comforter – the Holy Spirit

Commandments – the Law of God, God's Word

Communicate – giving, partnering with a ministry by supporting them financially

Communication – a person's ability to say what is in their heart, Words, preaching the Gospel, giving to ministries

Communion – the Lord's supper, fellowship, a covenant relationship, God speak and fellowshipping with man

Company (Companies)– the army of God, the household of God, a group of people, to have fellowship with someone, local churches

Compass (Compassed, Compassest, Compasseth) – being surrounded by something, cover or fills a large place, to travel

Concubine (Concubines) – woman without a husband, a part of the church who have not given themselves completely to the bridegroom

Concupiscence – lustful desires, a longing for that which is forbidden

Coney (Conies) – us as unclean but hiding in the Lord our God, our weakness turned into His strength

Confusion – a thing outlawed by God, embarrassment, disorder

Conquer (Conquering, Conquerors) – sons of God going throughout the whole earth, the overcomers, to prevail, to overcome

Conscience – soul of man, moral consciousness, the place in each of us that knows right from wrong

Consecrate, Consecrated, Consecration – dedication, to hallow, to sanctify oneself wholly, to make holy, made or to make holy

Consolation (Consolations) – comfort, solace, hope for comfort

Consumption – judgment to God, to emaciate, destruction, to utterly consume

Contempt (Contemptible) – despising, to disrespect, to disesteem, vile, shamed

Contend (Contended, Contendest, Contendeth, Contending) – to fight with or for, to struggle for, to defend, to wrestle

Contention (Contentious) – strife, quarrel, fight, to struggle

Controversy – a fight with, a contest personal or legal, an argument with

Conversation – behavior, lifestyle, citizenship, words of your mouth

Convocation (Convocations) – an assembly, public meeting, holy gathering

Cord (Cords) – binding, to twist, the love of God

Corn – the Word of God, Jesus the bread of life, mature Word, harvest, increase, the body of Christ, inheritance, revelation; the Hebrew word for corn, *dagan* – increase, grain, and comes from a root word, *dagah* – to spawn, to move rapidly, become numerous

Cornelius – Gentiles hungry for Jesus, a giver, opening of the Gentile world

Cornerstone – Jesus Christ our foundation

Cornet (Cornets) – a call to gather, worship

Corrupt (Corrupted, Corruptly) – to decay, to ruin, spoil, destroy

Corruption (Corruptible) – destruction, marred, to decay or ruin, to destroy

Cost (Costly) – sacrifice, how much it will take, expensive, the price that must be paid

Counselor (Counsels) – given advice, Word of God, Holy Spirit, Jesus, leadership, evil advisors

Course – predetermined path, direction

Courses – orders of worshipping priests, God's people, each of us has our individual turn to worship God

Court (Courts) – Tabernacle or House of God (which has three divisions – outer court, holy place, and most holy place), place of God's presence

Covenant – solemn oath between God and man, a promise God made to us and a promise we made to Him, Old Testament and New Testament, agreement between two people or peoples, the Word of God, God's presence in the covenant (ark), cutting of the flesh, agreement

Cover (Covered, Covering) – protection, to fill or surround, clothing our nakedness, our sins forgiven, headship

Covering (Head Covering) – submission to authority

Covert – hiding place, Jesus, the sons of God in the last days

Crackling – fool's laughter

Crane – mourning, loneliness

Creep (Creepeth, Creeping) – earth or flesh, demons, false balance

Crib – the House of the Lord

Crimson – the blood of Jesus, sacrifice for sin

Crooked – sin, deformity of the flesh, twisted not straight, sin in your life that excludes you, satan

Cross – salvation, redemption, suffering, death to bring life, self-denial, the Lord Jesus

Crown (Crowned, Crownedst, Crownest) – Jesus, reward, honor, authority, rulership, paid a price to get it

Crucified (Crucify) – Jesus our Salvation, death to self.

Crumbs – Gentiles (the Nations) hungering for very small portions of the Word of God, Nations desperate to hear the Good News

Cruse – container of anointing, container of the Holy Ghost, Supernatural provision, Holy Spirit filled believers

Crystal – transparency, innocence, purity

Cubit (Cubits) – measurement, full stature, maturity, the area of the Lord working through us, God's divine order of things, His sovereign detail of life; the cubit is a measurement from the elbow to the tip of the middle finger; the actual Greek word, *pechus* means – "the forearm"

Cucumbers – temptations of the world that causes us to backslide, longing and lusting after the old life before salvation.

Cud – chewing the Word of God, meditating on the Scriptures.

Cummin – Word of God beaten small, looking at every aspect of a passage of Scripture to get the maximum revelation out of it; also a type of giving of the revelation that one has received; cumin is a seed producing herb when harvested is threshed with sticks.

Cunning – skillful person in any field, work of a skilled person, people who use evil tactics to deceive

Cup – the gift from God inside you, a container of blessing, the cup of the Lord (communion), cup of life and health, cup of devils and abominations, cup of suffering

Cupbearer – servant of the king, bringing wine to the Gentile nations and kings

Curtain – the coverings of the House of the Lord, leadership who protects the House of God, the beauty of God's people and the glory inside them, Jesus hung for our sins; the colors of the curtains were: white – righteousness of Jesus, blue – heaven origin of Jesus, purple – royalty of Jesus, scarlet – suffering and humanity of Jesus; Cherubims on the curtains – the glory of Jesus' image on the house of God.

Cush – darkness, sin, father of Babylon.

Cushi – redeemed from darkness and Babylon, running with a message (the Gospel), a faithful messenger, ministers of the Gospel, Jesus the messenger of the New Covenant

Cut – covenant, judgment of God, to remove idols, to sever the flesh, the remnant formed by God

Cymbal (Cymbals) – praise and worship, noise without true substance

Cyrus – God our King, Jesus who sets the captives free

D

Dagger – weapon

Dagon – a false god, antichrist, picture of our God defeating the enemy's god and leaving him helpless

Daily – principle of faithfulness in searching the Scriptures, principle of continuance

Dainties – the enticements of the enemy, something that would make us desire evil, or false doctrine

Damage – hurt received or hurt done

Damn, damnable, damnation, damned – judgment given, ungodly and unrighteous, those to whom judgment has already been given

Damsel – the bride of "Christ, the local church, a young sister, a virgin

Dance, danced, dances, dancing – to rejoice enthusiastically, to give glory to God, to be free in worship, to rejoice in victory over a win, to celebrate

Dare – not wanting to put yourself in a position to cause something to happen

Dark, darkness, darken, etc. – evil, night, sin, blindness, to confuse, to deceive

Darling – the soul, also God's bride, Jesus' soul

Dart – wicked tactics of the enemy, false doctrine, something that destroys

Dash, dasheth, dashed – to hurt oneself, to damage a body part, to bring judgment

Daughter – female offspring, child of God, child of Zion, member of the body of Christ

David – the Lord Jesus, the bride of Christ in love, boiling in love towards the Lord, a great worshiper, overcoming army, a king and a priest, the faithfulness of God to forgive us, one whose heart is right with God and who strives to keep a deep and personal relationship with the Lord

Dawn – the coming of the Lord, the breaking of the morning, the release of the sons of God

Day – light, brightness, openness, the day of the Lord which is a thousand years, also the day of the Lord being the day of the sons of God, a period of time

Daysman – an intercessor, a mediator

Dayspring – the Lord Jesus, the one who brings the daytime or light out of darkness

Deacon, deacons – a servant, one who's already doing the work, an office in the body of Christ

Dead – no life, no anointing, the end of physical life, spiritually dead, a point where no life remains, emptiness

Deaf – inability to hear the voice of God, inability to hear period

Dealt – the workings of God, the workings of people, judgment given, the way people have been treated

Dear, dearly – cared for deeply, chosen one, honored one

Dearth – famine, emptiness, hunger, spiritual drought

Death – cessation of life, no spiritual life, dying to self, bowing and humbling yourself

Debase – to humble yourself, to make yourself small in your own and other's eyes

Debt – something owed, something God has forgiven, something you have to work for

Decay, decayed, decayeth – a breaking down, falling down, slothfulness, a tearing down of that which was strong at one point

Deceit – deception, lies, trickery, false doctrine, false dealings

Deceitful, deceitfully, deceitfulness, deceived, deceivableness, deceive, deceived –someone who uses wicked tactics to change our opinion, someone who is diluted and believes a lie, someone who has convinced themselves over a period of time through sin that something is righteous when it is wrong

Deceiver, deceivers, deceiveth, deceiving – a person similar to the antichrist who seeks to cause us to go away from our righteous position, to change our minds by using evil and simple tactics and false doctrine to make us believe something that is not of God

Declare – to speak steadfastly, to be bold and say what God is saying, to say boldly what God has done and is doing

Decline (Declined, Declineth) – backsliding, slothfulness, a falling away from a point of righteousness

Dedicate (Dedicated, Dedicating, Dedication) – to submit to the Lord, to give to the Lord, to present to the Lord as in dedicating a child or a building, to sanctify and allow God's presence to take rule

Deep – the unknown, place of darkness, the deep place of God, the deepest place in the heart of God or in the heart of a human being, can also mean water or sea

Defile (Defiled, Defileth, Defilest) – to contaminate, to make impure that which was pure, to bring a mixture, to make unrighteous that which was righteous

Delilah – demon, sensual or sexual demon, the spirit of Jezebel, one that seeks by feminine wiles to bring a man of God down, also someone who can't get along with others, a noncohabitant

Demas – a Christian who forsakes the things of God and his walk with the Lord in the end

Desert – place of the dealings of God, a dry and desperate place, a place where all men and women of God must walk through in their lifetime and become victorious

Desolate – empty, barren, wasted

Desolations – a place that has been judged by God and left barren and empty

Despise, despised, despiseth – to set at nought, to count for nothing, to dislike, to be envious or jealous of

Destitute – someone who is afflicted and tormented, someone who is in famine, emptiness, without provision

Destroyer – satan and demons, someone intent on doing harm and bringing an end to someone's walk with God or confusion to one's walk with God.

Devil – adversary, enemy.

Dew – the Word of God, the anointing of God, God's Word gently falling and being received welcomingly by a child of God.

Diadem – signet of beauty, someone who is blessed of God, carrying the rod of God

Dig (digged, diggeth, diggeths) – to search, to do whatever you need to do to find the will of God or something from God, willingness to work, to search

Diligence (diligent, diligently) – a faithful man, someone who has gained authority through obeying the Lord, faithfulness

Dim – almost blindness, vision darkened, something that was once bright and shining that now has slackened

Diotrephes- ambitious believer, someone who always tries to have the preeminence and authority, an ambitious spirit, a controlling spirit

Discern – to see through, to look through, to be able to tell the difference, to rightly divide, to be able to separate or distinguish

Disciple – a disciplined one, a student of the Word, someone who is far more committed than those in the multitude

Discord – that which brings disharmony among brethren

Discretion – wit using wisdom and common sense to guide one's affairs

Diseased (diseases) – sickness, anything that takes away from the ease of life, maladies brought by satan, sickness

Distress (distressed, distresses) – narrowness of room, a crowding in, pressing out of measure, times of great trouble

Diverse – many or different

Divination – witchcraft, a false spirit of discernment, a familiar spirit, evil, occult practices

Divisions – separations, factions, something to divide the body of Christ

Doctrine – God's holy Word, a set of preordained and orderly teachings in the Doctrine and person of Christ, soundness in the Word of God

Dog (dogs) – evil workers, a backslider, someone who is not very highly esteemed, a company of end time saints, ignorant and unlearned people

Door – an opening to something, Jesus as the door, a person or minister being the door, an entrance way into something more revelatory, more light, or a closing of something both natural or spiritual , a closing of light to darkness, the entrance into all things heavenly

Double-tongued – someone who speaks out of both sides of their mouth, someone who doesn't mean what they say, someone who has hidden motives, untrustworthy

Dove – the Holy Spirit, one who is faithful forever, the Bride of Christ, harmless, loving

Dragon – the serpent, the devil, lucifer

Dream (dreamed, dreamer, dreams) – a holy vision or purpose from God, someone who is working toward a particular vision, someone who has a tended seed, lives in visions

Dry – no anointing, barren, empty, no spiritual refreshment, adverse to the presence of God

Dunghill – a place of poverty, a place of scouring, a place of refuse, a place where God brings His overcomers out of

Dust – speaks of the earth, lowness and frailty, the carnal nature, the carnal mind, mourning and grieving, Abraham's seed

Dwarf – immaturity, that which is insufficient, that which has not grown, unable for ministry

Dwell – to abide, to inhabit, to live in, dwelling place, dwelling places, place of abiding, house of the Lord, places made available to the Lord, His people

E

Eagle (eagles) – the overcomer, a warrior, the Lord Jesus, protector, the sons of God

Ear – hearing from the Lord, your ability to hear from God, willingness to listen to the voice of God

Early – sunrise, first thing in the morning

Earring (earrings) – something planted on our ears, an ornament, an ornament of the voice of God in our lives, the gift of the discerning of spirits, the ability to hear the voice of God

Earth – speaks of the flesh, the world, man, man's flesh

Earthquake – speaks of the dealings of God, the judgments of God, the shakings of God

East – speaks of the coming of the Lord, the returning of the Lord, the sun rising

Eat – to receive the Word of God, to receive something that is taught

Eater – something that attacks us, the enemy

Eden – paradise, the garden of God, the place that the manifested sons will enter into

Edification – to build up, to increase, to cause to be built up

Egg – something birthed, something in its birth form that has not broken forth yet

Egypt – the world, the flesh

Eight – the number for new beginnings

Eighteen – the number for bondage

Eighty – the number for the fulfilled life

Elder – someone with authority in the body of Christ, someone who is a watchmen, a leader in ministry

Eldest – the oldest one, the most mature one, many times the one whom God causes to serve the younger

Elect – God's chosen, God's anointed, God's people

Eleven – the number in Scripture that means disorder, disorganization, and confusion

Eli – the old order, the old system of religion, the backslidden priesthood: the ones who have lost the glory, one who will not command his sons

Elihu – Jesus, a mature believer, one who speaks for another

Elijah – the overcoming saints, the caught up saints, men and women of God moving in power and miracles, unafraid to speak truth to power

Elisha – the double-portion ministry, a true son, one who moves in power, authority, and miracles

Elizabeth – speaks of a worshipper, someone who keeps their oath and covenant before the Lord, the last day mothers and fathers in the Lord who birth the ministry prior to the sons of God coming forth; they birth the John the Baptist ministry

Elkanah – the Lord Jesus

Elm Tree – a place to hide your sin, a place of backsliding, a place of committing adultery

Embrace – to receive someone, to make yourself vulnerable to someone by receiving them completely and lovingly

Emerald – speaks of prosperity, speaks of the priesthood and the city of God

Emerods (hemorrhoids) – speaks of the judgment of God upon the world

Emptied – speaks of being poured out, allowing everything that God has done in you to come out of you so that he can fill it again

Empty (emptiness) – nothing is left, everything is gone

Enchantment (enchantments) – speaks of witchcraft, things people say to cause demons to manifest themselves

End – speaks of the finished, one side, all that God has done, and all that God wants to do

Enemies – enemies tactics, trials, burning, dealings of God, our adversaries

Engrafted (engraved) – something that has been laid upon your heart, written upon the tables of your heart, written by the Spirit of God upon your heart

Enlarge – to be expanded, to be multiplied, to go beyond the borders that you've known before

Enlightened – means that the Word of God has touched you, revelation has entered your life, means darkness has receded as the light has shown

Enoch – the overcoming saints, the saints that are caught up with the Lord, dedicated believers

Ensign – a banner waved, a banner and sign signifying a tribe or the people of God, a symbol of protection and a standard lifted high

Entangle – to be caught in a yoke of bondage, to be lured and caught in a trap, to trap someone

Enter – to move into something new, to be brought into something you have not known before, to go through

Entire – completion, to the uttermost, full-ended, speaks of the uttermost and farthest parts of the earth as our inheritance from God, speaks of our uttermost salvation, the entire earth waiting to hear of our uttermost salvation

Envy – jealousy, something that God is against, something that the Lord does not want in us because it breeds strife

Ephesus – one of the seven major churches in the body of Christ, one of the seven local churches, one of the seven churches

Ephod – a symbol of the priesthood ministry, a symbol of worship, personal worship to the Lord

Equal – something that is balanced, something that is even on either side

Err – to miss the mark, to sin, to mess up, someone who refuses reproof

Esau – the flesh of men, profane, profanity, speaks of hairiness or that which grows of the flesh, one who comes behind

Espoused – to be engaged, someone you're going to marry, someone you know will be your husband or wife

Establish – to lay a foundation, to prepare to build a building, to make ready, to teach people the Word

Esther – the Bride of Christ, the fasting and interceding saints, willingness to lay your life down

Eternal – that which is ageless, that which is of God, that which is forever

Ethiopia – speaks of Kush, the black of Africa, black people

Eunuch – one who has separated himself to the Lord, someone who has separated himself personally and sexually, one who has given himself to the Lord in every way

Eve – the Bride of Christ, one that comes out from the body who then is given to the body

Evening – that which is first, that which is dark, that which is at the end of the day

Evidence – the word "proof", faith

Evil – that which is dark and not of God, sin, unredeemed mankind, man in general, that which is of satan

Examine – to prove, to test, to allow God to deal with you in any and every way

Excellency (excellent) – that which the Sons of God are after, that which is God is after in our lives, the Sons of God; Jesus Himself; a type of that which always surpasses that which is expected

Eye – vision, sight, omniscient, all seeing

Eye Salve – anointing, eye service, doing something that you don't mean from your heart just to please men

F

Fable – that which is a false story, something made up, and old wives tale

Face – the presence of God, the inner countenance or true inner being of someone

Fade – to depart, to diminish, fall, desolation, to stumble, to sin, to give up, that which is of wickedness, familiar, ungodliness, something that is known, departed from something

Fail – to disappoint, to not accomplish, to not finish what you started

Faint – to become weak, weary, to give up

Fair – beautiful, lovely, precious

False – that which is not true, bad teaching, a lie, feigned

Family – speaks of fellowship, love, communion, covenant together

Famine – judgment, scarcity, no food spiritually or naturally

Famish – no strength, no food, devoured of the word of God

Fan – separation, purging

Fashion – to be made after something, to be made liken unto

something
Fast – to cover the mouth, to go without food, to separate yourself unto God, a time of seeking the lord without eating, to stay close by
Fasten – to join yourself to something, to be connected to something, to be tied to something
Fat – symbolic prosperity, blessing, riches, abundance; foolish, simple minded, a glutton
Father – beginning, leader, elder in body of Christ, God the Father, true discipleship
Fatherless – those without a father ministry, those without a parent, no leadership or structure in their lives
Faultless – no sin, no accusation, to be clean
Favor – that which is blessed, the latter rain, God's choice
Fear – to stand in awe, to be afraid, to trust deeply in God
Feather – symbolic of covering
Feeble – weak, impotent, no strength
Feed – someone who has been nourished, someone who has been taught the word of God
Feet – symbolic of our walk, our conduct before Lord
Feign – to fake, to pretend, lying, false
Fellow Heirs – speaks of brothers and sisters, disciples together, those who shall inherit together the blessing of the Lord
Fellow Helpers –members of the body of Christ, disciples flowing together, working together in ministry
Fellow Laborers – both working for the gospel, preaching together in unity
Fellowship – communion, community, covenant, deep relationship with one another
Fence – an enclosure, something to guard and protect
Fervent – that which is hot, passionate, on fire
Fetter – that which puts us in bondage, keeps us in bondage
Fever – sickness or disease. Something that brings heat; worry
Field – the world, the place of planting, hearts of men, place of ministry
Fiery – that which is stirred up
Fifteen – rest, and acts of grace
Fifty- jubilee, liberty, deliverance, Pentecost
Fig – the fruit of the nation of Israel
Fig tree – national and political Israel
Fight – to engage in battle, to defend, to stand up for what you

believe in, to strive for truth, wrestling matches with the flesh, brothers and sisters, or with the world

Fill (Filled) – that which is completely saturated, overflowing, and complete

Filthiness – uncleanness, ungodliness, sexual perversion

Finger – that which God has pointed out, something he is dealing with; work

Finish – to complete, perfection, the end of the race

Fir or Fir Tree – men, picture of joy and happiness

Fire – burning, purging, God himself

Firmament – heaven, the sky over us

First Born – the most important child, the blessing upon the child, first fruit; first fruits – that which comes to fruition first; first fruits – that which matures quicker, the remnant

Fish – men in revival

Fishpools – the beauty, clear deep expression and passion of the bride

Fist – rebellion and/or determination

Fitches – preaching the gospel, the word of God

Five – grace

Fixed – steadfast, attached to something, nailed to something, mind made up, determined

Flame – that which burns, the presence of God, our spirits within us

Flatter (Flattering, Flatters, Flattereth) – trying to impress, something to be aware of, something that the strange woman and false doctrine do

Flax – symbol of the weakness of man

Flesh – the human nature, actual physical flesh of man, soul and body of man together

Flies – evil spirit, satan's kingdom

Flock – symbolic of Gods people, local church

Flood – large number of people, Spirit of God coming out of our hearts or spirit of God within us, deluge of the glory, judgment

Floor – earth, foundational, that which to build upon, the ground

Flourish – the blessing of the Lord, to grow, to be blessed, to prosper

Flow – the ability to work with and join with others, to be in harmony with

Flower – fading glory of man, fruitfulness, growth, grinding, the Word of God, broken body of Christ

Foal of an ass – the Lord Jesus, sacrifice

Fold – a flock, the local church, a group of believers

Folly – foolishness, stupidity, sin, that which is known that is not of the Lord, someone who is backslidden, given up on the Lord Jesus, someone who is in sin, someone who is sick

Food – any kind of sustenance, the Word of God

Fool – silly, perverse, fat, antichrist

Footmen – demon warfare, level or rank of demon warfare

Footstool – mercy seat, place of God's feet

Force – to take hold of, to pressure someone into doing something, to use violence

Forehead – our minds; mind of Christ or the world, pride

Foreigner – Gentile, stranger; someone without citizenship

Foreskin – heart, desire for worldly things that have not been cut off or removed, needs to be circumcised

Forest – symbolic of the nations, the world, men, large number of men, tress

Fornication – disobedience, sexual perversion, spiritual adultery

Forsake (Forsaken, Forsaketh) – to leave, to abandon midstream, to not go on with God

Fortress – a stronghold, place of protection

Forty – trials, testing, probation, chastening

Foundation – beginning of the word of God, foundation in the scriptures that which all of us must receive, knowing God in a general sense

Fountain – God's Bride, Holy Ghost that flows out of us, symbolic of life, source and God is the source

Four – number of creation, and that which is created, something to do with the earth

Foursquare – the city of God

Fourteen – doubling of perfection

Fowl – sacrifice, demon spirit, Babylon

Fox – cunning, evil man, satan himself

Fragments – that which is left over, that which remains, things left from the dealings of God that need to be considered

Frankincense – worship, suffering, purity

Free – that which is loosed, unbound, unreligious, flowing in the Spirit of God

Free Will – that which comes from your own heart, something voluntary

Frog – symbolic of demon, unclean spirit, judgment of God

Fruit – increase, multiplication, that which is grown

Fugitive – Cain, someone backsliding and wandering from the Lord

Furnace – trials, testing and dealing of God

G

Gainsaying (Gainsayers) – those who are argumentative, those who like to come against the truth; strife and contention

Gall – bitterness and poison; Jezebel spirit, or an un-flowing spirit

Gap – an opening or a gulf; to be made up and filled by someone as a bridge, a place where slothfulness and laziness take place, an opening in which satan and the enemies of God can enter

Garden – growth and fertility, the soul; the Bride of Christ, the place the where God deals

Garlic – the best things which the earth can offer, things that try to make us backslide

Garment – covering, evil or righteous, something defiled or beautiful, symbolizes the righteousness of the saints, where a person is at spiritually speaking, it shows where a person's righteousness is at.

Garnish – beautiful and artistic decorations in the heavens, the arrangements of the sun, stars, and moon, the flowery words used by Pharisees used to describe the greatness of the dead prophets, while they themselves do not obey their teachings

Gate – entrance, power, and authority, the place where elders meet, something that opens and something that closes, something that can be guarded

Gather – to bring together those of likeminded faith, bring together those who are ready to work towards a particular goal, and bring together those in fellowship of like precious faith; a day that is coming when God will bring together all the peoples, righteous and unrighteous, of the earth; there will come a time where God will bring into oneness all that belongs to Him

Gaze – to be transfixed, slothfulness, unwillingness to move out

Gehazi – an unrighteous servant, unrighteous son, son with sin in his life

Generation – lifespan of people, a forty year period, an entire block of time period in the Lord

Gentiles – the nations, heathens, the world

Gentleness – the Lord Jesus, characteristics of the Holy Ghost, what God expects from His people

Ghost – rendered spirit, speaks of the Holy Spirit.

Giant – demons, Nephilim, enemy, imposing and large enemies that try to intimidate us

Gideon – Jesus, our deliverer, the warrior sons of God

Gift – a bribe, something used to influence, a judge, the talents and abilities that the Holy Spirit has given someone; refers to money

Gilgal – circumcision and rolling away of the flesh, place we must enter into before entering into the Promised Land

Gin – a trap

Gird – to prepare yourself, to get ready, to strap on, warfare garments, to prepare yourself mentally and spiritually

Girdle – strength for activity, strength to be able to do something, established, strengthened, firmed up, prepared

Glass – transparency and the character of the Lord Jesus manifest in our lives; speaks of the Word of God and seeing through it dimly; being sinless, righteousness, holiness, and purity

Glean – gather that which has been left, to search the Scriptures, to harvest, to weed through, to work through, and to find that which God has for you

Gloominess – day of depression, day of darkness, time of great oppression

Glorious – something that you exalt or exult in, to be excited about something or to glorify something

Glory – weight, the characteristics of God, the character of God, the manifest presence of God, the nature of God, the goodness and beauty of God

Glutton (Gluttonous) – someone who is fat, a drunkard, slothful, lazy

Gnash – to attack with the mouth, an attack from an enemy using vicious words

Gnat – an insect that typifies the estimation we place upon sin, unpleasant and little things in our lives that we do not object to; something that is a pestilence and causes trouble

Goat – a sin offering, sin, sinners, and that which is filthy

Godhead – the name of the triune God, the threefold God, the name given in Scripture to define our threefold God

Gold – the nature of God, of the glory of God, and of the character of God; a symbol of being a king, God, and the Kingdom of God

Golgotha – place of crucifixion, place of sacrifice

Gomorrah – wickedness, idolatry, immorality, homosexuality, pride

Goodman – master of a house; the Lord Jesus, someone in authority

Goods – things that we have obtained in God, things we have worked for, and God has prospered us with; speaks of having the actual anointing and things of God in our life

Gospel – glad tidings, the good news, that which we are to preach to the world, the truth of Jesus' death, burial, and resurrection

Gourd – of that which the earth can produce that's temporary

Government – the Kingdom of God, the rule and reign of God, the authority of God; an established rule or reign

Grace – the divine enablement of God, unmerited favor, the ability of God where our ability runs out, the mercy and favor of God

Grapes – the fruit of the vine, of our inheritance, that which comes from the Promised Land, fruit that abounds, and harvest

Grass – symbolic of the frailty of the flesh, the frailty of human beings, the temporariness of life, and that which can burn

Grasshopper – multitudes and the people; also symbolic of not thinking very highly of oneself and being introverted, representative of smallness of size in relation to others

Grave – to be extremely concerned about; mourning, depression; something very hard to deal with emotionally; also, Hell or the place of the dead, the unseen realm

Graveclothes – religious clothing, outward appearance of someone religious, Babylon

Graven – something stamped or marked into our hearts or lives, something stamped or marked in history

Graves – death, place of the dead, the spirit realm, and hell

Gray – honor, old age, maturity, dignity

Greeks – Gentiles, those who do not know the Lord Jesus, worldly people

Green – prosperity, life, growth, affluence, blessing

Greyhound – the Lord Jesus and His swift way of doing things; swift actions

Grind – oppression, servitude, work, slavery

Grisled – the colors of God's judgment, a curse

Groan – that which comes forth from a man in pain; symbolic of deep wounds and scars; to moan in pain

Grope – to not be able to see where you are going, lack of vision, surrounded by darkness yet still trying to walk

Ground – the place of sowing, the place where the Word of God is planted, speaks of permanency, stability, and something that is established

Grove (Groves) – idolatry, false worship, something that God will judge

Guest – someone who is not admitted to the wedding, but is someone who knows about Jesus without knowing Him personally; someone who is not a part of the Bride

Guilt (Guilty) – someone who is condemned, someone who has been judged, feelings that come from certain judgments, whether right or wrong

H

Habitation – symbolic of the dwelling place of God, dwelling place in general, a place someone inhabits

Hagar – a handmaiden, mother of the flesh

Haides (Hell) – hell, unseen realm, place of the dead, place of darkness

Hail – symbol of announcing the Lord, call to worship, a symbol of divine judgment

Hair – covering, symbol of the glory of man or beast, speaks of the flesh; symbolic of strength, worship

Hairy – that which is fleshy, earth, and earthy

Hallowed – something that is blessed, something that is sanctified, something that has been set apart

Ham – the flesh, judgment, sin

Haman – satan, lucifer, the enemy, that which persecutes the children of God

Hammer – the Word of God, pounding home divine truth; to judge something harshly

Hand – works, strength and power, action, possessing something

Handful – something of purpose, small but enough to make a difference

Handkerchief – a point of healing

Handmaid – a servant, one who is obedient, the daughter of the Lord, the daughter ministry

Hang – symbolic of judgment, nail in a sure place, sons of God

Hannah – the local church, grace, that which births prophets, that which births the sons of God

Happy (happiness) – temporal joy or way of thinking, not depressed or sad

Hard (hardened) – something stiff and stiffened, something that overtime has become bitter or resentful, not of the Lord

Harden – someone who is rebellious, deliberately refuses to listen to God's word, stiff neck, allow sin and rebellion to cause their heart to backslide; to allow over time a heart to regress and turn from the Lord and His purposes

Hare – symbol of satan, demons, uncleanness

Harlot – spiritual adultery, idolatry, Babylon; the false church, strange women

Harness – that which is used to control and manipulate; the Spirit of God controlling and using our lives for good

Harp – praise and worship, something to release worship upon, that which you use to glorify God

Hart – symbol of gentleness, sensitivity, worship, desire

Harvest – symbol of the end gathering, reaping of the righteous and the wicked, reaping of any kind of crop, gathering together of that which has been sown

Haste – something done without proper preparation, something done far too quickly without waiting on the Lord first

Haughtiness – pride and arrogance, refusing to humble yourself

Hawk – symbol of uncleanness, a scavenger, an enemy, a wicked man

Hay – little worth, that which is to be burned up, disobedient to God

Head – leadership, rulership, lordship, husband, the Lord Jesus, realm of thoughts, mind, and intelligence Speaks of the mind, and the mind of Christ

Heady – thinking more highly of yourself than you ought to think, being high minded, allowing your intellect to rule

Heaps – a storage place, storing up God's provision, abundance of provision

Hear (heard, hearing, harken) – to listen to, to take heed to, to be willing to submit yourself, to surrender to another's voice

Heart – center of your being, place of the emotions, will, affections, feelings; it is where everything begins

Heat – trial, persecution, burden, and pressure from the dealings of God

Heave – to wave back and forth before the Lord, to lift, worship, sacrifice, offering

Heaven – speaks of the mind, place in the spiritual realm, dwelling place of God, and the place where satan's seat is located (there are three heavens)

Heaviness – depression, darkness, condemnation, guilt, a tormented soul

Hedge – symbol of protection, restraint, restriction, protection, covering, an enclosure

Heel – power to crush, that which the sons of God will latch onto to come forth in God, that which shows you have authority over something

Heifer – the bride of Christ, sacrifice, consecration, dying to self, purification

Heir – one who is destined to inherit, one called by God to receive a portion

Hell – the unseen world, a place of separation from God, the place judgment, place of darkness

Helmet – symbol of salvation, protection for your mind and emotion

Hem – something to latch onto which bring healing, place of worship

Hemlock – something that is poisonous and bitter

Hen – symbolic of motherhood, one who gathers or protects; symbolic of leadership, women ministry

Herb – symbolic of suffering and bitterness, that which is eaten during Passover

Herd – a flock, a group of animals, that which God has blessed you with (congregation members), a group of people joined together for the same purpose

Heresy – that which is false doctrine, that which is not of the Lord, that which brings judgment

Herod – satan, the enemy, a false king; glorying in the flesh

Hewed – something being worked out and built into our lives; speaks of that which is cut down and built that is not of God, speaks of God cutting and dealing in the lives of his people

Hidden (hid) – that which is secret, the secret things of the Lord, that which is kept secret, that which is unrevealed, that which must be sought after, mystery, kept from others

Hide – to protect, to keep, to keep out of sight from those unworthy of seeing

Hiding – symbolic of secrecy, symbol of sin; symbolic of the secret place of the most high, place of refuge

Hiding Place – secret place of the most high, place where man meets God, God's protection and provision, God's promise of a place where he will surrounds us and keep us

High – speaks of pride, power, place of leadership and honor, an elevated place

Highway – journeying place of the sons of God, King's highway (the highway of the Lord). It's our pathway as we walk and the pathway of the Lord

Hills – symbolic of something high and lofty, elevated, symbol of the earth and what it produces

Hinds – swiftness, agility, a deer, running after the lord, having a heart for God

Hinnom – burning, place of judgment, a place where evil is purged

Hissing – to torment someone, to talk about someone, to harass someone

Holiness – that which is sanctified, that which is glorious, that which is of God, that which is righteous

Hollow – a place out which the Spirit of God will flow, a place of the dealings of God in our walk, a place where God touches in our walk with Him

Honey – symbol of sweetness, something good, the word of God, predigested revelation

Honeycombs – that which is sweet, that which drips, the word of God, and a place of great revelation (predigested revelation)

Hoof – a walk that is divided, someone who walks with the world and with God; something that is not of the Lord

Hook – speaks of God catching the enemy, trapping the enemy, dealing with His people

Hooks – speak of that which joins something together in the house of God

Hophni – an evil son, the tabernacle ministry gone bad, the people despising the offering of the Lord

Horn – strength, power, defense, speaks of personal life

Horse – symbolic of preparation, strength, power, conquest, judgment

Hosanna – praise and worship, honoring the Lord Jesus, extoling Him as King

Hospitality – fellowship, openness, the love of God shown

Hour – the appointed time has come, an appointed time, a day far off

House – home, dwelling place, local church, house of God, dwelling place of the Lord

Housetop – bringing the heavenly to earth, opening the windows of heaven, a place to pray, a place of clarity and clearness in the Spirit, a place to flee from judgment

Hundred – speaks of fruitfulness and full measured

Hungry – a deep desire for God, a place in the human heart that recognize its need for God that can only be satisfied by Him; a place in our lives that cannot find satisfaction other than the Lord Jesus

Hunter – that which is of the flesh, searching for something

Husband – the Lord Jesus, headship, covering, protection

Husbandmen – a caretaker, vinedresser, farmer, one who cares for and brings forth the people of God, one who plants, one who oversees

Hymn – a song about God and about the things of God

Hypocrite – a phony, someone who is fake, someone who says one thing and does another, someone who is not true to themselves or to others

Hyssop –symbolic of the blood, purification, that which cleanses and purges

I

Ice – judgment, the judgment of God

Ichabod – the glory being lost

Idle (Idleness) – carelessness, thoughtlessness, slothfulness, laziness

Idol – a false god, worshipping something other than the Lord Jesus

Ignorance – willing stupidity, slothfulness, not knowing the Scriptures; not knowing something either willingly or not

Image – an exact duplicate in kind, also a false god; a picture of

Imagination – the realm of the soul, unrestrained thinking

Immanuel – God with us, the messianic name, the Lord Jesus

Impossible – something God does not understand, something God can always do and does all the time

Impotent – weak, unable, crippled, no Word

Impudent – proud, haughty, stubborn; thinking more highly of oneself when there is no reason to

Incense – worship, prayers, fragrance

Incline – to heed to, to hearken, to listen to

Increase – addition, prosperity, the blessing of God

Infidel – an unbeliever

Infirmities – weaknesses, sicknesses

Inhabit – to indwell, to fill up, to live in

Inherit (Inheritance) – that which we receive as a reward, our reward, what we are called to obtain

Iniquity (Iniquities) – lawlessness, sin, something Jesus paid the price for

Inn – the local church, the birthing place for Jesus, ministry

Innermost – the deepest part of a man, the reigns of a man's soul

Innocency (Innocent, Innocents) – purity, uncontaminated

Innumerable – without number, more than enough

Inspiration –that which God excites or inspires, revelation

Intercession – an intense praying

Inward (Inwardly, Inwards) – that which is inside of man, the spirit of man, the hidden man

Iron – the judgment of God

Isaac – the Lord Jesus, the manifested sons of God, willing sacrifice

Ishi – husband, the Lord Jesus

Ishmael – the flesh, that which we do in haste without waiting before the Lord

Isles – symbol of the Gentile nations in the earth

Israel – the last days church, the Israel of God, a spiritual name

Issachar – discernment, wisdom, understanding

Itching – people who are not satisfied with hearing sound doctrine, longing and looking to hear something new

Ivory – innocence and purity, throne, white

J

Jacob – Jesus and the sons of God, believers in their Adamic nature, the spiritual replacing the natural, and how God can redeem us from the flesh

Jael – women ministry defeating the enemy, the bride of Christ defeating satan

Jambres – opponent, one who strives against, the ministry, witchcraft, competing against the ministry

Japheth – the father of Caucasians, white people and their contributions in the Bible

Jasper – type and a symbol of the glory of God, brightness, beauty, and the gifts of the Spirit

Javelin – one of the enemy's darts, that which tries to smite worshippers and stop worship

Jaws – symbol of strength, power, and the Word of God as the jawbone of an ass

Jehoshaphat – leadership in the body of Christ, the overcomers, one with a revelation that worship defeats the enemy

Jeremiah – a weeping prophet, one who repents for the rest of the body, an intercessor, those who don't see themselves as ministers, yet the calling of God is on their life

Jericho – symbol and the bride city, the place we need to overcome so we can be free; place where God causes the walls to fall down

Jerusalem – symbol of the heavenly city of God, the dwelling place of God, also speaks of the saints living and dwelling in a foundation of peace

Jesse – the father, the father ministry, those that birth worshippers and worship ministries

Jethro – godly family member, skilled counselor, one with counsel in their mouth

Jewels – the gifts of the Spirit, symbol of special treasures, also speaks of the people of God, His bride

Jezebel – a non-cohabitant, someone who can't get along with anybody else, ambitious, manipulating, domineering person, as well as the spirit of antichrist and Babylon

Joab – leadership in the body of Christ, also faithful servant to the man of God, warrior

Job – the persecuted saints, trials, patience, enduring suffering, the overcomer

John – the beloved, favored disciple, one with a revelation of love, suffering believers who die to themselves and overcome in the end; ones who truly get the revelation of Jesus Christ

Joint – individual members in the body of Chris

Jonah – backsliders who eventually obey the Lord, the death and burial and resurrection of Jesus Christ, also ministry among the nations

Jonathan – close and dear friend, covenant brother, also a type of one who recognized the anointing but could not come out of Babylon

Jordan – the rivers we must cross in our life, the adversities we must cross, dying to self, going down, humility, and descending; surrendering our souls to God

Joseph – most important type of Jesus in the Old Testament, type of the rejected saints, those with the gift of God who are despised, also means addition suffering brings true overcoming

Joshua – the Lord Jesus, a true son, a leader taking us into our inheritance in the last days

Journey – our walk with God, the places God takes us to, the ups and downs of the Christian life and of our walk with God

Jubilee – the year of the Lord, liberty, freedom

Judah – praise

Judas – the antichrist, a betrayer, one who is concerned only for money, leadership that has ulterior motives, one who went out from us but was not of us

Judge – faithful watchman, faithful elder, one who is unmoved by gifts, one who serves God and judges God's people righteously

Judgment – neither good nor bad, but simply a sentence pronounced, what each of us will receive at the end of our lives for the good and evil we've done in our lifetime

Juniper – depression, disappointment, defeat

Just – that which is honest, pure, balanced, and righteous

Justification – part of our threefold salvation, our initial salvation, speaks of eternal salvation

K

Kedar – darkness, flesh, (son of Ishmael), black

Kernels – symbolic of the word of God

Key – the symbol of authority or power; to bind, to loose, to lock or to unlock

Keys to the Kindgdom – authority to enter in, authority to shut

Kidney – the inner most part of a human being/person; the unpleasant things in our life which should not be made known

Kill – to destroy, to murder, succession of life, to destroy life

Kindle – to initiate or start something, starting false fire.

Kindness – traits of Holy Spirit, gentleness and mercy of Christ; what God requires his people to show to one another

Kindred – family, brotherhood, members of the body of Christ

Kine – the years of plenty, the years of famine, the dealings of God

King – authority, power, rulership; symbolic of our king the Lord Jesus

Kinsmen –our redeemer the Lord Jesus Christ

Kiss – a sign of intimacy, worship, vulnerability, that which seals a relationship

Knee – bowing and submission, acknowledging Christ's Lordship

Knit – to bind together, to sew together, to join hearts

Knock – to seek God, to continue to seek the Lord

Knop – characteristics and anointing of the Holy Ghost

Know – intimacy, sexual intercourse (Adam knew Eve his wife)

Knowing – speaks of our calling, to know God intimately, highest call to man

Korah – rebellious son, son of Esau, son of the flesh, pride, arrogance, rebellious

L

Laban – unrighteous family member, someone who deceives and use trickery

Labour – that which we do for God, work, struggle under a heavy burden

Labourer – those who are workers, those who work for the Lord

Lack – not having sufficiency, poverty, inability, not having provision, not having enough

Lad – the Holy Spirit, the sons of God, the laborer that is willing to help and lay down their lives

Ladder – connecting heaven and earth; seasons in God in order to get to perfection, the progressions in God toward heavenly perfection, each individual rung in a place in God that we must attain to in order to progress to reach the end of the ladder, which ends in the heavenly realm

Lady – symbolic of the local church, symbolic of an elder in the local church

Laid -to teach, to put certain truths in believer's lives, that which has been established

Lamb – symbol of our Lord Jesus. Speaks of gentleness, submission, sacrifice, humility, and also can speak of ignorance

Lame – that which is imperfect, cannot walk correctly, cannot be used to its fullest extent

Lament – to be sorry for, repentance, regretting, intercession

Lamp – symbolic of light, revelation, the Holy Spirit, the word of God, and salvation, it is also symbolic of the spirit of man

Land – symbol of earth, something to stand on, a dwelling place, and something promised by God

Landmark – the old paths, known ways of the lord, places in God, recognizes the rights of others

Languish – to wallow, not pressing on

Laodicea – the last day church, where the people rule instead of God, the spirit that exists in the last day church

Lap – that which everything is cast into

Lappeth – the overcoming worshippers, type that will do whatever it takes to have the presence of God

Lasciviousness – wickedness, perversion, uncleanness

Latter – speaks of the last days, that which comes at the end

Lattice – a thin veil that separate us from the manifest presence of

God, and knowing him intimately, it is something that we must move in order for God's presence to come into our lives

Laugh – symbol of joy, gladness, the moving of the Holy Spirit, also a symbol of mockery

Laver – word of God, place where priest wash and cleanse themselves, the word of God exposing the sin/darkness in our lives, water baptism

Law – the word of God, particular commandments, statues, and precepts in it, religious rules and regulations that are not birthed of the spirit of God

Lawful – that which is of the Lord, that which follows the righteous path, that which is right

Lazarus – a friend of God, knowing the Lord intimately, the sons of God being resurrected while on earth

Lead – to take the authority, to take people where the spirit of God wants them to go

Leaf – symbol of prosperity, growth, life, an individual within the larger body of Christ, willingness to die to self and become one with the body, individual aspects of the power of the Holy Ghost

League – place where people are in covenant together, joining together

Leah – learning to praise God despite, learning not to depend on man

Leeks – that which the world tries to offer us to backslide, speaks of the world foods, temptation

Lean – speaks of hunger, trying time, and having more prowess as you go through the dealings of God, to put your face and trust in another, to recognize your need for the Lord Jesus and to submit

Leap – miraculous healing, response to God dealing with us, expression of joy

Leaven – symbol of false doctrine, evil practices or teaching

Lebanon – symbol of beauty, great fragrance, strength, something high or lofty, something to attain to

Lees – speaks of slothfulness, settling down, sitting down

Left – speaks of the judgment of God, the dealings of God, the adverse dealings of God

Legs – speaks of a man's walk, the balance in his life, human strength

Lentils – that which will cause us to give up our birthright, something we must fight for/stand for even against overwhelming odds

Leopard – a symbol of swiftness, vengeance, something that cannot change

Leprosy – symbol of sin, sickness, disease

Letter – symbol of the law of Moses, the particular laws in the word of God, and the religious observance of the law

Leviathan – satan, the enemy, the enemies ways and tricks, the enemy of God's people

Levite – a priest, someone who is called to ministry (full-time), someone who is joined to the lord in a richer way to be used by him

Liberal/Liberality – someone who entreats to give, someone who is willing to bless, speaks of a giver who is open to sow seed

Lift – to enable someone to do something, praise and worship

Light – symbol of revelation, Holy Spirit, Jesus the light of the world, that which is holy and good, separated from darkness, and a symbol of the body of Christ

Lightning- a symbol of a flash of revelation, something heavenly, supernatural, symbolic of the majesty of God, the Lord speaking from Heaven to earth, always associated to something else such as: thunder, earthquakes, voices

Lilies – symbol of beauty and of splendor; something that is innocent and pure, gentle, bride of Christ

Linen – speaks of moral purity, that which we attain to in God, righteousness

Lion –symbol of the Lord Jesus, an aspect of his character, royalty, Judah and praise, boldness and courage, symbolic of satan (fake lion)

Lips – speaks of the word of your testimony that which comes out of the heart of man, used to express intimacy, usually speaks of the words of your mouth

Little – small in your own eyes, something that is not very impressive or important, small in the eyes of men

Lively – that which is stirred up or built up in the Lord; someone that is excited and going on with God

Liver – the place the enemy will attack, a very vulnerable place naturally and spiritually

Loatheth – to despise or not think very much of

Loaves – the word of God, revelation, or higher level of the scriptures, certain doctrine within

Locks – covering and anointing upon your life

Locust – symbolic of evil, destructive, destroying; rank of demons

Lofty – that which is high, speaks of pride and arrogance

Loins – speaks of your mind, speaks of sexual aspects of men and women, symbolic of strength, the deepest part of a man soul, a place of strength and vitality, a place of tremendous power, and the source of life

Long – to desire greatly, to care for deeply, to want to be with

Longsuffering – speaks of patience, willingness to put up with what others will not

Loose – to release, to untie, the devil being taken out of someone's life, free

Lord – symbolic of the Lord Jesus, rulership, satan and his rulership (in an evil sense)

Lordship – speaks of rulership or having authority over

Lost – to lose something/ or give up something precious to you, to suffer deeply because of a failure, or something that is no longer in your life, someone who doesn't know where he is going: no purpose, leadership, or direction; the unsaved world

Lot – backslider, a Christian that is in it for themselves and not for the kingdom, one who is willing to live with the little sins in their lives

Love – intense affection and feelings for, either eros (physical love), phileo (soulish/friendship love), or agape (God kind of love)

Lowliness – speaks of meekness, humility

Lucifer – satan, the enemy, how pride can destroy someone

Lucre – unclean money, unclean payment for services

Lukewarm – barely alive in God, slothfulness, indifferent to go on with God, happy with the status quo

Lust – evil desire, wanting something desperately

M

Maid – A servant, someone who serves the Lord

Magicians – That which are evil men, evil workers, false

Mahanaim – It is the coming together of heaven and earth or the place where heaven and earth meets

Male – the spirit of man, the beginning of creation

Man – the image and likeness of God, the natural, God's highest creation

Man of God – someone who represents the Lord Jesus, an example of holiness, purity, and of Christ's likeness

Manger – a poor place. It is also the glory of God found in a fleshly and worldly atmosphere

Manna – the Word of God, also a type of "What is it?", a word given by the Spirit of God, the golden pot of manna is also the holy place revelation

Mansion – a room or a place in God

Mantle – symbolic of a spiritual covering, also the anointing of another man

Marble – symbol of kingdom beauty, foundations

Marishes – the places that are murky, the lowlands of life, where it is hard to walk and to go on with God, also the place where healing never comes

Mark – a sign, identification, something to distinguish something, a symbol like the mark of the beast or the image of Jesus

Marriage – symbolic of union, two becoming one, marriage of the bride and the Bridegroom

Marrow – Speaks of sustenance, the Word of God, the flesh and body of a man

Martha – Christians who are interested in doing, not sitting. It is also a type of unbelief

Mary – one who sits under the Word of God, a worshipper. It is one who has revelation of God's purpose

Maschil – It means understanding or a teaching

Master builder – an apostle

Meal – the Word of God

Meal offering – offering before the Lord

Measure – reveals how far, how long, how wide, how short, how small something is, the plumbline of God in our life, holding us up to the example of the Lord Jesus

Meat – symbol of the Word of God, a heavier type of the Word of God, also provision

Meats – A type the law or the things in the flesh or abundance in the things of the flesh

Meek/meekly – It always speaks of humility, kindness, gentleness, the Spirit of Christ

Melchisedec, Melchizedek – speaks of a priesthood, the royal priesthood, speaks of the Lord Jesus, righteousness, and peace

Melody – singing the song of the Lord, the voice of thanksgiving flowing through us, always keeping a heart of worship

Member – A person in the body of Christ or an individual physical member of your body

Mephibosheth – those who cannot walk with God on their own, their walk with God is crooked, they need help, but yet the Lord loves them and they still eat at the king's table

Merchandise, merchandising – trafficking things that are not of God, things that keep us away from our walk with God and the things of God

Mercy seat – symbol of the atonement, the meeting place between God and man, the place of mediation, also the place of the manifest presence of God and the mercy of God

Messenger – the Lord Jesus, someone carrying truths

Michael – warrior, those who fight for the people of God, the archangel

Midnight – the darkest hour of the day, the end of the age, also the beginning as well as the end, the time when we should worship the most

Mile – used to describe when we do more than what is expected of us, more than is required of us

Milk – the Word of God, foundational principles, simple and basic truths

Millstone – An unnecessary weight placed upon God's people's hearts. It is a great weight

Mind – It speaks of the soul of man, emotions, feelings, affections and the will of man. It is also an enemy of God

Miracle – a sign of the supernatural power of God, that which the natural cannot perform

Mire – symbol of man's works and the filth of man, the things men get caught up in that cause them to not go on with God

Mix – A mixture of the people of God and the people of the world. Something bad mixed with something good

Moab – the flesh, the world

Mock – to stand in judgment of, to make fun of, to be sarcastic

Moment – A short time, something that happens instantaneously

Moon – symbolic of the bride of Christ, having no light of her own, symbol of light in darkness, also the sign of the Son of man, also a sign of the church shining in the darkness

Mordecai – the Lord Jesus, an intercessor, a faithful witness

Morning – symbolic of the resurrection, symbolic of the sunrise, a new day

Morsel – a very small portion

Moses – Christ, deliverer, prophet, sent one, lawgiver, also those who don't make it completely into the promised land

Moth – symbolic of demon powers, symbol of destruction, that which hinders

Mother – a mother in Zion, a woman of God, someone who cares for and gathers God's people together and nourishes and protects them

Mountain – symbolic of the kingdom, strength, majesty, stability, also obstacles

Mourn – To grieve, to be sorry, to be depressed, to be afflicted, to weep

Mouth – symbolic of your testimony of the words you speak both good and evil

Mule – stubbornness and rebellion, the nature of man

Multitude – Those who come to hear the Gospel and to receive blessings, but don't necessarily become followers of the Lord or disciples

Myrtle (Myrtle tree) – Symbolic of the blessing of God, that which remains vibrant and radiant throughout the winter

Murmuring/murmur/murmured – To complain, to talk about, to grumble, to despise, to be in rebellion against the Lord

Music – joy, praise, worship

Mustard – seed, the smallest seed that grows to the greatest height

Mute – that which cannot speak, the flaw in the life of someone who is not able to say what is in their heart

Muzzle – to keep from flowing, to keep from having provision

Myrrh – symbol of suffering and bitterness, bitter experiences, also the fragrance of the Lord, the dealings of God in our life

Naaman – the world responding to the power of God, the world coming to Jesus

N

Nabal – a fool, rebellion, stupidity

Nail – symbol of something fastened, something steadfastly placed, a peg, the sons of God, also the Word of God

Naked – exposed, stripped, undone, innocent, without a covering

Name – symbolic of character, distinction, title, position, a revelation of the person, who they really are

Naomi – a backslider, one who goes wherever the provision is regardless of whether it is God or not, one who eventually returns home, also bitterness and repentance

Napkin – a touching point for healing; resurrection, and covering

Narrow – the ways of a holy walk with God

Nativity – place of birth, place where you came from, natural, that which is of the earth and flesh, born of man

Naughtiness – sin, unrighteousness, uncleanness

Navel – our stomach, speaks of the Word of God being digested into our life, also speaks of strength and power

Nazarite – separation, consecration, dedication, vow

Nebuchadnezzar – pride, Babylon, also worldly leaders bowing to the King of kings

Neck – symbolic of foundation, strength, beauty, also humility, as well as stubbornness, rebellion, hardness of spirit

Needlework – the work done by the Holy Spirit in our life. It shows how we've grown in God, the workmanship of the Spirit of God and the dealings of God in our life

Nehemiah – a true pastor, true man of God, one willing to intercede and pray for others

Neighbor – all people being our personal responsibility

Nest – dwelling place, a home, also a place of comfort that you refuse to leave, a gathering place

Net – symbolic of a trap, symbolic of a catcher, symbolic of the tactics of the enemy

Nettles – speaks of slothfulness, a covering that is not of God, showing or exposing a lack of a real walk with God

New Song – Is freshness in worship, the song the sons of God will sing in the last days

Nicodemus – worldly leaders sympathetic to Jesus, also someone who has great insecurities, afraid to openly confess Jesus

Nicolaitans – the priesthood ruling over the laity, something God hates, when men try to take authority and rule and reign over God's people unrighteously

Night – without light, no revelation, darkness (spiritual and natural), tribulation, a period of the dealings of God, a period of obscurity, no vision, blindness

Nimrod – satan, Babylon, the antichrist

Nine – the number for finality, also a symbol of judgment

Nineteen – speaks of divine order in judgment

Ninety – number for rebirth

Noah – righteousness, a true saint of God, obedience, someone who is willing to do the will of God in spite of persecution and voices

Noble – that which is esteemed in the eyes of men, something honored, something precious in the sight of the Lord, a leader (good or bad)

Noise – the sound of worship and praise, the sound of something happening, a move of God

Noon – the middle of the day, the sun at its height

North – symbolic of judgment, power, God's throne, also a place of darkness

Nose – symbolic of discernment and breath

Nourish – to build up, to minister to, to teach, to cover, and to protect

Number – an individual digit, the totality of something

Nurse – speaks of a pastor, a father ministry, someone who is loving and precious and kind

Nuts – the bride of Christ and all the varying shapes and sizes of people that are within it

O

Oak – type and symbol of strength, the sons of God, men as trees walking, men walking in their righteousness

Oath – symbolic of covenant, promises made

Obedience – submission, following the Lord in all things, a wise son

Oblation – an offering of worship and praise, sometimes an offering that is not received from the Lord

Odor, odors – praise and worship, anointing, the fragrance of the soul of a human being in worship

Offering – a sacrifice given to the Lord, something given from the heart in respect and honor to someone, more importantly to God Himself

Office – the fivefold ministry, particular place of ministry

Offspring – the manchild, that which is birthed, the Lord Jesus

Og – speaks of giants and the line of giants

Oil – the anointing, healing, the Holy Spirit, also preparation for ministry and the seal of ministry

Ointment – similar to oil but somewhat different, anointing, a healing salve or balm

Old – that which is mature, aged, experienced, wisdom

Olive, olive tree, oliveyard – deals with the anointing oil of God, oil that is crushed and squeezed and broken, suffering that brings forth the anointing

Omega – the end or finished

One – symbol of beginning, symbol of God, the source of all, also means unity

One hundred fifty-three – the number representing revival, harvest time, the end gathering of souls

Onesimus – a faithful son in the Lord, a servant

Onion – that which the world offers, the church, to backslide, taking the place of manna from heaven

Ophir – the gold of God, the character of God, that which adorns the bride of Christ

Oppress – that which an enemy does, daily warfare, something to overcome

Oracle – speaking for another, the divine voice speaking through us

Ordain – setting in ministry, laying hands on someone and acknowledging who they are in God

Order – ministry, priesthood, military rank

Ordinance – a law or a statue given by God or men

Ornament – something that is added, that which is added to, or symbolic of gifts of God or characteristics of the Holy Spirit, an outward sign of an inward work; also speaks of religious baubles

Outcast – someone who has been rejected, put out, someone who has rebelled and been judged

Oven – symbol of fiery trials, testing, or judgmen

Overcome (overcoming, overcometh) – the sons of God, the Lord Jesus, using your faith, walking in victory, travailing, prevailing in faith

Overflow – to exceed that which is necessary, an abundance, an overflow of the Spirit of God, the total release of the river of God inside us

Overlay (Overlayed) – a covering of something, as in wood overlayed with gold or with brass. It speaks of something other than itself

Overseer, overseers – leaders in the body of Christ, watchmen on the wall, the fivefold ministry

Overshadow – symbolic of God's presence, the anointing, covering.

Owl – an evil spirit, a demon, a night bird

Oxen, ox – beast, servant, worker in ministry, one of the characteristics of the Lord Jesus as well as the sons of God

P

Pain – hurt (whether in the mind, body, or spirit), trouble, sorrow

Palace –symbol of heaven, God's dwelling place, also a very wealthy place

Pale – symbol of death, disease, and destruction

Palm tree – symbol of victory, resurrection, strength, worship

Palmerworm – a level of demon spirits, destructive powers of the enemy

Palsy – a physical ailment, something that is paralyzed and cannot walk on its own

Pangs – the feelings of some emotion, something about to take place, an emotional response

Paps – the breasts, a form of nourishment, where nourishment comes from

Parable – a spiritual truth in a natural story, called a dark saying

Paradise – symbol of heaven, the third heaven, the most holy place, bliss

Pardon – to free, to judge guiltless, to let go, to have mercy upon

Partition – a separation whether it be between rooms in buildings or Jews and Gentiles

Partridge – an offering, something sacrificed

Passover – judgment being passed over, the Lamb of God delivering His people, God's judgment being passed over His people because of Jesus

Pastor – a shepherd, one who cares for God's people, part of the fivefold ministry, ordained by God not by men

Pasture – a place of feeding ground, Jesus our shepherd, a place where the Word of God is taught

Path – the way of life, the narrow way, a walk with God

Pattern – that which God has shown, something we're to follow after and copy

Paw – symbol of unclean power

Peace offering – offering before the Lord, symbol of Christ as our peace maker and reconciler, also mediation, humility

Peacemaker – those who try to make peace, those who try to live honestly with their brethren

Pearl – a gate of God, God's people formed through suffering, symbol of the Word of God and the truth of God's Word, also that which is made over a period of time, hidden from the eyes of men, also speaks of Jesus as the pearl of great price

Peculiar – purchased, God's people

Pelicans – symbolic of loneliness

Pen – the tongue, speaking, saying or writing that which is in your heart

Pentecost – speaks of the baptism of the Holy Ghost, one of God's feasts, the second feast

Perceive – to understand, to discern, to have revelation of

Perdition – lost, ungodly

Perfect – that which is complete, whole, or finished

Perfecting (Perfection, Perfected) – that which is complete, finished, God has completed what He began in a person

Perfume – fragrance, worship, fragrance of our walk with God and our intimacy with Him

Perilous – ungodly, dangerous

Perish – to no longer live (whether spiritual or natural), also not necessarily death but destruction and emptiness

Perpetual – something that is continued, something that shall always be

Persecute – to torment, to accuse, to attack, to come against

Persuade (Persuaded) – to be fully convinced of, to have faith for, to trust in, to be totally assured

Perverse (Perversion) – that which is ungodly, something demonic, something unclean, something right that has been turned into something dark

Pestilence – the judgment of God, disease, an attack

Pharaoh – satan, the world, Babylon, religious leaders that do not know the Lord

Pharisee – speaks of self-righteousness, the law, the traditions of men, loving the praises of men more than the praises of God

Philistines – the enemies of God, those that break up the clod, those that use the flesh to attack

Pigeon – sacrifice, something that's mourning

Pilate – worldly leaders in the last days

Pilgrim – a sojourner, someone who is searching, looking for the city of God

Pillar – symbol of strength, firmness, support, leadership in the body of Christ, the overcomers

Pillow – that which you rest your head upon, that which your mind rests upon (whether it be God or intellect); the rock Christ Jesus

Pine tree – symbol of fragrance, beauty

Pit – symbol of bondage, prison, and darkness

Pitcher – symbolic of the human body, an earthen vessel, symbol of the sons of God being broken in the last days so that the light can shine through them

Plague – a pestilence, a disease, something that satan uses to attack and sometimes God uses to judge

Plainly – speaks of showing something or explaining something so it can be understood, to speak in a way that cannot be misinterpreted

Plant – to prepare a crop, to sow seed in the hearts of men as well as in the earth, speaks of giving and sowing seed financially

Pledge – to commit to do something, to give yourself to something

Plenteous (Plenty) – abundance, more than enough

Plow – to break up fallow ground, to teach the Word of God

Plow (or Plough in Greek) – speaks of teachers of the Word of God, breaking open, preparation for sowing, tilling the ground of men's hearts

Plowman – a teacher of the Word of God, someone who sows seed

Plowshares – something used to work, to bless, to build and grow something

Plucked – to be picked up, to be taken from among

Plumbline – the divine standard, symbol of measuring truth, accountability; the Word of God

Poison – symbolic of false and evil teachings, that which is not of God, planted to destroy

Pollute – to darken something, to make something unclean, to dilute

Pomegranate – symbol of fruitfulness, joyfulness, happiness, bursting with energy

Poor – symbolic of humility, distress, poverty, that which is in need

Porch – part of the house of God, a place in the house of God to congregate

Portion – an allotted amount given, something that belongs to another

Possess – to own, to have authority over, to have command over

Pot – speaks of the container out of which you eat something (whether natural food or the Word of God), all things are cast into it

Potsherd – a piece of broken clay or pot, also speaks of the Lord Jesus being broken on Calvary, something which is broken

Potsherd – symbolic of the natural man, clay, the earth, as well as something of the earth to scratch ourselves or to relieve an itch (whether soulish or natural)

Potter – the Lord Jesus, the workings and dealings of God in our life

Pound – symbol of responsibility and accountability, weight, something's worth, price, value, cost

Pour (Poured) – to cause to flow out, to cause to come down, an outpouring

Powder – speaks of utter annihilation or obliteration, all that is left

Power – speaks of strength, might, authority, and rulership

Precept (Precepts) – the Word of God, laws, rules, regulations

Precious – that which of great price to you, something dear to you, something you love greatly

Preeminence – to have the rule over, to always be important in the midst; ambition

Prepare – to plan ahead, to make yourself ready for all situations, to have studied and given yourself

Prevail – to overcome, to win a victory

Prey – something that is captured, something that can be taken

Prick, pricked – something that you press against that hurts, both emotionally, soulishly, spiritually, as well as physically

Priest – Jesus our High Priest, a mediator, an intercessor, someone who ministers to God for men, someone who ministers to men for God, someone who dwells and deals in the holy things

Principality – a place of rulership, place of government, also demon spirits

Prison – symbol of bondage, slavery, also hell, being bound in your mind or soul

Prisoner – someone who is in bondage, someone being held either for a righteous or unrighteous cause, bound

Profane – to make something godless or ungodly, to make something that was once lovely now dark

Prophecy – a tiny part of the knowledge and wisdom of God spoken, also the testimony of Jesus when you know Jesus' presence is in a place where prophecy is taking place

Prophesy (Prophesied) – one who speaks for another, to speak in the name of the Lord, to speak the Word of the Lord

Prune – to scale back, to try to cause to grow in a more meaningful way

Psaltery – an instrument of praise and worship and rejoicing

Publican – a sinner, someone who is not walking with Jesus, someone outside of the kingdom of God

Publish – to make known, to speak about

Puffed (up) – proud, self-righteous, thinking more highly of yourself than you ought to think

Pure – that which is holy, clean, and lovely

Purge – to cleanse, to remove that which is ungodly, dark, and evil

Purify – to cleanse, to make holy, to remove all darkness

Purple – the color for royalty, wealth, prosperity

Q

Quail – not being satisfied with God's provision, lusting for more from what God has provided
Quake – the coming of the manifest presence of God, fear
Queen (Queens) – the bride of Christ, a rank within the body of Christ
Queen of Heaven – idol, heathen goddess, harlot, Babylon
Quench – to put something out, to put a stop to
Quick (Quicken, Quickened, Quickening) – to make alive, to give life to, to revive
Quit – to be emphatically like a man, to act like
Quiver – a place of protection, household or family

R

Rabbi – master, teacher
Race – Symbolic of that which every Christian enters into upon their salvation. It also speaks of our walk with God and running after the prize
Rachel – the bride of Christ, doubly loved woman, also the impatient person, those in the body of Christ who desire children more than they desire the Lord, one who dies birthing a king, but who doesn't know it, one who doesn't understand that suffering is from the Lord
Rags – Poverty, our (human) righteousness
Rahab – harlot, a worldly person who helps and blesses the kingdom of God
Raiment – Covering, that which we've gained in God
Rain – A symbol of the blessing of God, the outpouring of the Holy Spirit; God's Word and the blessing of God
Rainbow – Symbolic of God's covenant with men and earth. It is also symbolic of the mercy of God
Ram – A sacrifice, symbol of substitution. It also means stubbornness
Rank – order, placement in God
Ransom – Speaks of the Lord Jesus, provision, substitution, sacrifice
Raven – A symbol of evil, satan
Ravished – someone's heart that has been stolen away, a heart that has fallen absolutely in love with the Lord Jesus, also someone who has been taken advantage of and raped
Reap – Harvesting, a reward, that which you've taken after planting be it good or bad

Reason – speaks of our intellect and intelligence trying to understand things with the carnal mind rather than the Spirit of God

Rebel, rebellion – to go against the things of God, to disobey God, to be in a place of disobedience

Receive – taking in and hearing what God or someone is saying, to believe the Word of the Lord

Recompense – payment or reward given

Reconcile – to make peace with, to have mercy upon, to walk in peace with someone, to forgive, Jesus redeeming mankind

Red – The color of suffering, sacrifice

Redound – to go back to

Reed – Something frail and unstable

Refine – Symbol of purifying, trying and testing. It is God removing the uncleanness out of something

Refuge – A symbol of Jesus, our refuge. It is a place you run to for protection and safety

Rehoboam – a stubborn son, one who will not listen to his elders

Rehoboth – to make room for or to give place for

Reign – To have rule over another, to have authority, God's sovereignty; to enjoy life, to walk above and not beneath in this lifetime

Reins – Symbolic of the motives and inner workings of a person's heart

Remission – speaks of the removal of and forgiveness of

Remit – to cancel out, to make of none effect

Remnant – that which is left behind, the faithful few, the overcoming remnant, the sons of God

Rend – A symbol of tearing, ripping, a symbol of grief, anger; a symbol of division and schism within the body of Christ

Rend – to tear

Renew – to bring a fresh anointing to, to stir up, to bring revelation, to enlighten

Rent – It speaks the torn veil, the opening to the presence of God for us

Repent – to turn back, to change direction, to turn to the Lord Jesus

Rephaim – speaks of giants, the valley of giants

Replenish – to refill, to restock, to bless again

Reproach – that which we bear for the Lord Jesus, the sufferings we go through because of our walk with God and the cross of Jesus Christ

Reproof – a rebuke, to be corrected, or instructed

Rereward – speaks of that which follows you, that which backs you up

Rest – A divine peace, a Sabbath in God

Rest – Symbol of peace, refreshing, a cessation from work. It is also a symbol of relaxation. Symbolic of the peace of God resting upon someone

Restore – to build back up, to get back that which you had before, to return to former glory

Reuben – being unstable as water, an unfaithful son

Revelation – taking a cover off, God opening up the Word of God to us, hidden and secret truths being understood or revealed, God opening His mysteries

Revive, revived, reviving – to stir up, to quicken or make alive, to restore, to renew

Reward/rewards – That which we've gained in God, payment due or rendered, that which we've obtained in this life and the payment thereof

Rib – a woman, that which comes out of the body of Christ, that which God form out of the body of Christ – the Bride

Riches – Possessions evil or righteous; rewards, the blessings of God and the blessings of worldly rewards

Riches – That which is a blessing, the blessing of God; worldly distractions, the gifts of the Spirit, the true things of God, the deeper things of God

Right – That which is on the right hand; deals with the blessing, victory, power, the glory of God, that which is good

Ring – Eternity, endlessness, the eternal circle, speaks of someone who has authority and power in another's name

Ripe – That which has reached a place of fruition, the hungry heart; wickedness at its height

Rise/rise up – awakening to God's purpose, an answering to the call of God, also means evil arising in the earth

River – A symbol of a life-giving flow, the Holy Ghost, the presence of God

Roar – an animal when it is hungry seeking prey; it also speaks of crying out.; speaks of the enemy seeking God's people; God shouting; prophetic utterance

Roast – to go over that which you have studied; to search it out

Rob – to steal from God

Robe – Symbolic of covering; righteousness

Rock – Symbolic of Christ Jesus; symbolic of a foundation in God, a symbol of the Word of God

Rocks – Foundational principles in the Word of God; a place of hiding; obstacles in our lives

Rod – A symbol of royal authority, chastening, guidance, judgment, shepherding and correction; a weapon.

Rod (Aaron's) – Symbolic of the choice of God, God's eternal priesthood, fruitfulness

Roe – deer, gentleness and the Bride of Christ. Loveliness

Roll – the Word of God, the truths of God that we are to eat

Rome – That which is of the world, of the flesh, worldly government, the enemies of God

Roof – Covering, oversight, that which blocks the heavens

Root – Symbolic of the source, that which is deep within the earth or in the heart of man; it could be somebody's offspring

Rooted –something that planted deep in the ground, the Word of God planted in hearts of men, a heart filled with the Scriptures and established in the Lord

Rope – Symbolic of bondage or that which we tie up and wrap around

Rose – A symbol of Christ, but also His Bride

Rot – speaks of that which at one time was good and a blessing but has now become a stench in the nostrils and has gone to waste

Royal – Speaks of kingly, something in authority, something given by God

Ruby – Preciousness, value, glory; suffering

Ruddy – speaks of health, vigor, youthfulness; that which is beautiful

Ruin – Symbolic of man's fall into sin; something that was once alive and wonderful, but has now fallen into disarray and slothfulness

Run – Swiftness, movement, following a vision (run with a vision), carrying the message of the Gospel

Rush – symbolic of a weed or sins that grow up into a defiled heart

S

Sabbath – Symbol of rest, cessation from work, it speaks of the Kingdom rest from labor of all kind, spiritual and natural

Sack – Someone who carries the treasure of God within it

Sackcloth – Symbol of mourning, sorrow, repentance, great weeping

Sacrifice – A symbol of slaughter, the substitutionary death of another; that which costs something; pointing to the Lord Jesus

Sadducees – a Jewish sect who didn't believe in the resurrection. These are religious and Phariseical Law-oriented people

Saint – A born again child of God; someone who has received the Lord Jesus as their Savior

Salt – A preservative, symbol of incorruptibility; covenant or that which endures

Salute – To greet someone, to hail someone in the Lord

Salvation – the Lord Jesus Himself, God's plan of deliverance for mankind

Samaritan – Speaks of the half breed, one of the mixed nations

Samson – deliverer, savior; the believer who has serious issues in his life

Samuel – a true prophet, priest and judge; one whose words never fell to the ground

Sanballat – satan, the opponent of the things of God and the things of the Lord

Sanctification – A second part of our salvation experience; to be set apart, to be purified, to be cleansed; the Holy Spirit and the Word of God are the main avenues of this happening

Sanctuary – A symbol of God's dwelling place among men, the tabernacle of the Lord; God's dwelling place in heaven, the place of God's presence

Sand – The multitude of seed, the earthly seed of Abraham; unsaved multitudes

Sap – the anointing, the presence of God, the character of God, the Spirit of God inside the believer

Sapphire – A symbol of beauty and of hardness

Sarah – the Church, also of the Bride of Christ; someone who learns obedience by the things which she suffers; one who has a name change and becomes a princess

Satan – Our adversary, the enemy, the devil.

Satiated – To be completely and utterly filled and overflowing

Satisfied – For everything in your life to be met, to be at peace, to be more than happy, having your needs met

Saul – a believer and leader who started off good, but ended up bad; one who despises worship and tries to slay worship leaders; an anti-Christ to slay the anointing

Savor – The anointing, worship, our worship towards the Lord Jesus; a fragrance suitable to His nostrils

Scales – Symbolic of justice and something weighed in the balance and plumb line

Scapegoat – Christ Jesus, our sacrifice; one who bears the sins of another

Scarlet – The color of suffering and sacrifice

Scattered – To be spread abroad, to be moved from your original place, to be without a home

Scent – That which smells; an odor, be it wicked or godly in the nostrils of God; something that can be discerned

Scepter – A symbol of power and authority; speaks of the rod of God, kingship, rulership

Schoolmaster – the law

Scorn/scorners – To despise, to laugh at, to make fun of, to cause someone pain or hurt because of their belief and walk with God

Scorpion – evil spirits and evil men, that which stings and brings pain

Scribe – Someone who is an intense studier, one who writes the Word, about the Word or teaches the Scriptures; a faithful servant

Scroll – the Word of God, that which is the Word to be eaten and assimilated into our lives

Sea – A symbol of masses of humanity, the wicked nations.

Sea of Glass – A symbol of peace and tranquility before God's throne, as well as the transparency of the people of God

Seal – covenant, the image or mark of God; also, the mark of satan; a symbol of covenant

Seal – The presence of God saying that something is right; His anointing upon something is His seal; also the Holy Spirit, the promise

Season – A time period where a proceeding word comes forth in our life. It can last as long as it needs to until the Word of God is fulfilled in our life; a time of the dealings of God; it could also be a time of blessing

Seat – A symbol of throne, power and authority

Secret – Something that is hidden purposely, something that needs to be revealed

Seduced – To be tricked, to be lied to; most of the times it is dealing with false teachers and false prophets and/or demons and wicked spirits trying to get us to give heed to something that's not of God

Seed (1) – offspring, the fruit or posterity of the righteous or wicked

Seed (2) – The Word of God, a financial offering

Sepulcher – death and decay; a place of hypocritical and religious leaders

Seraphim – an order of angels; a picture of the redeemed sons of God in worship

Serpent – satan, evil spirit; to be sly and cunning, the devil

Servant – A faithful brother/sister who is willing to give his/her life in service to their Master, who does it lovingly and freely with a perfect heart and unforced

Seven – The number of completeness and perfection; wholeness

Seventeen – It is the number for spiritual order

Seventy – The number for spiritual order

Seventy five – A symbol of separation, cleansing and purification

Severity – The opposite of goodness; the dealings of God, the wrath of God

Shadow – Symbolic of covering and protection; the presence of God, the glory of the Most High

Shaken – That which can be moved; something in our lives that is not permanent and not settled, something that needs to be removed out of our life

Sharpened/Sharpenest – Something with an edge; the tongue; the sword; words that hurt

Shave – A symbol of being stripped of your strength and power

Sheaf – a person surrendering to the Lord lifting up their hands to their presence in a wave offering

Sheaves – Those people we lead to the Lord, people whom we have brought in to the Kingdom of God

Sheepfold – A symbol of God's people, Israel or the Church

Shepherd – the Lord Jesus. It is also a pastor, one of the five-fold ministry offices, an elder over God's flock

Shewbread – Deeper Word in the Holy Place, the bread of His presence, bread of His face; a revelatory Word from the living God

Shibboleth – that which only those who know the Spirit of God can understand

Shield – A symbol of protection, the guardianship of the Lord Jesus, the Lord protecting and surrounding us

Shiloh – peace and peacemaker. It is also the Lord Jesus

Shimei –One who rails against authority, someone who is in rebellion and throws accusations and curses; someone who God sends

Ship – A symbol of merchandise, trafficking, business among nations; that which carries the Gospel

Shipwreck – Not only speaks of the dealings of God, but things ministers must go through. It is also speaks of someone whose faith has been destroyed

Shittim – Speaks of wood, the flesh, that which is natural

Shod – Prepared with the Gospel

Shoe – Symbolic of your walk with God; treading, the Gospel of peace

Shortened – Not strong enough, not good enough, cannot bring help

Shoulder – strength, support, government, that which someone can depend on, that which holds somebody up

Shown/to shine – Shining with the glory of God, the potential for pride, but for those who are really humble will never see it, unlike satan or lucifer did

Shut – Closed, not allowed in, only Jesus can open that door

Sickle – the Word of God, separating the chaff from the wheat, harvest tool

Sighing – A voice of grief, a voice of sorrow, an exclamation of disappointment

Sight – Revelation, perception, discernment, understanding; the eyes being able to see

Sign – A miracle, an emblem, something dramatic or miraculous

Signs – miracles and emblems showing the Lord's handiwork

Silver – Color of Redemption, the price of a soul; a payment made by the Lord Jesus

Simple – Foolish, a scorner, someone who doesn't know or understand, has no revelation

Simplicity – That which is simple, uncomplicated

Sin – Missing the mark, disobeying the Lord, transgressing the commandment of God

Sin offering – the Lord Jesus been made sin for us; an Old Testament sacrifice of an animal

Singing – thanksgiving in worship, praise, an attitude of joy, making melody in your heart

Sink – A time of depression or great need, of big distress

Sion – A mountain, a people, the place where the presence and glory of God comes down and rests upon the hearts of true worshippers. It is also the people of God and Israel

Sister – The Bride of Christ, your fellow member of the body of Christ

Sit – A symbol of a finished work, of rest. It speaks of authority, a throne

Sieve – A symbol of sifting, shaking; the separation of chaff from the wheat. It also means testing and proving

Six – The number of man or satan

Six six six – The number of the anti-Christ, the mark of the beast; the fullness of satan in the fullness of man (six being the number of satan and of man, both created in the sixth day); the fullness of satan in the fullness of unredeemed man is the anti-Christ

Sixty – The number for pride

Skins – A symbol of covering, protection and sacrifice

Slack – Slothful, when you do not perform what you are asked to do, when you do not do it on time, unfaithfulness

Sleep –Rest, resting in the will of God, death, slothfulness

Sleight – The cunning race of men, false doctrine, men trying to deceive us

Slimepits – Symbol of man's sinful works and the judgment of God upon them

Slippery – the walk of the wicked that is full of pitfalls and trouble

Slothful, slothfulness – extreme laziness, someone who will not do what they know they are supposed to do, foolishness, waiting for someone else to do it for them, watches their building or walk with God decay because of their lack of faithfulness.

Sluggard – The exact same thing of the above; someone who gives in to sleeping; someone who desires but does not work, finding reasons and excuses not to work.

Slumber – Sleep; sleep that is slothful; laziness

Smoke – A symbol of blinding power, both good and evil; the glory of God, the cloud of glory

Snare – That which is used to enslave, to bring into bondage; an instrument to catch and to harm, usually demonic

Snow – Symbol of whiteness, purity, brilliancy; the treasures of God

Soap – Symbol of cleansing and of washing

Sober – Watchful, vigilant, not given to drunkenness or foolishness or outlandish behavior

Sockets – That which holds things together; support and strengthen. Connection

Sodom – immorality, homosexuality, violence, idolatry, pride and disobedience

Soldier – A good brother in the body of Christ. Someone who is a faithful servant who serves the Lord truly

Sole – The foot

Solemn – That which is quiet and sober as a solemn assembly, quiet and waiting upon the Lord

201

Solomon – the Lord Jesus, the Beloved of the Lord; someone who starts off good and ends up bad

Song – A symbol of joy and praise

Songs – Melodies of thanksgiving, of praise; melodies of deliverance, melodies to encourage us to overcome; one of the songs of the people of God

Sore – A hurt spirit, judgment, disease, a broken heart

Soul – Human life, affections, the will, emotions, desires, the mind; the female part of man

Sounded/soundeth/sounding – To speak or sing, to make noise so as to be heard

Sour – A symbol of false teaching, leaven and immaturity

South – The blessing of the Lord, prosperity; the opposite of North, which is judgment; the goodness of God flowing to us

Sow – A symbol of scattering seed, to plant into the earth, to give an offering, to give money, to bless someone's life

Sower – One who teaches and preaches the Word of God; one who sows the Scriptures into people's lives and teaches them

Space – A time allotted or given for someone to repent or to make a decision

Spare – To save, to keep from judgment

Sparrow – Something very small of small value in the eyes of men, but large in the eyes of God

Spear – that which pierces and thrusts through

Spew – To spit out, to get rid of

Spice – Part of the ingredients that make up the perfume and fragrance of the Lord; worship

Spider – Symbolic of wisdom and wise activity

Spikenard – Fragrance, our worship to the Lord Jesus; worship from the Bride to the Bridegroom

Spikenard – Worship and fragrance to the Lord; our worship to Him

Spirit –The Spirit of God, the third aspect of the Godhead; also, the human spirit

Spirits –Human spirits; all manner of evil spirits

Sport – To be foolish

Sporting – Making love to your wife

Spot – a blemish or an imperfection; sin in our life

Springs – An overflow of the presence of God, an outburst of the glory; speaks of happiness; God's presence coming down to the desert

Sprinkle – A symbol of cleansing and purifying; a scattering of the cleansing virtue of the Lord Jesus

Stablish – To make firm, to make absolutely certain something is, to cause everyone to know that this was birth of God

Staff – Symbol of the rod of authority, of strength, of guidance and protection; also, a weapon

Stagger – To move in unbelief

Stammering – Speaking in tongues

Standing – Uprightness , standing fast in your position, holding fast your position

Star – Symbolic of Abraham's heavenly seed, the spiritual Israel; ministers of the Gospel and pastors; the morning stars would be the symbols of angels

Stave – That which carries the presence of God, that which holds something up (similar to a staff)

Steadfast – To be firm, established, immovable, faithful, one who continues

Steps – Places and ranks in the Kingdom of God; stairs that we take each one, a new place of revelation (glory to glory, faith to faith)

Steps – Spiritual progression or digression depending on which way you are going; your walk with God if you are going forward; if you are going backwards you are obviously backsliding

Steward – A manager, one who deals in the things of God, an overseer

Stiff-necked – Stubbornness, resistance to authority and rebellion. An inability to submit oneself

Stink/stinketh – Someone who has not gone on with God and their sin remains in them, therefore they begin to smell in that slothful state

Stocks – Punishment, correction

Stone – Christ himself, the cornerstone; accusations or accusing words; a symbol of stability and strength; a foundational truth; God's people

Stony – Things in our life we allow to come in to block the Word of God from bearing fruit and coming forth in our life

Stoning – A symbol of the law and death; the outcome of the law

Store – Provision made, laying up provision

Storehouse – the local church, a place where your provision is

Stork – A symbol of loneliness, a bird in flight

Storms – Distress, trouble, the dealings of God

Straight – A good direction that is not crooked, going in a straight line, following the Lord

Strait – That which is full of difficulties, question mark on how to do, how to respond

Strange – Speaks of that which is false, demonic, not of God and will be judged by God

Stream – A divine flow of the presence of God; related to blessings; can also speak of ministry

Stretch – To go beyond what you normally do. To reach out. To do more than usual

Stripes – Punishment received for walking with the Lord, the righteous receiving reproach for their walk with God; judgment given by God

Stubble – That which is useless and worthless, bound for the fire

Stumble – To trip, to fall into some kind of sin

Stumbling block – obstacles, things that snare us and cause us to fall or make us stumble; sin or things in other people's lives that make us sin

Subjection – Under authority, brought under, broken

Submitted – Willingly surrendering, bowing yourself in humility to one another

Substance – Your provision, that which God has blessed you with, that which you have both spiritually and naturally

Suffer/suffered/suffering – To allow, to go through something, to go through the dealings of God knowing that in the end God will reward with glory

Summer – One of the four major seasons of God that will continue forever; speaks of a time of blessing, a time of restoration

Sun – God the Father, a symbol of glory, brightness, light

Supper – A symbol of the broken body and shed blood of Jesus; symbolic of the marriage supper of the Lamb, the Passover supper. They are all important suppers and are worthy in their own right of note

Supplication – intercession and prayer where you ask the Lord for that which is needed, not only for yourself but for others

Sure – That which you can count on, that which you know it will be there; something that is trustworthy and faithful

Swaddle – To care for, to nourish little children no matter what age they are (spiritually speaking)

Sweat – man's human efforts, works of the flesh

Sweep – the Holy Spirit going through and looking and finding that which is missing in our lives

Swelling – That which rises up and reaches a point of explosion

Swim – Flowing in the things of God, letting the natural go and trusting entirely on the Holy Spirit and flowing with Him

Swine – That which is ungodly, a symbol of uncleanness, ignorance, hypocrisy, a symbol of unbelievers

Sword – The Word of God, an instrument of war and judgment, weapon in the spirit realm

T

Tabernacle – Symbolic of God's dwelling place; the house of God and the sanctuary of the Lord

Tabernacles – Speaks of the Feast of Tabernacles, the great ingathering of the Lord, harvest time

Table – communion, the fellowship of the priesthood. Supernatural food

Tabret – Tambourine to praise and worship, rejoicing in the Lord

Tail – Symbol of the end of that which stings, that which brings death, the devil

Talebearer – A scandalmonger, someone who gossips and stirs up strives with words; strife with words; reveals secrets

Talent – Symbolic of a responsibility that God has given us; a gift God has given us; something we have to be accountable for

Tapestry – That which someone makes a covering of; the working of God in our lives; could speak of something very religious and false doctrine

Tare – Symbolic of false teaching, a child of satan; someone who used to be a Christian and now is not; false things that are sown among the people of God

Tarry – Simply means to wait until

Taskmasters – Rulers ruling over the people of God; could also speak of demons

Taste – To enjoy the presence of the Lord, to be in His presence; satisfaction; the blessings of heaven and experiencing them now

Taught – Someone who has a foundation, someone who has been taught the Word of God and is established in the Word

Teacher – Part of the fivefold ministry, one of the gift offices of the Lord. It is one who labors in Word and doctrine, one who lays out the Word of God in a systematic way

Tears – Symbolic of sorrow, sadness, grief; symbolic of humility

Teeth – Symbolic of your mouth and speaking; sharpness, devouring words

Temperance – Self control

Tempest – A storm, an upheaval, an outpouring of God's judgment; sorrow and affliction

Tempestuous – Means roaring and loud; stirred up activity all around

Temple – Symbol of the dwelling place of God; a dwelling place of the human body, the body of Christ Jesus; a place of worship

Temporal – That which is subject to change

Ten – Number for law and order

Tentmaker – An occupation of the Apostle Paul; speaks of working while in the ministry

Terrible – Very good, very awesome, very powerful, very mighty; also speak of that which is not good and is awful

Testimony – That which you say or report

Thick – Speaks of darkness, clouds, great coming together

Thief – the enemy; that which steals something that does not belong to them

Thigh – A symbol of strength

Think – Symbolic of reasoning, having a mental understanding and not thinking by the Spirit of God; the carnal mind

Thirst – An indescribable longing for God, an indescribable longing for water; the human heart which is not satisfied; unbelievable longing for God

Thirteen – Is the number in Scriptures for rebellion, backsliding, sin, depravity

Thirty – Number for maturity and preparation for ministry

Thistle – Symbolic of the curse and uselessness

Thomas – the believer that doubts and must see rather than believe

Thorn – Symbolic of the curse of that which slothfulness bears; a hindrance to the people of God

Thousand – The number for perfect fruitfulness and rest, the millennium

Three – The number for the Godhead and resurrection

Three hundred – The number for a faithful remnant and deliverance

Threefold – the Lord Jesus and the husband and a wife; represents our salvation, justification, sanctification and glorification. represents the threefold plan of God, the threefold principle

Threshing – A symbol of separation, judgment, chastening. trampling of the foot; a symbol of God separating the wheat from the chaff.

Threshing floor – A place of intercession, a place where God separates and divides; the place where things are beaten into submission; a place where we make our choices to serve the Lord in a greater way

Threshold – The doorway; the Lord Jesus

Throat – A symbol of swallowing either good or evil; it can also speak of the mouth or words

Throne – A symbol of authority, kingship, rulership, sovereignty, power, dignity, mercy; the dwelling place of God

Thumb – Works, the priesthood and the anointing upon it

Thunder – A symbol of God speaking; what happens after revelation flashes, a move of God

To shout – praise and worship, an exclamation of victory, an exclamation of faith, high praise, high victorious praise

To sigh – intercession, grieving, sorrow

Tongue – Symbolic of language, speech; that which cannot be tamed; a blessing or cursing

Tooth – Symbolic of biting or devouring; also refers to the mouth and speaking

Topaz – Symbolic of beauty, something of value; a precious gem

Tower – Symbolic of safety, strength, protection; the Lord Jesus Himself; that which we run to

Transparent – Speaks of gold, the life of God, the gold of God, the divine nature; someone who has become dead to the world

Trap – Something the devil leaves for us, snares to catch us

Travail – intercession and praying; a longing for something of the Lord; a time of great suffering and sorrow that somebody goes through; the birthing of something

Treasure – Symbolic of the true riches of God; great character; Wealth

Trees – Symbolic of men, nations; symbolic of the Lord Jesus Christ Himself, as well as the Church

Trespass – Sin and disobedience; the trespass offering, the Lord Jesus Christ

Tribe – Divisions within the body of Christ or the children of Israel these are certain characteristics of a particular people within the people of God

Trumpet – Prophetic pronouncement, prophecy; symbolic of gathering, of the coming of the Lord Jesus, of the coming of judgment or blessing

Try – To test, purify, the dealings of God

Turtledove – A type and symbol of the Holy Spirit

Twelve – Number in the Scriptures for divine order and divine government

Twenty – Number for expectancy

Twenty Four – Number of priesthood and heavenly government

Twilight – To have just enough light to deceive you; dusk and deception

Two – Number of witness, division and separation

U

Unaccustomed – Learning to submit, rebellion

Unadvisedly – Not controlling your tongue, disobedient to the word of the Lord

Unawares – Not watching, unprepared, not ready

Unblamable – Purity, innocent, giving, no reason for accusation

Uncertain – Not knowing, unsure

Uncircumcised – Not being in a covenant with God; uncleanness, rebellious, and returning God's rule and authority, the heathen

Unclean – sin, impurity, not righteous, abominable, demonic, defiled

Uncover – Having no head, nakedness, exposing sin

Unction – The anointing within, the witness of the Spirit of God; our human spirit

Undefiled – Purity, innocence, not stained by sin

Unequal – Not being balanced, not together in the same spirit

Unfeigned – Sincere, not hypocritical

Unicorn – Symbol of strength, wild beast

Unlearned – Those who do not understand the message of the gospel, or those who have not been taught

Unleavened – Symbol of purity, no false doctrine, Word of God free from error

Unruly – Rebellion, not submitted to authority, untamed

Unskillful – Immaturity in the word of God

Unspotted – Having no stain of sin, righteous, the Lord Jesus our sacrifice

Unstable – Double-minded, no foundation

Untoward – Not knowing where to go, no direction, and no true purpose

Up – Going on with God, progressing in the faith, exalted by God
Upright – The righteous, walking holy before the Lord.
Uriah – A faithful man, champion, one of the remnant
Urim – the guidance of God, revelation
Usurp – A spirit of control, manipulation
Utterance – God's anointed speech
Uzzah – ignorance of God's ways, trying to control the Holy Spirit
Uzziah – an idol, one who keeps you from seeing the Lord

V

Vagabond – Fugitive, wanderers
Vail – A covering, a partition that divides
Valiant – the sons of God
Valley – Symbol of the dealings of God, place of judgment, place of decisions
Vanity (Vanities) – Emptiness, something transitory, something evil or false, useless, senseless talk, idol worship
Vapor (Vapors) – Ascending, worship, presence of God, transitions of life
Vashti – rebellious Christians who do not want to attain to brideship
Vermilion – Symbol of false covering
Vessel – Human being; a container for God's blessing; something used of the Lord
Vial (Vials) – A carrier of God's anointing, judgment, prayer and worship
Vine – Israel and the church, fruitfulness; Jesus himself
Vineyard (Vineyards) – God's people, Israel and the Church; the bride; our souls
Viper (Vipers) – The devil and his demons, false teachers, false doctrine
Virgin (Virgins) – the body of Christ, God's people in the Old and New Testament, Christian's who are virtuous
Vision – Earthy and heavenly goal or purpose for our lives
Visions – heavenly sight, spiritual eyes opening, and an appearance of the Lord or angels
Visitation – A move of God, God visiting his people
Voice – God speaking; prayer, a sound of words good or bad
Void – Emptiness, to break covenant, a dark place
Vomit – Symbol of bad doctrine, sin
Vow – Sacred oath to God

Vulture – Symbol of uncleanness; satan

W

Wages – That which is attained from labor, reward, eternal rewards, payments whether good or evil

Wailing – Uncontrollable weeping, uncontrollable sorrow and bitterness of heart

Wake – To come alive, to open your eyes

Walk – Our journey with God, our conduct, our behavior, our lifestyle

Wall – Symbolic of protection, separation, security whether righteous or evil

Wallow – The wicked who revel in their own sin and iniquity, slothfulness, unwillingness to rise and walk

Wander – To backslide, to go from one place to another without taking root, no vision, no purpose

Want (To Be in Want) – To be desperate, to be in need, poverty, to desire something but not be willing to pay the price for it

War – Symbolic of destruction, death, carnage, the battle between good and evil, the battle or wrestling match between our soul and spirit, fighting between good and evil

Warmed – To bless somebody but completely meet their need

Warn – To speak to people and tell them of that which is coming whether they listen to you or not

Wash – To cleanse yourself, to purge yourself, purification, the washing of the water of the Word, using the Word of God and the Spirit of God

Wash Pot – Speaks of the flesh

Watch – Symbolic of leadership, wakefulness, alertness, being on guard considering evil and the world around you

Watch Tower – A place of intercession, a place of guarding and protecting

Watchman – A leader in the body of Christ, a leader that is good or evil, a prophetic ministry

Water – A symbol of people, the Word of God, the Holy Spirit, symbol of washing and cleansing, symbol of eternal life, the baptism in the Holy Ghost

Water Pots – Speak of humanity being filled with the Holy Ghost, the miraculous

Waves – The presence of God flowing over us, deep calling unto deep, those who live for the presence of God and the glory of God, the judgment and punishment of God, ungodly teachers and their teachings

Wax (To Wax) – To become or to make yourself liken to

Way – Speaks of the walk and manner of life in which we live whether saved or unsaved, the narrow way

Weak – Unable, insufficient, not strong, people who have not given themselves to the Word of God or the presence of God

Wealth – Speaks of prosperity, treasures, the blessing of the Lord, also the danger of riches

Weaned – To be birthed, to be fed, to be able to stand on your own, to be nurtured, to be taught the Scriptures

Weapon – That which is described as the Word of God, the armour of the Spirit of God

Weary – Worn out, to be depressed, mentally and physically worn down, in need of the presence of God

Web – Symbol of worldly and ungodly ties and chains that weigh us down, to be caught in a puzzle

Wedding – the marriage between the bride and the bridegroom or a man and a woman, the loving relationship between a man and a woman

Week – Seven days, seven years, seven-thousand years

Weight – Symbolic of the glory of God, or a symbol of a burden, heaviness, alone, depression

Well – A source of life, refreshment, water, and the presence of God, something that must be dug, a place prepared for the glory to fall

Well Beloved – Doubly loved, special one, loved one, the Bridegroom

Wellspring – A place and a fountain that brings forth life, the presence of God, light

West – Symbolic of evening, the going down of the sun, the day closing, backsliding

Whale – That which is under the command of God, used to judge us as well as protect us

Wheat – Symbolic of the Word of God, bread, the staff of life, Jesus, saints

Wheel – Symbolic of the glory, transport, speed, the circle of life, a remnant

Whip – A tool used to bring judgment, to bring hurt, and to bring pressure upon people

Whirlwind – A hurricane, a sweeping power, something that cannot be resisted, the judgment of God; a move of God

Whispering (Whisper, Whispers) – Backbiting, gossip, talking about others

White – Purity, innocence, holiness, righteousness

Whole – Completeness, thoroughness, all the way through, from beginning to end

Whore (Whoredom) – Spiritual idolatry, adultery, false doctrine, the false church, Babylon, immorality, someone who has stopped following Jesus and has backslidden

Whoremonger – Someone who dwells among whores, an adulterer, someone who is committing spiritual adultery as well as physical adultery

Widow – Someone who is separated to God completely, someone who seeks the Lord earnestly, and someone who God uses miraculously

Wife – the local church, the Bride of Christ, a woman married to a man

Wild – That which is of the flesh, someone unrestrained, stubborn, rebellious

Wild Ass – Symbolic of the adamic nature, stubbornness, self-willed, rebellion, depravity, the natural man

Wilderness – The dealings of God, a place of emptiness, a place of testing and of trial

Wiles – The tactics and tricks of the enemy

Willfully – Someone who does something with malice, forethought, and purpose in mind

Willow Tree – Symbolic of weeping and sorrow

Wind – symbolic of the Holy Ghost, the breath of life, the power of God, false doctrine, evil teachings, that which is natural

Window – Symbolic of Heaven, openness, blessings raining down from Heaven, the presence of God coming through

Wine – the Holy Ghost, resemblance of someone flowing in that which God is doing, present truth, the blessing of God, prosperity, true teaching of the Lord

Winepress – The place that presses out the Holy Ghost or the new wine, a place where true doctrine is produced, also a place where false doctrine can be pressed out

Wineskin – the local church, a person in the body of Christ, that which holds wine (it can be good or bad depending on what it is holding)

Wings – Speak of that which catches the heavenly breeze, divine transport, super natural defense, protection, God's covering

Wink – To encourage sin, to overlook sin, ignorance

Winter – Time of hardship, sorrow, darkness, hardness, difficulty, age and growing older, time close to its end

Wisdom – the Lord Jesus Himself, the fear of the Lord; someone who has applied knowledge to their life

Wit – To know and to understand

Witch – Someone that uses witchcraft and enchantments, someone rebellious, speaks of idolatry, Jezebel, something that is an abomination to God

Witness – Someone who testifies to something, someone who boldly declares something, those who declare something has happened, the Word of God

Wolf – Symbolic of evil, satan himself, false ministries, false teachers

Woman – the church, a virgin, also could be the false church, the harlot, Babylon, the soul

Womb – Place of birthing, a place from where the sons of God come forth, a place where everything begins

Wonder – A sign, a miracle, that which testifies of the power of God

Woods (Wood) – The flesh and humanity, Christ in his human nature, saints

Wool – the flesh and human works, used by false priests

Word – Jesus personified, the Word of God

Work – Labor, that which you do for the Kingdom of God and for the Lord Jesus, your labor in the Kingdom, or your labor just in the world or in the flesh

Workmanship – Something that has been created, something that has been skillfully done, something beautiful that has taken time to create; the Holy Spirit's work in us

World – Age, the actual world in which we live in, a time period, the carnal world around us, the fleshly nature of men

Worm – Symbol of that which is despised, used as an instrument of judgment, that which is small that works its way in to destroy, condemnation, despising oneself

Wormwood – Symbol of bitterness, satan, satan's power, death

Wound – Suffering that someone is experiencing that is causing great affliction and sorrow in his life to which there is no remedy, a deep sorrow brought about through something that has happened in someone's life that only God and the Word of God can heal

Wrestle – To fight with the powers of darkness, to fight with God and the presence of God

Wrinkle – A spot or blemish or anything in our lives that brings dishonor and disgrace to the presence of God and to the Lord Jesus, something that Bride of Christ is to have no part of

XYZ

Xerxes – bridegroom, God, King

Year – prophetic time period, symbolic of time, time in which God moves, a season

Yearn – To long earnestly for, cry out for something

Yellow – Sin and uncleanness, the glory of God

Yesterday – a prophetic time period, time past

Yield (Yielding) – To humble oneself, to bow, to give way to

Yielded – Increase, fruit

Yoke – Bondage, being tied to someone in a bad way, to be bound to something or someone, submission

Yoke fellow – Tied to a colleague, joined together

Yonder – Going farther in the Lord, a place apart from the rest

Young – Immaturity, not yet grown in the Lord

Zacchaeus – the wealth of the world being given to the righteous, also type of the world whose hearts are crying out for more; a sinner who truly repents; one who really wants to see Jesus

Zacharias – the priesthood who do not really believe; the believers who are shocked when their prayers are really answered

Zadok – the Lord Jesus, highest rank or order in the body of Christ

Zamzymmims – evil giants, Nephilim, the devil

Zarephath – Place of God's provision, the dealings of God, receiving the word of God and anointing in time of a spiritual famine

Zeal – Spiritual fervor, spiritual desire

Zealous – Spiritual desire, being on fire for God, strong desire

Zebedec – the father of a remnant, a father who brings forth good sons

Zechariah – Prophetic restoration, prophetic encouragement

Zedekiah – a hireling, Babylonish minister, ultimately destroyed by Babylon

Zephnath-peaneah – Jesus, character change, the remnant in the last days, overcoming adversity and prospering in spite of suffering; Joseph

Zerubbabel – Jesus; prophetic ministry that leads God's people out of Babylon

Ziklag – Place of encouraging yourself in the Lord, restoration, overcoming oppression, overcoming depression

Zion – God's dwelling place, remnant worshippers, the Lord Jesus sitting on the throne of his people's heart Authority, God's throne, God's government, God's mountain

Zophor – accuser of the brethren, gossipers, busybody, counsel of the ungodly

List Of Biblical Numbers And Their Meaning

1 - Unity, God, That Which Is First
2 - Witness, Division, Separation
3 - Godhead, Resurrection
4 - Creation, That Which is Created
5 - Grace, Spiritual Ministry
6 - Man, satan
7 - Perfection, Completion, Rest
8 - New Beginning
9 - Finality
10 - Law, Government, Completed Cycle
11 - Disorder, Disorganization, Confusion
12 - Divine Order, Divine Government
13 - Rebellion, Backsliding, Sin, Depravity
14 - Doubling of Perfection
15 - Rest, Acts of Grace
16 - Fullness
17 - Spiritual Order
18 - Bondage, Binding
19 - Divine Order In Judgment
20 - Expectancy
21 - Divine Perfection
22 - Double Disorder or Confusion
23 - Death
24 - Priesthood, Heavenly Government
25 - Grace Intensified
26 - Rebellion Intensified
27 - Finality of What God Does In The Earth
28 - Eternal Life
29 - Departure
30 - Maturity, Preparation for Ministry
31 - Offspring, Seed
32 - Covenant
33 - Promise
34 - Birthing Of A Son
35 - Hope
36 - Enemy

37 - Word of God
38 - Slavery
39 - Disease
40 - Trial, Testing, Probation, Chastening
41 - Deception
42 - antichrist
44 - Lake of Fire
45 - Inheritance
46 - Second Death
48 - Dwelling Place
50 - Pentecost, Jubilee
56 - Seeing the Heavenly
60 - Pride
66 - Idol Worship
70 - Spiritual Order
77 - Vengeance
80 - Fulfilled Life
90 - Rebirth
99 - Sealed
100 - Fruitfulness, Full Measure
120 - End of all Flesh
130 - Appointed Seed
144 - The Bride, The Remnant
153 - Revival, Sons of God
200 - Insufficiency
300 - Faithful Remnant, Deliverance
390 - Bearing Iniquity
400 - Divine Probation
480 - Building of the Temple
600 - Warfare
666 - antichrist, Fullness of satan in Fullness of Man
888 – Jesus
999 - God's Wrath
1000 - Perfect Fruitfulness, Rest
1081 - The Abyss
1260 - Tribulation
144,000 - Perfection of Divine Government

List Of Biblical Directions And Their Meaning

East - Coming of the Lord, Place of God's Glory
North - Judgment, Place of God's Throne
West - Darkness, Backsliding (Moving away from the Lord)
South - Blessing, Refreshing, Prosperity
Right - Blessed, Special, Chosen, Strength, Victory
Left - Judgment
Up - Ascending in God
Down - Humility, Spiritual Decline, Judgment
Forward - Growth, Vision, Direction
Back - Backsliding
Straight - Spiritual Purity, Having Direction, Going on with God

List Of Biblical Colors And Their Meaning

Green - Life, Prosperity
Silver - Redemption
Blue - Heaven, Heavenly
Grey - Maturity, Honor, Experience, Old Age
Red, Scarlet, Crimson - Sacrifice, Suffering
Purple - Royalty, Majesty, Wealth
Black - Judgment, Darkness, Famine, Sin
White - Purity, Holiness, Righteousness
Yellow - Sickness, Sin, Glory
Gold - Glory and the Divine nature & character
Amber - Glow of God, Glory of God, Brilliance of God and His Presence, God's Fire
Brown - That which is of the earth, flesh
Vermilion - A False Covering
Pale - Death, Hell, Shame
Bay - Spirits wandering over creation in the last days
Grisled - Judgment on Creation

ABOUT THE AUTHOR *Samuel Greene, Ph.D.*
One of the callings the Lord gave Brother Sam years ago was to help write sound doctrine for the remnant and Spirit-filled believers. Since 1976, Brother Sam has been teaching the Word of God daily out of which has come dozens of teaching manuals and books. These study manuals are part of an eight year Bible College curriculum taught at churches and Bible Schools all over the world. Below is the list of available manuals and books:

www.NWMin.org

FOUNDATIONAL SERIES (Hebrew 6:1-3)
Volume 1 - Searching The Scriptures *(ISBN: 978-0-9831696-4-2)*
Volume 2 - Repentance From Dead Works *(ISBN: 978-1-937199-18-0)*
Volume 3 - Faith Toward God *(ISBN: 978-1-937199-41-8)*
Volume 4 - Doctrine Of Baptisms *(ISBN: 978-1-937199-17-3)*
Volume 5 - Laying On Of Hands *(ISBN: 978-1-937199-14-2)*
Volume 6 - Resurrection Of The Dead *(ISBN: 978-1-937199-37-1)*
Volume 7 - Eternal Judgment *(ISBN: 978-1-937199-39-5)*
Volume 8 - Doctrine Of Perfection *(ISBN: 978-1-937199-36-4)*

PRESENT TRUTH SERIES
Eternal Salvation *(ISBN: 978-1-937199-40-1)*
Fasting *(ISBN: 978-1-937199-42-5)*
The Grace Of Giving *(ISBN: 978-1-937199-44-9)*
Scriptural Happiness *(ISBN: 978-1-937199-45-6)*
The Kingdom Of God *(ISBN: 978-1-937199-65-4)*
The Kingdom Of Darkness *(ISBN: 978-1-937199-47-0)*
O Worship The Lord *(ISBN: 978-1-937199-50-0)*
Prophetic Utterance *(ISBN: 978-1-937199-52-4)*
Teach Us To Pray *(ISBN: 978-1-937199-57-9)*
Dealings Of God *(ISBN: 978-1-937199-34-0)*
Walking Before Him *(ISBN: 978-1-937199-59-3)*
Women In Ministry *(ISBN: 978-1-937199-60-9)*
Healing *(ISBN: 978-1-937199-46-3)*

REVELATIONAL SERIES
Call Of The Bride *(ISBN: 978-0-9831696-7-3)*
Crowns Of The Believer *(ISBN: 978-1-937199-33-3)*
Glory Of God *(ISBN: 978-1-937199-43-2)*
Mystery Babylon *(ISBN: 978-0-9831696-6-6)*
Order Of Melchisedec *(ISBN: 978-1-937199-08-1)*
The Remnant Principle *(ISBN: 978-1-937199-53-1)*
Slaying Our Giants *(ISBN: 978-1-937199-55-5)*
Tabernacle Of Moses *(ISBN: 978-1-937199-56-2)*

SERMON ARCHIVES
Volume 1 - Doctrine Of First Things *(ISBN: 978-1-937199-12-8)*
Volume 2 - A Lamp That Burneth *(ISBN: 978-1-937199-66-1)*
Volume 3 - Precepts Of The Lord *(ISBN 978-1-937199-54-8)*

(cont...)

www.NWMin.org

THE GOD MANUAL *(ISBN: 978-0-9831696-0-4)*

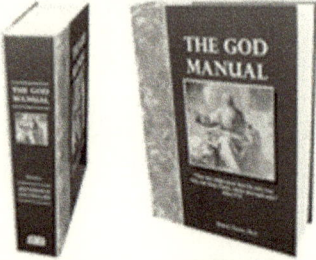

John 17:3 says, "*...that they might know thee the only tr*
God, and Jesus Christ, whom thou hast sent."

THE GOD MANUAL was written with hopes of seeking
reveal the correct Biblical image of who our precio
Creator really is. With 160 lessons, it exhaustively teach
almost every aspect, characteristic, and attribute of God v
can think of. In order to fulfill our calling to be conform
to Jesus' image, we must first know what that image is. O
prayer is that as you study these lessons your life w
forever be changed, your worship increased, you reali
that holiness is not an unattainable thing anymore, a
most importantly you fall deeper in love with Jesus. *T*
reference book is a must have for all teachers and devot
disciples.

160 Chapters, 1160 pages
revealing the tapestry of God's character,
heart, and being as found in Scripture

THE LITTLE BOOK DEVOTIONAL   *(ISBN: 978-1-937199-62-3)*

A 365 Day Spirit Filled Devotional!

This 365 day devotional is not your typical devotional. As disciples of Jesus, we are called to
know the mysteries of the Kingdom (Mark 4:11). This devotional has been written to provide
some answers to those that ask you of the hope within you (I Peter 3:15), to provide a place
for you to be instructed, encouraged, inspired, blessed, assured, and an avenue for you to meet
powerfully with the Lord Jesus every day of your life through His Word. I dedicate this book
to the body of Christ, and particularly to the remnant all over the world, who daily give
themselves to the Word of God, to studying it and walking it out, to worshipping Him with
passion, and for their great desire to become true living disciples. To that end, this devotional
has been written. God bless you, and may the Lord greet you every day as you open this book;
may it inspire you, encourage you and strengthen you, as it gives you fresh understanding of
God's heart and His ways.

OTHER BOOKS   by Samuel Greene, *Ph.D.*
Deeper Truth Dictionary Of Bible Types *(ISBN: 978-1-937199-35-7)*
The Call To Aloneness *(ISBN: 978-1-937199-25-8)*
Face To Face Communion *(ISBN: 978-1-937199-00-5)*
The Sound Of God *(ISBN: 978-0-9831696-2-8)*
The Israel Of God *(ISBN: 978-1-937199-15-9)*
I Am Black But Comely *(ISBN: 978-0-9831696-1-1)*
The Anointing Of God *(ISBN: 978-1-937199-16-6)*
A Stone's Throw Further *(ISBN: 978-1-937199-63-0)*
Digging In The Valley *(ISBN: 978-0-9831696-9-7)*
Hast Thou Considered My Servant Job? *(ISBN: 978-1-937199-19-7)*
Handfuls Of Purpose - Volume 1 *(ISBN: 978-1-937199-06-7)*
Handfuls Of Purpose - Volume 2 *(ISBN: 978-1-937199-13-5)*

www.ingramcontent.com/pod-product-compliance
Lightning Source LLC
Chambersburg PA
CBHW030506100426
42813CB00002B/356